THE

LADY'S REALM

a selection from the monthly issues:
November 1904 to April 1905

with an introduction by
Lady Georgina Coleridge

ARROW BOOKS

ARROW BOOKS LTD
3, Fitzroy Square, London W1

AN IMPRINT OF THE HUTCHINSON GROUP

London Melbourne Sydney Auckland
Wellington Johannesburg Cape Town
and agencies throughout the world

This selection first published by
Arrow Books Ltd 1972

Made and printed in Great Britain
by Acorn Typesetting & Litho Services Ltd.
Feltham, Middx.

Bound by Wm. Brendon & Son,
Tiptree, Essex.

ISBN 0 09 906740 4

Contents

Introduction
by Lady Georgina Coleridge

The thoughts of the ladies in 1904 must have turned constantly towards the realm of High Society, Court circles, and the right dress in which to appear at the right place, at the right time of year. The Editor of THE LADY'S REALM is well aware of the main interests of his readers and keeps them au fait, emphasising the more important points by plenty of italics – specially on the fashion pages – but these readers are educated women who also want to know what is happening in the world of art, drama, antiques, travel and even careers for women. What thoroughly professional contents even if there seem to be rather a lot of words on every page! ! The fiction serials run at great length so they had to be left out of this selection, but they are just as amusing as the feature articles which convey an incredibly clear message – No lady cooks, cleans or mends – She only visits dress or hat shops – She is interested in modern art and has plenty of time – So much indeed that using it up is a full-time job.

The pages of THE LADY'S REALM were designed to be turned gently, slowly with a happy contented sigh by readers who looked for inspiration towards Court Circles – where else could this piece of information be useful?

"Entertaining their Majesties:
   There is one little point with regard to dress which the invited guest must not lose sight of. While each one goes fully provided for all the necessary changes demanded by society rules and with due consideration to the situation of the mansion, time of year, functions arranged, etc., they should not at the same time omit to take both mourning and half mourning."

Also in the fashion pages which are largely devoted to special occasions in the rarefied atmosphere of High Society, we find the comforting news that "There is not a great difference between the Court bodice of this season and last except that fronts are straighter and points are sharper."

The Editor kept readers well in touch with new developments, devoting nine pages to the formation of the Ladies Automobile Club which met at Claridges Hotel so that: "Weary women members of the Committee will be at rest from the treadmill round of ordering the dinner."

He also dealt regularly with more serious subjects – like Careers for Women (not ladies, oddly enough) and in Sanitary Inspecting we hear that "It must not be imagined that the lady inspector is always received with open arms. Dirty over-crowded people do not welcome sanitary reform; and the position she holds is, to say the least of it, peculiar."

On a happier note in "How to furnish a flat with economy" – the reader must be encouraged to learn that "Flats have proved kindly promoters of matrimony."

Miss Alice Head, one of the first women to edit a magazine (and founder Editor of *Good Housekeeping*) remembers that her mother was a regular and devoted reader of THE LADY'S REALM, but she bought the junior version, *Girls' Realm* for the family. THE LADY'S REALM was reputed to have the highest standards, and did not talk down to women. Could the Editor have been among the first of the liberators? Miss Head believes the editor was a woman but the editorial message is always in the masculine gender – For instance in a note about the hundredth issue of his publication, he solemnly promises to continue providing news of the arts, the drama and, of course, society.

Really the main difference between the editorial approach then and now is the heavy emphasis on "High Society", the absence of coloured illustrations and of any direct reference to sex – otherwise the subject matter of interest in 1904 is just as relevant today.

In this delightful anthology a slice of social history is laid before us – this was how some of our ancestors saw life. It was specially interesting to me, looking quickly through THE LADY'S REALM of 1904, to find on page 206 a photograph of my grandmother, an Italian who married a Scotsman, and on page 210 a photograph of my great aunt, a Greek who married an Englishman. They are featured as foreign ladies who broke into High Society by marrying into the peerage. In a later issue even Americans had arrived, and one caption reads "The Countess of Suffolk . . .

Our newest Ameri can were handsome, rich and popula

It seems extraordinary t features could be based on such a theme, but it gave me ar added fel warmth towards a highly entert book to come upon familiar faces a its pages.

Have fun with THE LADY'S REALM there are so many more delicious little pieces of unconscious humour like my favourite caption: "Viscountess Falmouth is a daughter of Lord Penrhyn(*sic*) – Her ladyship entertained the King on his last visit to Cornwall."

Note:
Lady Georgina Coleridge is one of the most distinguished and successful woman journalists in the United Kingdom. Beginning her career as a freelance writer, Lady Georgina then joined *Harpers Bazaar*. Subsequently she was assistant to the fashion editor of *Country Life* and *Homes & Gardens*, before becoming beauty editor and then editor of *Homes & Gardens*.

By 1963 she was editorial director of *Homes & Gardens*, *Flair* and *Modern Woman*. Since then she has been publisher of *Ideal Home* and *Woman's Journal*. A former president and chairman of the Women's Press Club, Lady Georgina is currently Director of I.P.C. Magazines Special Projects Department.

ENTERTAINING THEIR MAJESTIES

BY MARY SPENCER WARREN.

WHEN Their Majesties the King and Queen signify their willingness to sojourn beneath the roof of any member of the British aristocracy, no greater honour or more signal proof of esteem and friendship can be accorded or received. That such visits are comparatively rare, renders the event all the more a mark of distinguishment.

Royal visits come about in various ways. A nobleman who may properly be described as on terms of intimate friendship with Their Majesties, may verbally or by letter ask " the great honour "; or, incidentally in conversation some prized possession, antiquity of residence, or beauty of neighbourhood may be mentioned, and the Sovereign may express a desire to see such, knowing full well that his expressed wish is the highest compliment he can pay. Or again, some function of great local interest is about to take place which Their Majesties have consented to grace with their presence, and the county magnate who is nearest resident may offer his castle or mansion for the Royal use.

But in either case, when once the visit is a settled thing, special and vast preparations have to be made. Few outside the charmed circle realise the magnitude of these necessary arrangements. Naturally much depends upon the host and hostess, and much also upon the place to be visited. Many of the ducal and other stately residences have a suite of rooms which practically are always in readiness; that is, they are never used but by Royalty, and they are furnished in accordance with the well-known tastes and wishes of these distinguished personages. These suites of apartments are generally quite remote from those occupied by other guests, in order that perfect quiet and retirement may be secured, as well as facilities for the transaction of government and other state business. Separate suites are provided for the King, the Queen, and any other members of the Royal Family present, and consist of—at any rate, those for Their Majesties—a sleeping apartment, a dressing-room, a bath-room, breakfast-room, study or writing-room, and a drawing- or reception-room; and very often there is a separate garden leading from these apartments, which for the time being is kept exclusively for the Royal use.

Another item which must be considered is suitable accommodation for Their Majesties' respective suites. It will be quite understood that the affairs of the realm must proceed as usual even when the King and Queen are paying visits; thus the private secretaries and other functionaries must be in attendance, King's messengers must come to and fro as usual, and the post and telegraph still bring their daily duties. Such business could not be allowed to accumulate, or endless confusion would ensue. A large staff of servants also accompany the King and Queen, in order that Their Majesties may be always surrounded by familiar faces, and by those who are fully accustomed to the régime of the Royal household, which runs like so much well-kept machinery. To lodge this staff of servants is a comparatively simple matter, undertaken generally by the steward or housekeeper; nevertheless, these functionaries in their turn have some nice points to consider, for there is much etiquette of place in the Royal household, certain of the staff taking their meals in certain rooms, and those in the hall each taking his or her appointed place at the table in order of precedence or length of service.

Coming to the mansions where " Royal

THE ARRIVAL OF THEIR MAJESTIES AT A COUNTRY STATION.

Photo by H. N. King.

THE STATE MUSIC-ROOM AT CHATSWORTH WHERE THE FAMOUS THEATRICALS TAKE PLACE.

apartments" are not, the work of preparation is magnified to a very appreciable extent, for redecoration and reupholstery must inevitably take place; also other rooms are depleted of choice articles of furniture, and much that is new is ordered in for the occasion. Then the artistic tastes of the coming visitors with respect to works of art and curios are considered, as is also their preference for certain floral decoration. Her Majesty is partial to orchids, roses, lilies-of-the-valley, and violets; while the King does not much care for flowers of very strong scents, and only a small quantity of any sort. This of course applies to the Royal rooms only, both the King and Queen being great admirers of the floral produce of the houses and grounds.

The next momentous problem to be faced is the making up of a house-party to meet Their Majesties. Firstly, it must be ascertained that Their Majesties wish for a house-party at all, and if the answer to this is in the affirmative, Their Majesties are consulted as to whether they have any special desires or wishes in the matter. In olden times Royal personages used to signify that they were about to visit So-and-so, and they commanded that Such-and-such be invited to meet them; but graceful courtesy has taken the place of imperative orders since the advent of the Victorian reign, and although the Royal wishes for the presence of certain persons may be expressed, and undesirables placed on the list which is invariably submitted may be erased, the King and Queen do not make up the party, but leave it to host and hostess, relying of course on their good taste in the matter. Of course, even in Society there are a few whom it is not desirable to bring into the Royal presence as (and the term is respectfully used) fellow-guests. The host or hostess may not be conversant with some little matter which may have come to the ears of the King's entourage, and so an undesirable may occasionally be included. Of course, the erasement of a name is practically social extinction. There are a few favoured members of Society who are continually receiving invitations to meet Their Majesties. Needless to say, these are not the dullards of society; they are, on the contrary, those who are clever or brilliant in some particular direction, or have distinguished themselves in some particular way.   At the same time, friendship and exalted birth is necessarily taken into consideration in the selection of guests.

It goes without saying that the majority of the invited ones are quite conversant with all the little nice points of etiquette necessary to observe when in the company of sovereigns. Their Majesties are fully desirous that their host and hostess and all guests shall be quite at their ease, and converse as entertainingly and amusingly as at other times.   But obviously a certain line must be drawn, for the King and Queen are, as it were, hedged off by quite a host of little observances, and the line which separates ease and intimacy from undue familiarity requires to be very finely drawn. Should any individual be invited who, perhaps from the exigencies of his calling in life, is not conversant with Court etiquette, he will find a friendly equerry quite willing to instruct him.

There is one little point with regard to dress which an invited guest must not lose sight of. While, of course, each one goes fully provided for all the necessary changes demanded by Society rules, and with due consideration to the situation of the mansion, time of year, functions arranged, etc., they should not at the same time omit to take both mourning and half mourning.   King Edward and Queen Alexandra are so closely allied to many foreign Courts, rendering occasions for mourning frequent and often sudden, while the news is so quickly transmitted, that one is never sure when mourning many be demanded, and it is etiquette that when visiting where the King and Queen are present every guest must appear in exactly the same degree of mourning or half-mourning.   This also applies to those who may be invited

to dinner and are not staying in the house.

Then the question of entertainment must be considered, for although there may be a variety of outdoor interests to fill up any spare time Their Majesties may have during the day, yet it is customary to provide something special for the after-dinner hours ; this, then, must be carefully thought out and previously arranged, so that no possible hitch may occur.   Lately, private theatricals have been quite the fashion, certain well-known members of Society having proved themselves remarkably talented, both in arranging and performing. Perhaps, however, a noted London company will be requisitioned, the transference of the whole of the actors and stage effects thither being

THE KING IS A QUICK SHOT, KEEPING TWO LOADERS BUSY, AND ALWAYS ENJOYS A DAY'S SPORT.

Photo by H. N. King.

THE BEDROOM USED BY HER MAJESTY WHEN STAYING AT GOODWOOD.

made at very considerable cost; or any special soloist, instrumentalist, or noted band performing in the country may be summoned for one of the evenings. All this immensity of preparation—the situation of the rooms, with correct decoration and fittings, the near proximity of the rooms of the personal suites of Their Majesties, the making up of a suitable house-party, and the entertainment of the exalted guests—brings many anxious moments to the host and hostess, and mere enumeration of these may perhaps give some slight idea of what it really means to entertain Their Majesties.

When the day of arrival comes, the host must repair to the nearest railway station to meet the special train conveying the King and Queen. Local volunteers may form a guard of honour, and the yeomanry of the district constitute an escort, but no band must be provided or procession arranged.

A carriage and four horses, ridden by postilions, must be in attendance, as well as other carriages for the suites and fourgons for the luggage. The hostess will meet her Royal guests at the entrance to the castle or mansion in the usual way.

During the stay of Their Majesties, the manner of spending each day of necessity varies. The visit, it may be remarked, generally extends to but three or four days, but occasionally lasts a week. Both the King and the Queen take their breakfast in their own apartments; in fact, unless it is the shooting season, Their Majesties often scarcely leave their rooms at all during the morning. Of course, it is quite understood that the Royal guests are perfectly at home in the house of their host, and dispose of their time as may be necessary in accordance with the demands of State and other business.

There may be a visit to some object or place of local interest, and then probably the King and Queen take luncheon with the other guests. As a series of small tables is now so prevalent, the rule is that Their Majesties and the host and hostess always sit together, others of the company being honoured by invitations in turns. Generally

Dinner is a very stately meal. The whole of the guests assemble in a saloon or drawing-room, and about five minutes previous to the hour—which is generally nine o'clock, in deference to the King's well-known preference—form up into an avenue, ladies on one side, gentlemen on the other. When the King and Queen enter, His Majesty

Photo by H. N. King.

THE KING IS AN EXPERT BILLIARD PLAYER. THE ILLUSTRATION SHOWS THE TABLE WHICH HE USES WHEN STAYING AT CHATSWORTH.

speaking, Their Majesties plant trees in commemoration of their visit, this being an afternoon function; but whatever takes place, the whole of the house-party meet for afternoon tea, which is quite the informal meal of the day, and always the occasion for a pleasant exchange of courtesies and cheerful conversation.

of course advances to lead in the hostess, the host taking in the Queen. These personages walk through the avenue of curtseying and bowing guests, who then follow in order of precedence, gentlemen offering their right arms to the ladies.

The King and Queen are waited upon by their own servants, these keeping their

Photo by Lafayette.

LADY MAUD WARRENDER IS A CHARMING SINGER,
AND IS FREQUENTLY A GUEST AT HOUSE-PARTIES
HONOURED BY ROYALTY.

Photo by Lafayette.

THE MARQUIS DE SOVERAL, THE PORTUGUESE MINISTER
IN LONDON, IS A PERSONAL FRIEND OF THE KING,
AND IS KNOWN FOR HIS BRILLIANT WIT.

position near Their Majesties' chairs, receiving the dishes brought to them by other servants. The meal is never unduly prolonged, the King being rather a rapid eater, and having a dislike to lingering at the table. The exit from the dining-room, then, is generally made within one hour of entering it, the ladies going to the drawing-room, the gentlemen to

Photo by Alice Hughes.

MRS. WILLIE JAMES, ONE OF THE MOST POPULAR HOSTESSES
IN SOCIETY, IS A TALENTED AMATEUR ACTRESS AND
TAKES A PROMINENT PART IN THE CHATSWORTH
THEATRICALS.

the smoking-rooms. The stay in the latter, though, is generally brief, the ladies being presently again joined. Now the circle is often enlarged, leaders of Society or local celebrities having received invitations for whatever entertainment there may be, and some of these additional guests are, by previous arrangement, presented to Their Majesties. During a recent visit paid by the King and Queen to one of their distinguished subjects, there was a large torch-light procession, an illumination of some ruins and the park, finished up by a grand pyrotechnic display. As has already been said, however, the form of entertainment varies very much.

Perhaps the best part of one day may be spent in visiting some neighbouring town to perform a public ceremony, or inspect some manufactory or place of celebrity ; or, again, the time may be taken up with shooting. If the latter, the whole of the gentlemen drive or motor to the selected covers, and a special cob of the King's is led over by a groom for His Majesty's use if required. The King is a quick shot, keeping two loaders busy, and always enjoys the sport exceedingly. The Queen and the ladies of the house-party drive over for luncheon, which is laid in a specially erected tent.

When His Majesty in turn becomes host and entertains at Sandringham his guests are always sure of good sport, for under the management of the head keeper the Royal preserves have now become some of the finest and best stocked in the kingdom.

The game-room at Sandringham holds six thousand head, and is the largest in Europe, save that of the late Baron Hirsch in Hungary. The room presents a wonderful sight after one of the King's shooting parties,

when it is filled with pheasants, partridges, hares, rabbits, and wild-fowl, which are finally despatched to charitable institutions. The King is a genial host amongst his

BEFORE GOING AWAY THE KING GENERALLY PLANTS A TREE IN COMMEMORATION OF HIS VISIT.

sporting guests, and occasionally relieves the tedium of a long "wait" in the covers by some good-natured jokes. Seated on his shooting-stool, which is fixed in the ground by one long leg, and gives the King the

Photo by H. N. King.

THE KING'S RETIRING-ROOM WHEN HIS MAJESTY IS A GUEST AT GOODWOOD. UNLESS IT IS THE SHOOT-
ING SEASON THEIR MAJESTIES SELDOM LEAVE THEIR ROOMS DURING THE MORNING.

appearance of being seated in the air, he looks the picture of a jovial country gentleman. Imagine a bright January morning, with an invigorating breeze sweeping inland from the North Sea through the pine-woods. About eleven o'clock the shooting party groups itself in the grounds. Behind the sportsmen stand some forty beaters, making a picturesque group in their blue blouses and low felt hats trimmed with Royal scarlet, and armed with formidable-looking quarterstaffs. The King is very strict about the wounded birds being immediately put out of their misery by the keepers, and never likes to see one of his cherished breed of golden pheasants amongst the killed.

The Truth About Man

By a Spinster.

ILLUSTRATED BY FACTS FROM HER OWN PRIVATE HISTORY.

The author of "The Truth About Man" is a well-known novelist, who prefers not to disclose her identity. She desires in the first place to beg Man's pardon for the truth she is about to reveal in these papers. She confesses that, notwithstanding his faults, she has always found Man adorable—for a time—and only wishes there were more of him to adore. For it is the fewness of him that constitutes at once his power and his peril.

As he believes that the views of "A Spinster" may not be shared by all the readers of THE LADY'S REALM, *the Editor has decided to offer a prize, month by month, for the best criticism of "The Truth About Man." Particulars will be found on page* 120.

CHAPTER I.

The Spinster, suffused with blushes, reveals herself to the world as a feminine Free Lance, and craves indulgence on the score of her mission.

WOMEN are of three kinds: those who gamble with an eye to the main chance; those who play for love of the game; those who look on. The first always marry; the second sometimes do; the third do not.

The woman who marries early can be no authority on the ways of Man in general, unless she becomes a widow, for the widow is proverbially the most knowing, as well as the most wily, of her sex. But the duties of catering for a lord and master, managing a household, rearing a brood of little human chicks, leaves scant time for scientific investigation into masculine psychology on the part of a young wife. She is generally found to be content with Man, as a husband and breadwinner, and has no desire to probe him as a problem. With the Widow and the Spinster it is different. They have more time, more opportunities, and their interests are more diffused. To them Man reveals himself.

When I use the word "spinster" in this

sense, I do not mean it to include that class of women whom I have dubbed the Lookers-on. They are very numerous, and some of them are quite happy, in the sense that a nation without history is said to be happy. But, for reasons I shall presently try to explain, they have no love affairs, and see Man only from the outside — a suit of clothes encasing a male human biped. It is not because they are plain, or foolish, or poor, or disagreeable, or un-lovable ; on the contrary, they are often ideal women, but they have no power either to attract or understand Man. Perhaps, in some cases, he does not attract them, and of course he does not understand them. No man did ever yet understand a woman of any kind, not even the simplest, nor ever wish to do so. Indeed, nothing annoys him more than a woman's attempts to elucidate herself ! He positively dislikes the inter-pretive woman, but he has no such active feeling for her I have called the Looker-on. He simply passes her by without notice, and she is left standing to watch the game. Very rarely does one of this class marry, and then, as it were, by accident. The reasons for their celebacy I shall endeavour to show.

But there is another type of spinster, " one of whom I am which." It is she who regards marriage, not as a prize, but as a snare to be cleverly avoided while she sports round the rim of it. Believing that " to travel hope-fully is better then to arrive," she looks upon such arrival at the altar as a stern conclusion to a delightful frolic, rather than as a goal to be reached with all possible speed. A revolter against the tame commonplace, a pursuer of mirage, she cherishes freedom, loves constant activity, lives every moment of her life, and revels in the joy of being wooed. She is, in short, the Free Lance of the feminine world, and to her adventurous eyes many mysteries are laid bare.

From the early days in her career, when she discovers the sneaking inclination of schoolboys for her vicinity, when bashful youths with red ears, simpering smiles, and stammering tongues begin to present them-selves at her garden gate to thrust drooping, ill-arranged posies into her unwilling hands, she is made aware of her destiny. From

the first inner curdling of sensation—half fear, half delight—she experiences at the touch of a timid boyish kiss, she is led to realise the mysterious relation that lies be-tween her and Man. Later on she proceeds to analyse this relation and thereby gains considerable insight. From understanding herself she begins to understand him who shares with her the world.

Of course, as a young girl, she set out with the firm intention of marrying. That she should never marry is to her a hypothesis as unthinkable as that the sun should set in the east ! But something—maybe the shatter-ing of her first passion, a failure to meet her conqueror, or, perhaps, merely her own high spirits and a natural shrinking from bondage—prevents her from fulfilling the destiny she has anticipated. So she goes on and on, as Henley says,—

> Lover follows lover,
> Dream succeeds to dream,—

until she recognises the fact that she is a Spinster. At first it gives her shock ; then she recovers and goes gaily forward with her eyes wide open, an Adamless Eve who tastes, without devouring, the fruit of the tree of knowledge, and learns one thing well—the ways of Man.

Now, I cannot answer for every spinster of my type, but it will surprise none of them to hear that I have been vouchsafed inner glimpses of the consciousness of at least fifty-seven different men who have made love to me, more or less. I have been able to study their behaviour, analyse their probable feelings, and draw certain con-clusions. As I am neither beautiful, wealthy, nor gifted with those unholy powers of fascination which we read of in certain novels, I may conclude that my list is com-paratively short. But, on the other hand, it has been varied. All sorts and conditions of men have honoured me with these glimpses into their mental interiors.

I can therefore, I think, claim to have a certain mission in life that may excuse my position as a Free Lance and my plunge into the print of these pages. My mission is : first, to show Man to himself, as he is, and warn him against certain rocks ahead ;

secondly, to teach innocent young spinsters how to deal with him ; to caution them against those errors into which I have fallen and, in fact, serve as an awful example. For here am I still a spinster when I might have been enjoying all the privileges of a married woman, the proud dignity of a wife, the sole possession and unlimited company of one man ! Can I say more to prove my qualifications as a danger signal ?

CHAPTER II.

The Spinster divides Man into three, and states a few general facts before proceeding to subdivide him.

MAN, as a whole, may be roughly divided into three distinct species, which I will call —the Bold, the Shy, and the Tough.

The first is composed of those self-assured and amorous males who fall in love with, and woo ardently, every other woman they meet. The second is made up of the world's good fellows, who have a great reverence for all women, and silently adore one for life without telling her so, having no opinion of themselves. The third species is concerned only with getting on and making money, is absolutely indifferent to women, and marries only as a matter of expediency.

The first of these we unhesitatingly condemn—and find irresistible. The second we admire profoundly, praise without stint— and ignore utterly. The third we dislike, despise—and marry !

Now why the man who, upon a first introduction, takes a woman by storm, makes fervent love to her, snatches unwarrantable kisses, and so forth, should conquer her will, haunt and overpower her imagination, is a matter that many of us have pondered over, but no one, I think, has ever quite solved. It may be outside the psychological plane, on the physical one. Whatever the reason, the fact is well proved that, although the woman knows perfectly well that such a man is accustomed to lose his heart and find it about four times a month, that he will take all he can get and give nothing worth having in return, that his sudden flame will blaze out quickly and leave but dry tinder, that his self-confidence is chiefly

due to the invincible conceit of superficiality —although she knows all this, she knows also (if she dare face the truth and her own soul) that she must succumb to his mysterious magnetism, unless she can, by sheer force of will, avert the spell.

And it is the same with the cold-blooded Tough, the mercenary Getter-on, who can always marry the woman he wants. His coolness and indifference pique her, stimulate her ambition ; she often falls in love with him, as much against her senses as when she is carried away by the passion of the Bold against her reason. Why does she thus fall a prey to the egoist when the Shy, the good fellow, is waiting for her, ready to worship her, to be an ideal husband ? Why ?

Is it because we women are fools and blind, or only because we are powerless against " the Moving Finger " ?

I can but quote my own experience, my own helplessness. During the past I have been fully aware that several good fellows have silently loved me far, a thousand times, more devotedly than those who have sworn impossible vows and kissed my feet. I have known that I had but to give a sign and I should have a husband for other women to envy. That sign I would not give—I *could* not. Why, again ? Because these men have roused in me no sentiment, have fed no sense of romance, awakened no thrill of passion. Just as the child hates to be called in from dangerous play in the sunshine to the cool, dim shelter of the nursery, so have I disliked and shrunk from everything that is safe, comfortable, and unexciting. For this has been the nature of the Unideal Woman ever since Eve wanted to taste the fruit of the tree of knowledge.

And what about Man ? Is he more consistent ?

I have already alluded to the Ideal Woman who is so often a mere on-looker at the entrancing game *l'amour*. Why is it so ? Why has she so few lovers ; why does she so seldow marry ? For the Ideal Woman is Man's own special creation ; it is his fancy that has brought her into being. Under the rules he has laid down for her, she has come to perfection, and is universally regarded as the flower of womanhood. Is she not pure, gentle, unselfish, womanly, affectionate, and domesticated? Does she ever waste time or attention upon the adornment of her person, indulge in any contemptible vanities? Is she not fully prepared and qualified to fulfil all wifely duties in a manner beyond reproach?

Then why does not Man marry her?

Moreover, why does he persistently ignore her? I have watched the Ideal Woman in many places, at home and in society, with the result that I have come to the conclusion she is the one of our sex whom men most persistently avoid. They are quite civil to her when she is thrown in their way; they will even openly admire her demeanour, or the way she keeps house, or nurses her invalid mother; but they do not seek her out, they do not talk to her, and they do not marry her. There are, of course, exceptions, but I find this the rule. Who does not know, in her circle of acquaintance, a goodly number of Ideal Women who are confirmed Old Maids? I don't mean merely spinsters, but confirmed, out-and-out, hopeless and helpless Old Maids!

I am not, as I have already modestly hinted, by any means an Ideal Woman. I plead guilty to powder and a touch of carmine on occasion. I deliberately wave my hair with hot irons, and spend a most reprehensible amount of time in organising my wardrobe. I am nearly always in debt for frocks and hats I can't afford. I cannot cook, or nurse, or keep household books; I do not know the price of anything to eat, except caramels and fondants; I am positively useless, and not even beautiful or dove-like in appearance. Yet Man has assiduously sought me out, hovered about me, flattered my vanity, proposed to me, fallen at my feet, while the Ideal Woman, my superior in every way, has pined neglected in a corner.

Why is this? Above all, why does Man put on airs of superiority and demand, in every book he writes, every sermon he preaches, every speech he makes, the ideal qualities of womanhood that he does not in the least desire? Why points he the finger of scorn at the clever woman, the smart woman, the flirt, the small-waisted, high-heeled paragon of fashion? Is it because he really admires the quiet and serious girl, or likes to see uncorseted figures, square-toed feet, and home-made gowns of sober hue and cut? Not a bit of it.

But he thinks he does. He plays a continual game of make-believe, and the funny part of it is that he actually deceives himself. We must take care that he does not also deceive us!

(To be continued.)

A MOTHER OF THREE.

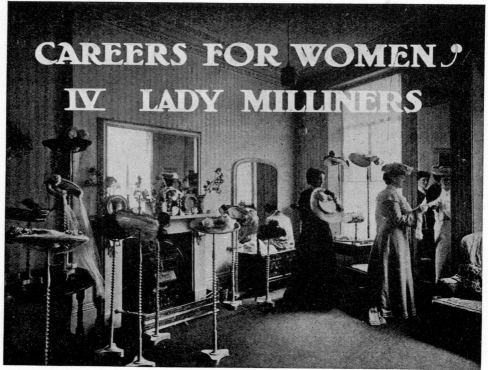

CAREERS FOR WOMEN? IV LADY MILLINERS

THE LADY CUSTOMER AND THE LADY MILLINER.

BY ANNESLEY KENEALY.

IT costs far more to start a milliner's shop than a tea-room. In fact, the tea-room is the Eldorado of the lady anxious to work, but with very little capital wherewith to play a waiting game. A tea-shop calls only for an outfit of crockery—and this you can get on credit. It is a ready-money concern, the coffee and cakes are paid for over the counter, and it more or less advertises itself, since it is most frequently on the ground floor, and its entrance is made as public as possible.

The lady milliner usually begins "upstairs"—handicap number one. For the average customer has a firmly rooted belief, which has absolutely no foundation in fact, that for each stair she mounts an extra shilling will be added to toque or picture-hat. The reason for the upstairs beginning is generally because the milliner-in-making has not a huge bank balance and is timid over spending money which she does not possess.

This is the essential difference between men in business and women in business. A man starts a "concern" and promptly outlays hundreds of pounds which are not his. For this is a sound business principle, and the main means of money-making. A woman, over-conscientious, refuses to set to work unless she has the wherewithal to pay her first six months' expenses snugly stowed away in a savings' bank. Ergo she begins modestly—ergo she makes small headway, and for a very long time her shop "takings" and returns are of the microscopic order.

Occasionally a woman arises on the business horizon who is not hampered by the fear of not being able to pay her way. But that kind of woman becomes a Madame Humbert. She is not content to woo Fortune through swathing chiffons and laces into bewitching picture-hats, or pleating box-cloth into smart travelling toques.

So the average lady milliner takes an upstairs floor, furnishes it artistically, interviews and buys from the travelling salesmen, whose business it is to scent out ladies setting up in business, trims or causes to be trimmed a score of tempting headgear of all sorts and conditions, and waits with a certain degree of fear and trembling for the belated buyer.

Friends furnish the first clients. When she " sets up " the lady milliner has a series of cards printed on which she announces her *début* as a business woman, her address and the range of prices for bridesmaids' hats, river creations, widows' weeds or Early Victorian bonnets. Her friends rally to the standard and buy. Sometimes for friendship sake they expect to buy at a reduced figure. But they tell their friends to come. And the friends form the snowball which rolls to success. Sometimes the snowball shrinks to failure. It all depends on the individual milliner.

In a private business the aim is to please each customer, and send her empty away rather than to insinuate her into buying a hat she does not like. Such private millinery ateliers work on totally different business lines from those practised by the big advertising shops of Regent Street, for instance. The motto of these, with their big and ever-changing *clientèle*, is—please your customer if you can—but sell a hat.

The private milliner will not sell her wares at the price of displeasing a client. For one reason she is a gentlewoman, " works for a connection," and does not badger her visitors to buy. Her next reason is that she wants to retain her customer's confidence, and sell her a really becoming hat or bonnet which will bring her back to buy more. For in buying bonnets, as in everything else, " a woman convinced against her will is of the same opinion still "—*viz.* that she looks a perfect fright in it. And if she is a woman with any sort of spirit, or of Eve's eternal

AN EMBARRASSMENT OF PRETTY HATS AT " DOLLY VARDEN'S."

Photo by J. Bulbeck & Co.

HATS, PARASOLS, AND COSTUMES IN THE LADY RACHEL
BYNG'S SHOW-ROOM.

build, she nurtures revenge in her heart against the person who talked her into buying it. Consequently the proverbial wild horses could not induce her to return to that establishment. At the same time, it is not enough to possess the talent of architecting a charming hat. You must add on the art of the saleswoman. Some people can design a headgear which would almost tempt a feminine angel to return to mortal spheres for the sheer joy of wearing such a creation. But the same master-builder of millinery might not be able to dispose of her lovely design. For the art of the saleswoman is born, and not made : that subtle admiring art which makes one feel, as the milliner lightly poises the prescription of feathers and frills on our heads, that this particular hat is just the last finishing stroke to make our style of beauty the toast of the town ! One does not quite know how the flattering suggestion is conveyed, but there it is. And the hat is bought, even though it were to involve the banishment to the debtors' side of Holloway prison of he who is responsible for our debts.

Some lady milliners adopt a *nom-de-plume*; others frankly place their names over the shop door. Among the latter is the Lady Rachel Byng, daughter of the Earl of Strafford. Her name, figuring as " Rachel Byng," appears over the door of a millinery and blouse shop at 26, South Molton Street, W. Lady Rachel combines with her hat and blouse business a school of millinery for gentlewomen, where a thorough training is given either for pupils who wish at the end of their course to start a business on their own account, or for ladies desirous of taking up millinery for the sake of home hat-making. Many Society ladies go through a term of millinery training so as to save on hat bills and at the same time suit their own particular style of beauty. Lady George Scott, for instance, is one of the best amateur milliners in London, whose hats of her own making are notorious for style and smartness.

The fees for lessons at Lady Rachel Byng's school are thirty guineas for six months, or eighteen guineas for a three-month

A CORNER OF HATS.

Lady Rachel has her office next door to the pupils' work-room, takes great interest in their progress, and does her best to find positions for them when they have taken their millinery diploma.

And Lady Rachel does not "play" at being a milliner, but works hard and interestedly in the profession she has adopted. Unfortunately she has made an adamantine rule that no photograph of herself shall be published, so that we are not able to pictorially present her at her chosen calling. A sale was in brisk progress at the time of the writer's visit, and as a striking object lesson that the more private millinery businesses do not charge high prices, may be mentioned the fact that a perfectly charming garden-party hat was ticketed at 5s. 6d., while many lovely specimens of high-class millinery were marked down to 15s. 6d. and one guinea.

"Dolly Varden," of 361, Oxford Street, is a type of millinery establishment which

term, the hours being from ten to six daily, with a whole holiday on Saturday. Afternoon tea is included, the pupils, of course, providing their own luncheon. There were four pupils at work in a bright work-room, all gentlewomen and daughters of professional men. Instruction is given by the manageress, and ranges from the elementary wiring of a straw hat to the most elaborate architecting of a "shape" of original design.

Some pupils develop a taste for evolving new designs; others are content to "copy" from models. Should a pupil intend to go in for millinery as a business, think of setting up a shop for herself, or entering into partnership, she is taught to take and keep stock, and may at her option be trusted to go into the city to match ribbon and velvets, or purchase millinery supplies, feathers and furbelows, chiffons, and flowers, etc. During the season, too, she may serve her apprenticeship in the show-room to the difficult art of selling. Blouse-making, too, is taught, the work being all hand-made and exquisitely done. A pupil of six months' standing was executing an order for bridesmaids' hats, and doing it most artistically.

MISS MONICA PURDON.
("Madame Monica.")

MISS LILIAN CLAPHAM.
(" Dolly Varden.")

fait with the French styles, these of course being modified, if necessary, to suit the differing British type. For the average Englishwoman does not look her best in unmodified Paris millinery, which needs some process of adaptation to the individual style of English beauty—which differs so essentially from that of the Frenchwoman.

The Parisian note of this showroom is marked *chic*. But "Dolly Varden," like other sister milliners, complains of the superstition which dies hard, that "private upstairs millinery" costs more than that of the ground-floor regulation shop.

An inspection of the little white tickets on the really charming hats and toques displayed in the artistic show-room distinctly shows that the prices tend to be lower than those of the regulation shop. And the standard of taste and workmanship, both in the hand-made blouses, skirts, and millinery, makes one all the more surprised that the prices are so moderate.

"Dolly Varden" possesses a school of millinery, the pupils being gentlewomen, for whom the very modest premium of fifteen guineas ensures one year's training from start to finish in their profession.

elects to carry on its decorative calling under a *nom-de-plume* suggestive of be-flowered and be-rosed damsels of a most dainty period.

This firm consists of two highly cultured and artistic ladies, Miss Lilian Clapham and Miss B. A. Earle, the daughter of a late distinguished professor at Oxford. The business began some three years ago, and has flourished exceedingly, owing to the artistic taste and high standard attained both in the millinery, the blouse, and the skirt departments.

Previous to the setting up of the "Dolly Varden" sign, Miss Clapham had been a lady dressmaker for some ten years, so that she started her more recent adventure with highly educated skill in modes and fashions, to say nothing of the business knowledge and training so essential to success.

One of the nice necessities of the business is a periodic visit to Paris, so as to keep quite *au*

PRETTY HATS FOR FAIR FACES.

BEFORE BUSINESS HOURS AT " MONICA'S."

Naturally enough, the pupil in her first six months not only absorbs an immense amount of attention from her teachers, but she spoils a great deal of costly material. But if at all clever with her fingers, she is able during the last six months of her training to recoup by her skill the time, trouble, and sacrifice of good material made in the early stages of her training. The most noticeable features about all the lady milliners' establishments visited are the charming and healthy conditions under which both pupils and apprentices work. There is no need for factory inspection in these bright, lofty, and spacious work-rooms ; and the terrible conditions of workers as shown in the Hon. Mrs. Alfred Lyttelton's powerful play *Warp and Woof* have no part and parcel in the establishments of the lady milliner. For such ladies work with a higher ideal than that of the commercial cent per cent—they bring their womanly sympathies to bear upon the workers in their service.

The only complaint Miss Clapham, the senior partner in the " Dolly Varden " firm, brings against her lady pupils is that just as they are becoming really skilful and useful

in their work they are sure to marry. So far, in this firm, the matrimonial act has repeated itself in the work-rooms with monotonous regularity.

One very special feature at this " house," and in fact in all the show-rooms of the ladies included in this article, is the rule that visitors are not coerced or influenced to buy. They may inspect and try on the hats, and if they do not care to make a choice they are not made to feel like criminals in the dock.

And how does the lady milliner guard against bad debts, the intricacies of credit giving, and the impositions of that type of woman who wants to combine the maximum of millinery with the minimum of bill paying ?

Other milliners, other customs. Some establish the rule of pay-day on the first of the month succeeding purchase. Many give long credit in safe quarters. But time, experience, and intuition soon teach one to diagnose the client who may be trusted to run up bills and she whose credit is somewhat shaky.

Then there is the customer who confuses

a milliner with a money-lender. She not only wants her hats on trust, but she seeks to borrow ready money, to be paid back when her quarterly dress-allowance is due, or to be put on the bill "To millinery and blouses supplied," etc. The lady milliner does not encourage the money-borrowing customer.

Another pitfall for the unwary is the buyer who does not intend to pay at present,

A cheque will be sent by return of post, etc. Sometimes, in the excitement of the moment, the ruse succeeds, and the lady gets the hat, while the milliner does or does not get the price of it.

Another device is to despatch a frantic telegram or telephone message, "Please send my hat immediately. Pay on delivery." When the hat arrives the lady has been called away from home, and could not leave

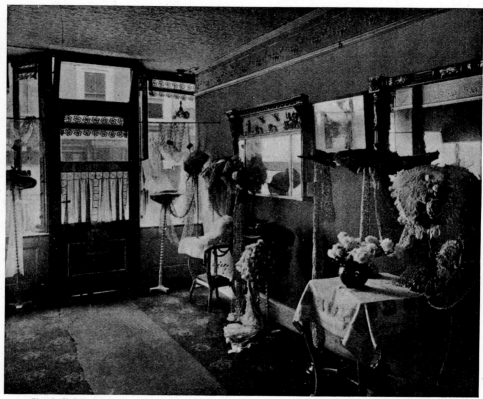

Photo by J. Bulbeck & Co.

THE MILLINERY DEPARTMENT AT THE LADY RACHEL BYNG'S.

and is not quite sure if her future is paved with good paying intentions, but who seeks by hook or by crook to get the ordered hat or hats into her possession. Possession is nine-tenths of the law, and once the hat is left at the house without the settling of the bill, it is not always an easy matter to recover. So a district messenger boy is sent to the show-room in hot haste. Mrs. So-and-So is hurriedly summoned on a trip to Paris, or has been ordered off to Harrogate to take the waters. She must have her new hat.

the money because she was not sure how much it would be, etc. Sometimes the messenger is induced to leave it; and then a long wait for the money—or, after the formula of girls who count cherry stones to see when they will be married—"This year, next year, never!"

Madame Jean Altoun, of 3, Blenheim Street, Bond Street, W., is a Scottish lady who conducts a millinery business in her own name, and who took a thorough training in a large business work-room. She either trims each hat throughout or else puts the last crowning finishing touch herself; and she constantly remodels millinery furnished by herself three or four times over, so as to bring the style up to the latest mode and whim of the moment. Madame Jean is the special friend of girls and Society women who want to wear the daintiest headgear and who nevertheless have only a limited dress allowance. She has been two and a half years in her business, and has never lost a customer. A chief speciality of this little millinery establishment is featherweight headgear, which is much appreciated by the modern woman who wears her hat from dawn to dewy eve—a tradition existing (so fond are some Society ladies of their hats) that they even take their baths whilst wearing them.

Madame Altoun receives pupils for a term of three months' training at an exclusive fee of from ten to fifteen guineas, her scholars ranging from ladies who want to know how to trim and remodel their own hats to those who intend making a calling of millinery.

Madame Jean forms a charming picture in her white serge gown against a background of tasteful millinery, and she takes individual pains to create her hats to suit their wearers.

"Monica," of 141, New Bond Street, is a millinery venture of two Irish ladies, Miss Monica Purdon and a sister, the daughters of Dr. Henry Purdon, the well-known skin specialist of Belfast. Miss Monica takes the greatest possible interest in the "face framing" art, and studies in her millinery creations to throw out all the prettiest points of a face. She advises none to enter the millinery business unless possessed of a desire for hard work and a faculty of resisting the joys of open-air life for a shut-in, indoor occupation.

The ladies of the firm Monica have the clever adaptability and artistic temperaments of their country; and another sister, Miss Isabel Purdon, is a successful professional violinist. The millinery of the Maison Monica is in charming taste and by no means costly, travelling hats ranging upwards from 15s. 6d. and picture-hats from one guinea. Pupils are taken for a six months' training term at an inclusive fee of ten guineas.

All the ladies engaged in the millinery business agree that it is a pleasant though an arduous life, and all speak in enthusiastic praise of the kindness of their clients. It is said that the calling is much overcrowded; but doubtless in this as in all other industries there is always room on the top!

There is no doubt that the lady milliner has raised her craft to a fine art, and that the pleasant and refined atmosphere of the "private upstairs show-room" gives a totally new tone to that most important of all dress matters, the choice of a new hat.

IS BRIDGE IMMORAL?

I.

BY MRS ROBERT TENNANT,

Author of " The A B C of Bridge."

THE basis of most of the attacks made on bridge from the pulpit or by the press is that it is a gambling game, and that it is entirely for this reason people spend so much time over it. Now this is a very foolish assertion to make, as it strikes those who only play bridge in moderation and for small stakes as singularly unjust: and that is the worst impression to produce if you want to stop people from doing anything. An intemperate ally often does more harm to a cause than an open enemy. In my own little circle, where we all love bridge, we play for quite small stakes, which never vary, and this is one reason why I think people make such a mistake in basing their attacks on bridge on the plea that it is mere gambling. I maintain in the face of all opposition that bridge is not a gambling game *pur et simple*. Before the game is begun the stakes are fixed, and however excited the players may become, they cannot alter them. If people are foolish enough to

start playing for more than they can afford to lose, that is not the fault of bridge. In all other gambling games, from roulette to pitch and toss, the stakes are elastic, and it is in the possible variation of the stakes that true gambling consists, because the stimulus of winning, or the sting of losing, temporarily affects the judgment and makes people imprudent and rash.

No! bridge is no worse than any other game that has become the fashion of the moment. Like all other pleasures it can be abused by excess, but it can also be enjoyed in moderation, and even its abuses are often much exaggerated. It does not do to believe all that is in the papers,—not even in the society journals.

It has at any rate the advantage of causing people to use their brains, some of them for the first time in their lives ; and that it is not a mere pretext for gambling is proved by the fact that it is constantly played for love— even in London—this I know for a fact ; and why people are to be prevented from enjoying a charming and intelligent amusement because others choose to lose too much money over it I cannot see. It has never been suggested, even by the most bigoted member of the Anti-Gambling League, that the Oxford and Cambridge boat race should be suppressed ; and yet, I suppose, a good deal more money changes hands over that one event than in a month's bridge-playing in London. But then every one can look on at the boat race, though every one cannot play bridge ; and here, I believe, we get at the root of the whole matter. I am quite sure that a great deal of the animus displayed against this clever game would, if we analysed it, be found to come from people who would give anything to play if Heaven had only endowed them with the requisite amount of brains. This not being the case, they are quite right not to attempt it, but have no right to abuse those who do. For my part, I am always pleased when people tell me they do not play bridge, when they give as their reason that they are not naturally card players. One of the legitimate objections to bridge is, that so many people have taken to it who have not got card minds, and so spoil the game for those who have. People who want to talk all the time are, I am sorry to say it, a nuisance, and as they can't care about the game ought not to play it ; but still theirs is an amiable weakness, and though it may be rather expensive to themselves and their partner, is preferable to the angry and envious spirit that makes unjust and one-sided attacks on others.

On no other subject would any attention be paid to criticisms from those who did not know what they are talking about. Surely accurate knowledge should precede judgement, or how can it possibly be called intelligent, or carry the slightest weight with sensible people ?

And now, having tried to give an answer to the most serious objections that are raised against bridge, let us dwell a moment on its positive and undeniable advantages. Just think of the change it has brought into the lives of certain middle-aged women, perhaps not very attractive in appearance, or amusing in conversation. Formerly their only diversion took the form of dreary teas enlivened by "a little music" (generally amateur), where they sat round the wall in a dismal circle, nobody taking much notice of them ; but now, if they are fair bridge players, how different is their lot ! They are eagerly welcomed when they appear with the joyous, "How good of you to be so punctual !" (In the anti-bridge days nobody cared whether they came or not.) You may smile at this, but anything that brightens the lives of middle-aged women ought not to be sneered at.

Then again, suppose you want to invite two or three people to dinner. Formerly the burning question immediately arose, "What are we to do with them afterwards ?" We all know that long, dull evening when the conversation becomes exhausted, and you see people vainly racking their brains as to what to say next. A furtive glance at the clock to see if a move can decently be made is rewarded by the horrible discovery that the clock has stopped ! and one is at last reduced to say timidly, "Could you tell me what time it is? We promised (any convenient relation can be introduced here) not to be late," and the hostess, much relieved, murmurs politely, "Oh ! must you really go ? Would you like a hansom called ?" and as you leave the room, you can almost hear her saying to her husband, "Thank goodness *that's* over."

But when bridge is the order of the day— or night—things are very different. The gentlemen do not linger long in the dining-room, but join the ladies with alacrity, longing for the fray. A well-assorted party assembles round the green cloth, and in this interesting game time flies so quickly that it is with astonishment and regret that midnight is heard to strike, and the guests reluctantly separate, having passed a thoroughly enjoyable evening.

I feel I cannot end this defence of bridge with more emphatic words than these. As the poet truly says :

Who can ask more, or dare hope for as much ?

II.

BY ADRIAN ROSS.

IT is but lately that I have become an authority on bridge ; and when I say an authority, I understand the word in the same sense as it was lately used in a newspaper paragraph, informing the world that an old lady, who had just died, was "an authority on the Anglo-Israelite question." This implied that the worthy dame was thoroughly well acquainted with a great deal of entirely baseless conjecture and rash inference, and in all probability was more learned in unhistorical science than any other professor of things as they are not and have not been. Probably she combined with Anglo-Israel the interpretation of prophecy, or the knowledge of things as they are not going to happen.

Somewhat of the same nature is my qualification for discussing the effects of bridge on Society. I do know, with fair accuracy, what bridge is ; it is a game of cards of the whist family, something like boston and solo whist and vint. It is played, usually, by four persons, one of whom is a dummy. It may be played for love, in which case victory loses half its charm, defeat two-thirds of its bitterness, and play all its responsibility. It may be played for a pound a point, in which case an injudicious no-trump declaration, if doubled, may make a perceptible gap in a lady's dress allowance, or compel her husband to have the old motor-car repaired for next spring. It might be played for a thousand pounds a point ; but this could only be done as an habitual recreation by American millionaires, and they prefer poker, at which they have been known to raise each other a cotton crop and open a jack-pot for a presidential election.

But though bridge may be a definite game, played for stakes which, while varying from nothing to infinity, are fixed in any single case, it is impossible to say as much for the Society which plays bridge. The question, "What is Society?" is one that is susceptible of a great many answers, and might be, and probably has been, set as the prize competition of a weekly paper.

I cannot think that the oldest and most honourable families of Society play bridge, or, indeed, anything more modern than a discreet and stately whist, with modest stakes given to the poor. The utmost that one could expect of the high-minded Duke of fiction would be that he should officiate as a dummy not required to make a declaration. That he should then sit and see tricks thrown away by a frivolous and reckless partner, and still retain his lofty smile and old-world polish of manner, would add a ring to his halo.

The Society that plays bridge, then, must be sought at a lower elevation. In the absence of scientific classification, it might be defined as a collection of families and persons with a certain standing in birth, position, and property. They can trace their ancestry to the Conquest in somebody's "Peerage," and to the Tudors or Queen Anne in fact. They have lands and spacious country-houses, to which they can go for the shooting, for the hunting, for intervals of rest and refreshment. They have money, or at least know where to get some. And finally, they must have, in the main, few duties except those classed as "social."

There is, of course, another Society that plays bridge. This is supposed to centre in Park Lane, and to have been concerned with South Africa. It plays bridge, possibly better than the country-house Society, and for larger stakes ; but it is not the same, though the two may shade into each other. More money it has, possibly more brains ; but its country-houses are rented, and its pedigrees are rooted between the paving-stones of German ghettos.

The Society, then, that plays bridge is that which makes up parties at country-houses, handed down from the ancestors of some of its members ; and it is in country-houses that bridge is supposed to rage furiously, and spread the passions of the gambler and the ruin of the spendthrift among the men and women—especially the women—of high, or smart, or some kind of Society. There is an anecdote illustrative of this fatal effect, which

I have heard from several friends, who assured me that it really happened; I have also seen it in various forms, and in recurrent cycles, in what I may call the anecdotal press. A guileless girl, staying at the country-house of intimate friends, it appears, was asked to play bridge; she declined, not knowing the game, but was promised advice and yielded. After sundry rubbers, she went to bed; but was informed next morning by her hostess that she had lost an amount variously stated as from sixty to a hundred pounds. The girl telegraphed to her father, who at once sent his solicitor or his butler, or somebody trustworthy, with a cheque for the amount in one hand and a wheelbarrow for his daughter's luggage in the other, and removed her from the haunt of vice.

How far this represents the habitual practice of hostesses, daughters, and fathers, I cannot say; but I do not think this reprehensible state of things, if it exists, will last long. Bridge is a game at which skill tells considerably, and its conventions and methods are being rapidly systematised. As with lawn-tennis, its vogue will die of its own excess. Skilled bridgers will soon refuse to play with the inexpert, for a foolish dealer is stronger than a wise dummy. Then the skilled will play with each other for the game more than for the stakes. Further, the confessed duffers, who have hitherto been favoured by the newness of the game, will sink back into hopeless inferiority, and cease to desire a sport at which they are bound to lose, luck being even. Then bridge will go the way of solo whist and lawn-tennis and ping-pong, and many another game—it will become unpopular by its perfection.

III.

BY MRS ERIC PRITCHARD.

It is perhaps a little unfair to be expected to give a definite answer to this very leading question, although many of us, no doubt, on the strength of our own personal observations and experiences, would like to reply uncompromisingly in the affirmative. Indeed, one would be but a poor fool if one did not recognise that the game is capable of harm when those who take part in it are inclined to seize unjust advantage of their neighbours. But to commit oneself to the general statement that the game of bridge is immoral is decidedly unfair to the player who simply plays to indulge a scientific fancy, or to while away a few idle hours before going to bed. If it may be permitted to me to hedge somewhat, I would reply that it is, to say the least, decidedly unfortunate that a game, which in itself is so intrinsically excellent, should have had such a lamentably bad influence on such a large section of Society.

In one way and another it has affected almost every grade of Society, from the so-called smart set to the suburban enthusiast. For example, to take only one instance; I am sure that most dressmakers have very definite opinions, and perhaps very genuine grievances, against bridge, interfering, as it undeniably has done, with the settlement of their accounts—for debts of honour, even among women, have claims which are prior to all others.

It is not so very long ago that women and girls used to regard week-end parties as occasions on which to see their friends, and to get the benefit of a change of air and new surroundings: now, however, we find that unless they are prepared to play bridge for fairly high stakes, they get appreciably fewer Saturday-to-Monday invitations; consequently, they are tempted to, and often do, play beyond their means. They sit up later than is good for them, and probably take to the soothing cigarette and a pick-me-up of some kind to keep up the excitement.

Undoubtedly bridge is a good enough game in itself, and being so excellent, it has become an absorbing one. This would not matter so much were it not for the fact that it offers opportunities for gambling—a vice which I firmly believe is inherently ingrained in the disposition of the woman of to-day. In fact, if what we read about the French Court and about Thackeray's ladies of a later date be true, it must have been so at those periods, and very probably at all periods. Then to my mind another argument against bridge is that it has proved a most successful damper to all intelligent and intellectual conversation, and by so doing has sounded the death-knell of the salon, and deprived it of its chief *raison d'être*, as an institution among the cultured entertainers of to-day. Then again, not only is bridge played in the evening and afternoon, but also sometimes on wet mornings in the country. This is very cramping to one's ideas, for few people can intellectually afford to concentrate all their energies on one craze. Consequently, to keep up the excitement these foolish people play for stakes, and attempt to make it into a business. A friend of mine, and one who is quite a first-class bridge player, who works hard all day, says he thoroughly enjoys a game of bridge for a couple of hours after dinner ; but he complains that if he is kept from his bed after midnight his work next day always suffers : and so, in order that he may derive the benefit to which his superior skill entitles him, he takes the businesslike view of compensating for the short duration of play by correspondingly raising the stakes. And this is a perfectly legitimate course for a man of brains and common-sense to take, but it is a dangerous precedent for women to follow. It is only exceptional women who possess the necessary brains and self-restraint to adopt this principle with success. As a rule, excitement of the game deprives them of their better judgment, and playing for long hours interferes with their health and has most disastrous consequences on their complexion. With the loss of such precious possessions, how can woman be fitted for the serious business of life ? Many girls have obviously spoilt their chances of matrimony through bridge playing. This extreme foolishness is more likely to occur in the case of the club girl, who spends her afternoons as well as her evenings in the cardroom. Unfortunately, girls are such excitable creatures that they cannot take to gambling, even in a mild form, without sacrificing most of their other duties.

Then there is the question, and it is one which is always arising : "Are women sufficiently scrupulous in their play ? " Is it not most degrading to our sex that men should have to submit, without protest, to irregularities of play on the part of women which, if they had occurred in the case of the male sex, would instantly lead to social degradation ? Therefore, I think a strong argument against the playing of bridge by women is that it often develops into gambling, and, to those so disposed, affords too many opportunities for mild cheating. These consequences and side issues of the game do not enhance the moral reputation of such of our sex who play. Last, but not least, bridge does not supply that little touch of romance which adds so much to the lives of most women. The bridge girl, at any rate, is not, as a rule, the apotheosis of innocent youth, neither is the married woman, in her anxiety to win her friend's money by means sometimes none too scrupulous, an ideal object for admiration. Women should always make a point of being seen at their best in the presence of the opposite sex, and the gambling woman, to my mind, is seldom seen to advantage. The immorality of bridge lies in the fact that it has deprived women of some of their most precious and subtle qualities—possessions which, ever since the world began, have been their best weapons of offence and defence.

The Care of the Complexion.

BY "NARCISSA."

HAPPY is she whose red and white has been laid on by Nature's cunning hand, for a good complexion is a most enviable possession, and should be treated as such, while strict attention to the laws of hygiene will improve a bad or indifferent skin in no small degree. Colour and expression have far more to do with beauty than mere regularity of feature. And unfortunately the complexion is the very first item in beauty's category to suffer from wear and tear. Worry, ill-health, fatigue, indiscretion in diet, exposure to wind and weather, leave undesirable marks upon the skin. The clear red and white tints become dull and blurred, fine lines form round the eyes and mouth, and the face that ought to be fresh for many a long day becomes prematurely aged. Or, if lines are escaped, various more or less disfiguring eruptions appear, which are extremely difficult to get rid of. Although very many delicate women have transparent complexions, yet, as a rule, a good complexion implies good health, and

FOR A DELICATE SKIN TAKE A TINY PORTION OF THE PUREST COLD CREAM AND APPLY IT TO THE FACE WITH A SOFT HANDKERCHIEF.

in order to have good health it is necessary to lead a hygienic life; which does not mean that it is necessary to become a faddist or a crank, but only to take ordinary precautions regarding diet, ventilation, exercise, and rest. A well-known lady physician, noted for her beautiful complexion recommends the following diet :—

For breakfast, *café au lait*, brown bread and butter, watercress, provided it comes from a source absolutely uncontaminated by sewage, or a baked apple, eaten with coarse brown sugar.

AFTER ALL TRACES OF CREAM HAVE BEEN REMOVED DUST THE FACE LIGHTLY WITH POWDER.

For lunch, eggs, fish, mutton or poultry, with plenty of green vegetables, milk puddings, and stewed fruit. Tea, if well made, and not allowed to stand more than three minutes, is not injurious, in spite of all that has been said to the contrary.

Dinner should be light, and not too late. The exigencies of Society make it difficult to lay down laws as to what should be eaten and what avoided. It is scarcely possible to ask a hostess what are the contents of the fearfully and wonderfully made dishes which grace the dinner-tables of to-day. It is merely possible to study menus, and choose the simplest fare therefrom. The less alcohol taken the better. A little good claret or light wine is harmless, but spirits and liqueurs are the complexion's worst enemies. Hot milk, on the other hand, is its greatest friend.

Next to diet, fresh air is essential; the bedroom must be well ventilated, and no gas or oil burned therein. The bedclothes must be light, and at the same time warm. Daily

AGAIN REMOVING THIS WITH A PIECE OF CHAMOIS LEATHER.

ture in washes and lotions so much money thrown away.

Just as there are all sorts and conditions of temperaments, so there are all sorts and conditions of skins, and the treatment that suits one person admirably has exactly the reverse effect on another. Therefore it is necessary to exercise discretion in carrying out the following suggestions, and to ascertain whether the skin is thick or thin, greasy or dry.

A thick skin is inclined to be greasy, and a thin skin to be dry. Happy is the woman whose skin is of tolerable thickness, for what her complexion may lose in transparency, it gains in durability, and remains fresh and unlined for years after her less-favoured sister has grown lined and faded. She can defy wind and weather, and dance all night without becoming unduly flushed. She of the thick skin can rely almost entirely on those finest of natural cosmetics, soap and water. The soap must be of the purest quality, the water either rain-water or distilled. If it is impossible to obtain this, then water that has been boiled and allowed to get cold, and heated again when it is required for use, is almost as good.

The following is a method that has been successfully carried out for years by a lady who possesses a fairly thick skin. Lave the face thoroughly in very hot water at night, make a lather of pure soap, and apply it with a loofah or indiarubber sponge, using a fair amount of friction. Then rinse off all the soap, and rub a little cold cream into the

exercise, whatever the weather, is a *sine qua non*, walking and riding being decidedly the best. Bicycling does not conduce to beauty, and, healthy as the sport may be, the woman who golfs in all weathers seldom, if ever, has a complexion fit to be seen.

Regarding clothing, let nothing be tight. It is possible to have garments which fit like a glove, yet do not restrict the circulation in any way whatever. It is also desirable that the feet shall be warmly clad.

So much for a somewhat dry dissertation on hygiene, without which local treatments are rendered well nigh useless, and all expendi-

face while it is still wet. Dry with a soft towel, remembering always to rub upwards, in order to preserve the contour of the face. In the morning, use cold rain-water, to which a few drops of lavender-water have been added. This tones up the skin, and modifies the tendency to greasiness.

The treatment for a thin skin is naturally diametrically different; the very touch of water irritates some people, and yet, especially in London, it is extremely necessary to cleanse the face in some way frequently. Tepid rain-water may be used night and morning, and oatmeal substituted for soap, but little if any friction must be used, and the face must be dabbed dry with the finest of fine towels. To thoroughly cleanse a delicate skin without soap and water take a little cold cream on a piece of soft rag, apply it to every portion of the face, removing it with a soft old handkerchief afterwards; then dust the face lightly with the purest of powder, and finally complete the process by removing all traces of this with a chamois leather. Many women object to the use of cold cream on the ground that it induces the growth of superfluous hairs. Provided the ingredients are mixed by a thoroughly reliable chemist, and animal fat and anything in the nature of vaseline avoided, the alarm is groundless. Nevertheless, it is as well to avoid applying cold cream in the region of the chin and upper lip.

In spite of all that has been said against steaming the face, if done judiciously it is most beneficial, especially where there is a tendency to acne or blemishes of any description. Irish and Devonshire girls are justly noted for the beauty of their complexions—owed, it is said, in a great measure to the moisture of the country in which they live; and it is hard to find a set of more charming complexions than those

A CERTAIN AMOUNT OF MOISTURE IS NECESSARY FOR THE WELL-BEING OF EVERY COMPLEXION, BUT DRASTIC MEASURES SHOULD NOT BE EMPLOYED.

owned by the girls working in a hairdresser's shop, who spend a greater part of the day over steaming basins in the process of shampooing; but the steaming must be done with precaution and care, not more than three times a week, and the following home-made contrivance is better than a more elaborate and costly apparatus. Warm a tall, narrow bowl, then fill it three parts full with absolutely boiling water. Let a towel form a sort of tent over the head, and hold the face over the bowl just near enough for it to come into contact with the steam, and remain in this position till the water has grown cool. Should there be any spots on the face the contents may be pressed out after this treatment; but the finger nails must be. protected with a piece of soft linen, and the places touched afterwards with a solution of perchloride of mercury, which any chemist will make up, the strength advisable being that which is technically known as 1-2000.

Of the use and abuse of cosmetics much might be said. The woman who would preserve her beauty through life will never use any preparation which has not been prepared by a thoroughly reliable firm. There is a ghastly tale of a fair lady who, in her endeavours to make herself yet fairer, anointed her face with a preparation which turned it a pale green. Powder in moderation is harmless, provided it contains no metallic substance. As a rule, creams and emulsions suit dry skins, and toilet waters, such as elder-flower, Florida, or rose-water, suit greasy ones; but there is nothing to beat domestic cosmetics, such as cream, cucumber, and buttermilk. Buttermilk which must be free from chemicals is, alas! not easy to get, and when obtained soon turns sour; but it is invaluable, especially for use after exposure to sun and wind, and is also an excellent remedy for nettlerash, allaying the irritation, and removing the unsightly lumps astonishingly quickly.

I have before me an old black-letter book which belonged to a beautiful great-grandmother, who died at eighty-odd years with a complexion like a rose leaf. She, I believe, never washed her face, but dabbed it with the finest of damask towels dipped in rose-water. The following are two recipes which she prepared

IN ORDER TO KEEP A THICK SKIN IN GOOD CONDITION IT IS NECESSARY TO APPLY FRICTION WITH AN INDIARUBBER SPONGE.

herself, and which may easily be prepared by any one.

The first is quaintly styled, "A very good medicine to make one's face both fair and clear." "Take a good quantity of rosemary flowers, and seethe them in white wine, with the rinde of a lemon, and wash your face often therewith, and

THE CHEEKS MAY BE RENDERED FIRM, AND A HEALTHY COLOUR OBTAINED, BY SYSTEMATIC PINCHING WITH THE THUMB AND FIRST JOINT OF THE FOREFINGER.

you can have none of the same water then take the cowcumber itself, and rub your face therewith. But first pare off the rind, and by often using of it you shall assuredly find both health and ease."

Some people, whether ill or well, are naturally pale. A fine colour, however, may be cultivated

also use for to drink of it, and it will make you look both young and fair. This hath often been proved."

For people who have too much colour and are subject to flushing the following is strongly recommended: "Take cowcumbers, and pare them very clean, and cut them in slices, and distill them with a little rose-water, and with the same water that cometh from them wash your face every day four or five several times, but if

by the following method: Dip an india-rubber sponge in cold water, shampoo the cheeks in circles for five minutes at a time for an hour before going out. In order to obtain a permanent colour, the cheeks should be pinched between the thumb and first joint of the forefinger, working from below upwards.

Next month I propose to treat of facial massage, and the various methods to obviate the effects of illness and the onslaught of old age.

The Realm of Society

Photo by Langfier.

THE COUNTESS OF MINTO,

The charming wife of the Governor-General of Canada. Lady Minto was over in England for a short time this season, and presented her daughter, Lady Ruby Elliot, at one of their Majesties' Drawing-Rooms in June.

IF "southerly winds" are rather conspicuous by their absence in November, so far as Great Britain and Ireland are concerned, we usually enjoy a surfeit of "cloudy skies," that other desideratum of Nimrods, according to the old song, together with some unwelcome variations in the shape of drizzling rain, sleet, and what in the country is called a mist and in London is known as a fog. Short of a black frost, however, hunting goes merrily on, whether the wind be in the south or the sky of the orthodox drab, until that period when, in the opinion of Leech's veteran sportsman, the perfume of the violets spoils the scent.

Curiously enough, although the presence of ladies at race-meetings is of comparatively recent date, Diana has always held her own in the hunting-field since the days when, falcon on wrist, she sallied forth with the rising sun to take a day's pleasuring. The racing-lady in the earlier years of the Victorian era was looked upon as distinctly "fast," although the late Queen herself attended the Derby more than once during the lifetime of the Prince Consort; but such adverse criticism was never extended to her hunting-sister, let her ride as hard and as "jealous" as she would.

It by no means follows that Nimrod invariably selects Diana for a helpmeet. Indeed, I recently heard a well-known hunting-man say that for nothing on

Photo by Langfier.

LADY LONSDALE,

Who is one of the finest horsewomen of the day. She is a daughter of the late Lord Huntly.

while their husbands and fathers are gaily pursuing the "little red dog."

Lady Lonsdale, who is one of the finest horsewomen of the day, and has a great knowledge of all things concerning the noblest conquest of man, was a daughter of the late Lord Huntly, and married Mr. Hugh Lowther, as he then was, in 1878. Like her sister, Lady Elena Wickham, Lady Lonsdale is never so happy as when leading a country

earth would he marry a woman who rode to hounds, as his pleasure would be spoilt by anxiety as to whether she was, or was not, breaking her neck, if he was fond of her, and the trouble of looking after her, whether fond of her or not. This view, though undoubtedly a selfish one, is that of the vast majority of men, where their own womenkind are concerned. But the hunting-woman who has a head upon her shoulders need not be a nuisance in the field by any manner of means, and it is scarcely to be expected of the wives and daughters of hard-riding men that they should sit at home occupied with "books and work and healthful play," as recommended by the late Dr. Watts (whose ideas, admirable as they were, did not quite reach the standard of modern requirements)

life, surrounded by her dogs, within easy reach of her horses, and as far away as possible from her magnificent town residence in Carlton House Terrace. She very much prefers Barleythorpe, Lord Lonsdale's hunting-box in Leicestershire, to her London house, and even to stately Lowther, and with her tall, slender figure and clear-cut aquiline features is never seen to greater advantage than on horseback.

Lord Lonsdale himself is a past-master in equine lore. His hunters are the very best that money can buy, and his carriage horses are equally well chosen. No equipages are more perfectly turned out than those used by Lord and Lady Lonsdale both in London and the country, whether it be the smart dogcart which conveys them to the meet, or the splendid canary-coloured state coach in which Lord Lonsdale attended the Coronation, seated in solitary grandeur, as Lady Lonsdale had been unable to accompany him, owing to illness.

Lowther Castle, which is always called "Lowther" *tout court* by its owners, is a huge, picturesque pile situated among the Cumberland hills, built of a kind of pink freestone, which time has tempered to a rich reddish tint. The entrance court is surrounded by an embattled wall, with bastions at the corners. Some idea of the enormous size of Lowther may be gathered from the fact that it is considerably larger than Chatsworth, and that at the time of the German Emperor's visit, a year or two ago, the eighty-odd members of his suite were put up without any difficulty. The castle is quite as imposing inside as out, the state drawing-room being one of the most magnificent apartments to be found in any of the stateliest homes of England. The furniture is of solid ivory, looted perhaps from Tippoo Sahib, to whom it once belonged, and among much valuable bric-à-brac and fine ormolu is to be seen a priceless Chelsea bowl, said to have been the first ever

manufactured. The dining-room is literally lined with gold plate, of which Lord Lonsdale has one of the finest collections in England, apart from that owned by the Sovereign. When a great dinner-party takes place the display of cups and salvers on the crimson walls is a sight not easily forgotten. Here also are to be seen many interesting Royal relics and souvenirs, including a gold snuff-box which once belonged to the Great Napoleon; an inkstand used by William III., who was more ready with his pen than with his tongue; and, perhaps most valuable of all to the owner, the cup presented to him by the German Emperor some eight or nine years ago. In the state bedroom, which is only used for Royal personages, is a carpet which was woven on the estate in the days when a carpet manufactory existed at Lowther. The hangings are of Japanese silk, beautifully embroidered, and the furniture originally came from the Palace of Versailles. The delicate set of toilet glass, which stands on a little table, once belonged to Charles II. The smoking-room is interesting because of its fine wood panelling and the pictures by Hogarth with which its

Photo by Elliott & Fry

THE DUKE OF BEAUFORT.

The Duke and Duchess usually spend the autumn at Badminton, which has long been a household word among sportsmen.

walls are adorned. A quaint custom obtains at Lowther, even when Lord and Lady Lonsdale are alone. When the wine is put on the table after dinner Lord Lonsdale raises his glass, and, addressing his wife, proposes "The Ladies," Lady Lonsdale responding with a like toast to the gentlemen.

About this time of year the Duke and Duchess of Beaufort are usually in residence at Badminton, which has long been a household word in sporting centres. The Duchess, who was Miss Harford, and married first Baron Carlo de Tuyll, became the wife of the present Duke, who was then Lord Worcester, in 1895. She is a charming, graceful woman, who has travelled in many lands, and since she has been chatelaine of Badminton has won golden opinions in Gloucestershire. As a hostess she stands unrivalled, and a year or two ago entertained Royalty at Badminton in the persons of the Prince and Princess of Wales. The Duchess was one of the first converts to automobilism, a form of sport which her father-in-law, the late Duke of Beaufort, who was so renowned in the hunting-field, and was one of the leading lights of the famous coaching club, would probably have looked upon as degenerate.

Oddly enough, although the great English estates had rarely changed hands until within the last thirty years or so, when they have been positively tossed about, Badminton has belonged to several families besides the Somersets. It was about the middle of the seventeenth century that the then Duke of Beaufort acquired the estate and built the present mansion, which covers three sides of a square. The great ballroom and the grand saloon are the finest apartments in the house, although the library is also splendidly proportioned. The stables, as befits the home of a race of sportsmen, are said to be the best in England, and were built by the late Duke, who left such a splendid sporting record behind him. The cellars at Badminton are very fine, and in olden days the genial custom prevailed of visiting the wine vaults after dinner, each guest selecting his own bottle from the well-stocked bins.

Hunting and pheasant-shooting in the same county are usually anything but conducive to harmony among the inhabitants thereof, as the hunting-man who preserves foxes is anathema to his shooting neighbours, whereas he who ventures to shoot or trap Master Reynard in order to protect his own game is looked upon as little short of a criminal by the hunting section of the community. Hence it follows that one sport obtains the ascendency, and more or less elbows the other out. In Leicestershire, Gloucestershire, Cheshire, Worcestershire, and the hunting counties generally, shooting is a secondary consideration, whereas in Norfolk and Suffolk, for instance, the reverse is the case. The first-named county undoubtedly holds the record as regards covert shooting : witness the splendid bags made not only at Sandringham, but at Houghton, Merton, Holkham, Melton Constable, and other places too numerous to mention. Lord and Lady Cholmondeley are not at Houghton this year, as the Hereditary Lord Great Chamberlain has let his magnificent estate to Colonel Ralph Vivian, who was Mr. Walter Long's tenant at Rood Ashton, which he gave up, as the shooting was not quite up to his requirements. Lord Walsingham has let Merton, the sporting record of which is almost unbroken, to Sir John Kelk, who recently sold his own place. Lord Leicester is at Holkham, where the King has shot many times and oft. The wild birds are a great feature at Holkham, as they come in hundreds to shelter from the severe weather, strict orders being given that the laws of hospitality are to be rigidly respected and the feathered guests left in peace. Considered from the point of view of the gastronome, the Norfolk pheasant takes front rank. The fattest and most satisfactory birds for the table are undoubtedly those from the Sandringham coverts, but as they never come into the market, only those who are privileged to receive the generous hamper, often containing as many as ten brace, which the King bestows on his private friends or the patients at the various hospitals, ever have the opportunity of tasting them.

LONDON & PARIS FASHIONS

BY MRS. ERIC PRITCHARD.

FOR some time past the leading tailors have held sway over autumnal fashions, but the furrier's art is beginning at last to gain the upper hand, while the *costumière's* skill is invoked on behalf of the *toilette-de-visite* and the evening frock. As I predicted last month, the *Directoire modes* have come to stay, but are subject to many alterations. Once more, as is generally the case in the world of fashion, it is the second instalment of models launched on the French and English markets that are the most generally becoming and will longest remain with us.

But many of the best-dressed Americans are not tall, and so with commendable wisdom have taken to the short basque coat instead of the threequarter *Directoire*, at any rate for practical wear. I would here impress upon my readers the mistake that is made by short women wearing a threequarter-length coat with a short skirt. Even a tall woman can hardly afford to cut her figure in this wise. I am glad, therefore, to observe that Worth, Paquin, Rouff, and Beer are making a distinct feature of the Russian blouse with the short basque, worn with the tailor-made skirt that clears the ground, for morning wear in the *Bois* and practical purposes generally. The short bolero in furs, especially in white caracal, is also popular, but as a rule short coats are cut with a basque all in one, or with a band at the waist. Besides these, we shall see a few smart little sacs in bright-coloured cloths, chiefly in the country and on quiet

occasions. There are some women who do well to always remain faithful to the bolero, for with a long skirt this style adds in appearance at least two inches to one's height.

THERE is no doubt that in London and in Paris dresses of faced cloth will be in vogue for smart morning wear as well as for calling ; these cloths are very soft and have a satiny surface. They are to be had in every possible shade : tomato-reds are much to the fore, invariably trimmed with velvet of a deeper tone. Deep blood-red and real scarlet will also be much *en evidence* as the winter advances, when we shall have tried somewhat of the autumnal bronze and green shades that Paris always affects with the fall of the leaf. Pastel shades never go out of fashion, and in blues, pinks, mauves, stone-grey, and a peculiar zinc colour, they lend themselves admirably to trimmings of sable, chinchilla, and mink. Some women look their best in these faded tones, which only require the richness of fur, a jabot of lace, and a trimming of velvet to give them a distinctive note.

AND now let us turn our attention to the cunning of the real sporting tailor. In the month of November riding habits are, of course, an important matter. One or two enterprising authorities in the hunting world are trying to bring in the tight-fitting, cut-away habit coat with a contrasting waistcoat. This is extremely smart for the Society leader possessed of a good figure, for wear in the shires ; but as a rule most true sportswomen prefer the semi - fitting, rather long hunting coat worn over a shirt or waist-coat with a hunting stock and, of course, the safety skirt. Dark grey whipcord still holds a prominent place, only sharing it with the regulation melton cloth. In fact there is but little variation in the sporting world. Here sartorial art has reached perfection, and beyond the revival of the velvet collar and fancy waistcoat there is nothing new to relate anent the question of riding habits. Some women prefer the coat that lies over the saddle, others like it to clear, and this, after all, is but a matter of indi-vidual taste. The success of a habit de-pends upon the cut, and nowhere can this garment be better built than in London. The same indeed may be said of all sporting clothes.

THEN the wants of

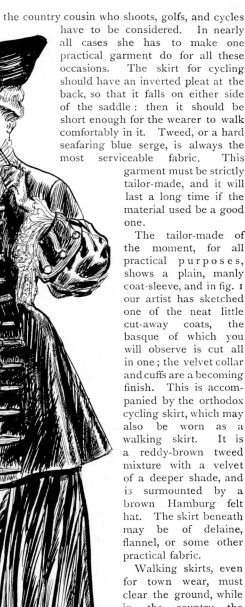

FIG. 2. A *TOILETTE-DE-VISITE* OF DARK GREEN VELVET IN *DIRECTOIRE* STYLE.

the country cousin who shoots, golfs, and cycles have to be considered. In nearly all cases she has to make one practical garment do for all these occasions. The skirt for cycling should have an inverted pleat at the back, so that it falls on either side of the saddle : then it should be short enough for the wearer to walk comfortably in it. Tweed, or a hard seafaring blue serge, is always the most serviceable fabric. This garment must be strictly tailor-made, and it will last a long time if the material used be a good one.

The tailor-made of the moment, for all practical purposes, shows a plain, manly coat-sleeve, and in fig. 1 our artist has sketched one of the neat little cut-away coats, the basque of which you will observe is cut all in one ; the velvet collar and cuffs are a becoming finish. This is accom-panied by the orthodox cycling skirt, which may also be worn as a walking skirt. It is a reddy-brown tweed mixture with a velvet of a deeper shade, and is surmounted by a brown Hamburg felt hat. The skirt beneath may be of delaine, flannel, or some other practical fabric.

Walking skirts, even for town wear, must clear the ground, while in the country the *trotteuse* skirt is still *de rigueur* : this, of course, should be accompanied by the neatest and smartest foot-gear. The great point to bear in mind about the short skirt is that it should be shorter at the back than in the front. Personally, I think that the *trotteuse* skirt looks best made with a frill below the knees. Many French women are wearing pleated skirts ; that is to say, they are arranged with stitched pleats at the waist, measuring about five inches in front and three at the back : in every case they are very full round the feet. Serge and rough cloth are the favourite fabrics for the pleated skirts, many of which are adorned with strappings or buttons, the latter being covered with velvet.

WHILE on the subject of practical dress, I must say a word about shirts and blouses. Delaine, silk and wool mixtures, canvas, and plain or patterned Viyella are much used, and many of these practical shirts are worn with detachable linen collars, plain or embroidered, and a smart little bow or jabot of silk. Those who cannot wear the linen collar should adopt the softer turn-over muslin collar, with a neat silk stock or bow. Shirts are cut with quite small sleeves, neatly finished with stitching, or made with a series of box-pleats or tucks.

OF course, the blouse is a different matter altogether. To wear with the smarter coats and skirts it may be made of guipure, lace, tucked silk, *crêpe-de-Chine*, or *chiffon-velours* ; but even here the sleeves are kept fairly small. Soft ruffles of lace at the neck and wrists are a distinctive feature of the more elaborate blouse.

Then there are some smart unlined blouses of bright-coloured cloth, trimmed with heavy guipure or crochet, and sometimes even with plain or coloured embroideries.

BUT to return to the magnificent fashions of the moment, for "magnificent" is the only word to express the sumptuousness of the fabrics, the beauty of the laces and embroideries, and the costliness of the furs now in use. We have chiefly adopted the *modes* prevalent in the days

of Louis XVI. and during the Josephine period, and these are synonymous with wonderful velvets and brocades. You cannot have a more suitable fabric than velvet for the winter *toilette-de-visite*, and the modern velvets are deliciously soft in finish and melodious in colour. Our

FIG. I.   A USEFUL CYCLING COSTUME IN RED-BROWN TWEED.

artist has sketched, in fig. 2, a beautiful *Directoire* costume in dark green velvet, quaintly trimmed with bands and buttons of dark green cloth. The *empiècement* at the neck forms a kind of collar at the back of the coat, and is of heavy gold braid over white cloth. The correct jabot is of old *d'Alençon* lace, which also forms the soft frills hanging over the hands. The hat is very simple and of *Directoire* shape in green velvet, trimmed with knots of gold. The coat, you will observe, is cut all in one, and it is lined with old brocade. The unlined skirt is pleated slightly in at the waist and falls by the weight of its own glorious folds.

There is no doubt there will be a revival of old brocades for lining coats of this period. The great *costumières* insist that we should be more or less correct in the carrying out of details, though they occasionally add here and there an entirely original touch of their own, which gives a *chic* finish and strikes a pleasing note of novelty.

A LESS extravagant, but very successful model had a skirt of tomato-coloured cloth, long and flowing, with a little *galon* trimming down the sides. The coat was also of cloth, with big revers, collar and cuffs of velvet of a deeper shade, edged with gold *galon* and big fancy gold buttons. The waistcoat was of white *moiré*, folded over an inner waistcoat of soft lace, the former being finished with smaller gold buttons.

FIG. 5. A LOUIS XVI. EVENING FROCK IN *VIEUX-ROSE* BROCADE.

This was worn with a felt eighteenth-century riding-hat in the same shade, with flutings of a deeper velvet and a beautifully shaded *Paradis* plume.

JACKETS of the Early Victorian period are being made of *peau-de-soie* and taffetas, trimmed with ruches and fringes, and resembling the old *paletôt* or redingote. They may be quaint, but they are rarely becoming, and I do not think they will ever really gain much sway. The real old polonaise trimmed with fringe and piping has been revived for smart indoor wear, but only by some exclusive *couturières*, to be worn by their equally exclusive *clientèle*. The success of such costumes depends upon their draping, which can only be arranged by the master hand, and must be composed of really costly stuffs.

AND what about the all-important question of millinery? Like the rest of fashion it is extremely varied, and a great deal is left to individual taste. Here and there we observe wild touches in the shape of quaint flowers, birds, etc. As for colours, all

FIG. 3.   A TRIO OF CHARMING HATS.
(*Sketched at Paquin's.*)

the curious dead autumn shades reign supreme, and how lovely they are in exquisite fabrics mixed by the master hand ! I simply revelled in the display of colours at Paquin's, of Dover Street, and I cannot do better than quote from that world-wide authority in the matter of autumn shading for headgear. The dyers and manufacturers of to-day, like the rest of the artistic, fashionable world, have taken a leaf from the book of the old masters, for the gorgeous golden browns, bronze greens, and claret and purple intermingled

are worthy reproductions of an old Titian or Vandyke.

In the page of hats here sketched by our artist at Paquin's it may be seen at what angle these French hats should be worn. The model on the right hand side is in white felt, with a beautifully shaded brown velvet rosette, with a quaint, gold-braided button in the centre, and the most attractive wide brown quill. Carefully note the arrangement of the rosette, and you will see that such an audacious trimming for a hat is very successful when treated

FIG 7. SOME DAINTY TOILET ACCESSORIES.
(*Sketched at 28, New Bond Street.*)

by Paquin. The delightful French hat on the left is also in white felt, with a crown of royal blue, and an edging of the same on the brim. Then quite a smart and novel felt either in cream or pale green, suitable for wearing with tailor-mades in town, is trimmed with sage green velvet round the rather high crown, and underneath the brim (which is also bound with velvet) lies the most cunning trimming, in the form of a shaded Argus quill. It is impossible to do justice to these three apparently simple hats, for such a lot lies in the colouring.

The hats all seem to fit closely on to the *coiffure* at the back, and show the most wonder-

ful arrangement of bows and rosettes. The intricacies of millinery are quite as marvellous as those of the picture-dressing of to-day.

I WAS glad to find that they are making a speciality at Paquin's of the silver fox stole, beautiful, thick, and oh ! so becoming, and, of course, here, too, Russian sable is to be seen at its best. As I predicted last month, chinchilla will be greatly used, especially on gorgeous evening wraps. Like ermine, it seems a fitting accompaniment of bright-coloured satins, silks, and velvets. Mink at its best is a costly fur, and ordinary folks have to be content with Persian lamb and white caracal ; the latter is popular among Americans, especially for smart skating frocks.

IN furs we see many *modes* of the Louis XVI. period. The once loose bolero is now cut with a pointed front, and is tight-fitting, with beautiful collar, and revers and cuffs of velvet, trimmed with old-world embroideries, and occasionally showing a gorgeous waistcoat of the same. Musquash, dressed like seal, forms very pretty Russian blouses and the new short basque coats : this is a cosy and excellent fur for those who cannot afford to pay high prices. Opossum, beaver, and golden otter are being used for loose sac coats. Few capes are seen, though many of the stoles resemble pelerines. Pretty little ties of ermine are worn at the neck, and these are often mixed with moleskin.

SOME gorgeous *paletôts* and long coats in fur are being made chiefly in the *Directoire* style, but many people still seem to prefer loose wraps for carriage and evening wear : not a few of us have to combine the two. Quite beautiful are the black and coloured tight-fitting velvet coats, trimmed with broad bands of chinchilla or sable. As I have already said, narrow bands of fur are being used on *toilettes-de-visite* and evening gowns. In fig. 4 our artist has sketched a *Directoire* coat in chinchilla, which could, of course, be copied in less expensive fur or in cloth. It fastens across with some beautiful enamel buttons, and has a waistcoat and revers of quaint embroidery, softened by the always attractive lace jabot.

FIG. 4. A *DIRECTOIRE* COAT OF CHINCHILLA WITH MUFF TO MATCH, WORN WITH A HAT OF VELVET
AND PLUMES.

EVENING DRESS is truly magnificent, though it is not so extravagant in the long run as would at first appear, because the picture frock carries but little date, and the lovely materials used will survive many visits to the cleaner. Our artist has sketched in fig. 5 a veritable Louis XVI. corsage in *vieux-rose* brocade with sleeves and fichu composed entirely of beautiful Brabant lace. Many of these Louis bodices fasten at the back, but the model here illustrated fastens in front (as it has a deep basque) invisibly under the bows. This brocade is very beautiful, and though it has a soft finish it is quite stiff. The skirt is amply full on the hips and at the back, though it hardly shows under the deep basque, which can be attached to the skirt or bodice as you please. Many of these brocades are embroidered in velvet, which necessarily makes them still more costly. This sketch is a splendid model for the woman possessed of a good figure. White and gold and green and gold are very favourite shades for evening wear in Paris, and a dramatic star has lately appeared in a most wonderful old silver brocade embroidered with real silver thread in a raised design of roses. The corsage is very

J.M. Pash.

similar to that in the sketch just referred to, but without the basque, and instead of the bows there are some beautiful old paste ornaments. The berthe is arranged with ruchings of Valenciennes and fine Brussels net. The sleeves are of the same length, but are a little more fussy than those in the sketch. Many of these details are matters of taste, so it is quite easy for most of us to be suited with this style of dinner-frock, unless, of course, one is very thin about the neck, in which case I advise the loose flowing lines of the Josephine period in preference to the Louis XVI. *modes*. Although the actual Josephine robes were a little stiff and hard about the *decolletage* and the puff at the top of the arm, our best *couturières* are altering these most cleverly, losing none of the quaint grace of that date, but adding soft touches of accordion-pleated chiffon or silk muslin, sometimes even allowing lace sleeves to hang in really picturesque style, which adds height and grace to almost any figure. The fichu is a welcome addition in many cases, and may be of the same soft fabric as the sleeves.

A LOVELY Redfern gown was in heavy, softest white satin Oriental, with a

FIG. 6. A SIMPLE BRIDGE GOWN OF LIBERTY VELVETEEN AND INDIAN MUSLIN.

narrow mink edging at the hem of a beautiful bolero of chiffon heavily embroidered in silver with cascaded angel sleeves of the same. Very pretty are some of these Josephine frocks carried out in the new shades of green, with velvet boleros embroidered in gold.

I DO not advise girls or even women on a limited income to attempt a too gorgeous style of frock, for young figures look so well in simple things. What is prettier than a white muslin evening dress, even for the woman of maturer charms, if she knows how to put it on ? I have had sketched in fig. 6 an attractive little bridge or quiet dinner frock in Liberty velveteen which can be had in a variety of glorious shades ; it is particularly lovely in the new tomato shades and in brown. If any girl who copies this be not possessed of a good lace fichu let her invest in fine Indian muslin or *point d'esprit* and make one of the same shape as that sketched. Both these fabrics wash beautifully, but I prefer Indian muslin, as it takes a soft, creamy tone and is peculiarly becoming as a finish to the *decolletage*.

The fichu is one of those delightful accessories which we can arrange to suit our individuality, and by its aid make our shoulders long and sloping or short and square. It can be brought high to the neck, and may be caught up in the front, at the side, or crossed over to the back just as the fancy of the moment or, indeed, of the wearer dictates.

THE sketch I have given you co..ld well be copied in cashmere—an old-fashioned fabric that has come rather into vogue of late—or even in summer gauzes. The girl with a limited allowance who has youth and a good figure on her side may present just as pleasing an appearance as richer women in more gorgeous raiment.

TALKING of figures reminds me that I would impress on my readers the fact that it is mostly a woman's own fault if she fails to possess a good figure, combined with comfort, for she has only to pay a visit to 28, New Bond Street, W., to get the best French corsets that are made. The famous "Tricot" corset, composed of the finest netted silk, moulded to the form of the wearer, still takes a foremost place in the favour of the Parisian, and in London, too, the most exclusive dressers generally prefer it. It can be had as low as 45s.

Then the real tailor-built woman is particularly partial to a most excellent corset, made of a very durable, but soft and silky stuff, daintily outlined with ribbon and coloured stitching. Delightful, too, is a dainty little *coutille* corset, very lightly boned, at 35s. Then the hunting, sporting, and athletic woman should never be without a pair of the famous silk elastic corsets, brought out by the firm on purpose to meet her requirements. Our artist has sketched, in fig. 7, a specimen of a favourite La Samothrace corset, which gives a rounded appearance to the hips and allows plenty of room in front.

AT 28, New Bond Street, W., one also finds attractive accessories in the way of cravats, belts, hand-bags, etc. These details play a very important part nowadays in the completion of a *toilette*. Many of the simple morning blouses and tailor-made skirts depend for their success upon a well-fitting waist belt. Perhaps the most popular is that composed of plain rucked kid, caught here and there with a slide or buckle. Narrow bands, of course, are worn with the short basque coat ; but with the blouse we still use the deep, pointed one.

THE hand-bag has become as much a necessity as any other accessory. In this we see specimens of old beadwork and quaint embroideries ; others in kid are decorated with silver, gold, and gun-metal ; while fine chain purses are adorned with blister pearls. These are so beautiful that I think they will never go out of fashion, and they are too expensive ever to become common. In fact, it is safe to say that anything good of its kind, and becoming to the individual wearer, can be used in conjunction with the varied fashions of to-day.

AN IDEAL BEDROOM AT MESSRS. LIBERTY & CO.'S, REGENT STREET.

THE HOME BEAUTIFUL.

BY ARDERN HOLT.

THE other day at Liberty's I was shown the plan of a room on the lines which are represented in the above picture. It is a most comfortable bedroom, in which its inmate might be tempted to linger many hours in the day. All the furniture is in walnut, intentionally finished with a dull surface. If you examine it, it appears to be arranged with fitments; but this is not so, and it is well, for they are apt to become landlords' fixtures, and consequently a great loss to the tenant. Each piece is quite complete in itself, and movable, therefore requires no fixing at all; yet has all the artistic appearance of regular fitments, with this advantage, that they can be passed from one room to another, or from one house to another, and can be arranged in a variety of ways, producing entirely new effects.

I want you to look particularly at the wall-paper, which displays various tones of soft grey-green, with a little mauve introduced. The frieze is of grass cloth stencilled in a conventional and quaint tree design, intermingled with flights of birds. This pattern

THE NEW DISC COLUMBIA GRAPHOPHONE.

in *appliqué* is carried across the linen window curtains, the lower part of which are of plain mauve in admirable contrast. The border to the carpet, the rug, the decoration of the toilet service, are all in harmony with the design, and the pretty tiles in the fireplace accentuate one good point, namely, that the grate, while consuming the minimum of coal, gives out the maximum of heat. It is hardly necessary for me to say that, being one of Liberty's suggestions for a sleeping-room, it is unique of its kind, and in a style which has made that wonderful house famous. We owe to it a new direction in art, both as concerns the dress of the day and the surroundings of our home life. There is never a discordant note; it is a new school not only well thought out, but carried out by masterly hands and active brains that secure success.

In those clever essays on social changes by George W. E. Russell, now so much talked of, he dwells a great deal on the power of home. "The State is built," he says, "upon the home, as a training-place for social virtue." This has to be cultivated ; not only must we make home beautiful, but we must make it enjoyable. Amusement, music, laughter, and joyousness generally should characterise it—a refuge from the worry and storm of life where its inmates are seen at its best. Worry should there be kept at bay, and healthy amusement cultivated at any cost, especially where there are young people. I find at family gatherings that the graphophone is a great adjunct to enjoyment, and the Columbia Phonograph Company, which has its headquarters here at 89, Great Eastern Street, E.C., is always formulating improvements and making fresh discoveries in the instrument which the young and old alike appreciate. Like the telegraph and the telephone, the graphophone marks an epoch in civilisation. It brings the amusements of the outside world—the music, the acting, and now even the literature of the day into our midst. For all sounds can be reproduced, and while you may listen to the Japanese National Anthem, the Port Arthur March, the very poem that His Majesty the Mikado composed and the cadets of the Military School at Tokio recited, you may also hear excerpts three minutes in length from such authors as Ian Maclaren, whose works have a world-wide reputation.

When George III. was king, England had a good deal to be thankful about, as far as the decorations of her homes were concerned. The best of upholsterers were teaching the rules of beauty, and there was a solidity in the results of their work which has survived the changes of the century and more that has intervened. A little earlier than his day beauty was still developing in the surroundings of home. French taste had shed its influence in its own country, and England had originated a notable school of design, from which we are now profiting. I am presenting to you some beautiful walls and ceiling, together with some fine furniture, which have been reproduced from the reign of William and Mary, as well as Anne and the Georges. Note the form of the back of the couch, and the pretty treatment beneath the seat. The canework at the back is partially hidden by crimson silk, which rather enhances the beauty of form. Any one desirous of decorating a house at its best in the Georgian and pre-Georgian times cannot do better than have recourse to Messrs. Graham & Banks, 445, Oxford Street. The charm of the wall and ceiling as backgrounds, as seen in the sketch below, will show you exactly what I mean.

A CHARMING OLD-FASHIONED INTERIOR SEEN AT MESSRS. GRAHAM & BANKS'.

THE · EDITOR'S · PAGE

THE coupons sent in for the Autograph Competition have now been carefully examined. No reader succeeded in finding correct solutions to the whole thirty-six, and some competitors were disqualified owing to disregarding the rules of the competition.

The first prize of a Fifty Guinea Piano is awarded to Miss E. Lambert, 91, Goldhurst Terrace, South Hampstead, N.W. The second prize, consisting of a Singer Cabinet Sewing Machine of the value of £16, is won by Miss Miller, St. Thomas, East Cowes. The third prize, it will be remembered, was a Columbia Graphophone with Thirty Records, which will now become the property of Miss Florence Hunt, 2, Felix Road, Stapleton Road, Bristol. The beautiful Leather Letter-Tray, which was offered as a fourth prize, is awarded to Mrs. F. Dobson, Ivy House, New Malden, Surrey.

The awards in connection with the additional Beauty Competition will be made in the Christmas Number, which will be ready on November 28, and will contain illustrated articles on nearly every subject that is of interest in a home of refinement, together with fiction by Stanley J. Weyman, Frankfort Moore, Rev. S. Baring-Gould, "Rita," G. B. Burgin, and others.

It will be noticed that the first of a series of papers entitled "The Truth About Man" is given this month. As the Editor believes that not all his readers will share the opinions of "A Spinster," he has decided each month to award money prizes to the two readers sending in the best original Defence of Man, written in reply to "A Spinster's" criticisms. The first prize will be One Guinea, and the second, Half a Guinea. Competitors must cut out the coupon on page 20 of the Advertisements, and forward this, together with their MS., so as to reach the Editor by the last day of the month in which the competition is given. Thus the last day for sending in criticisms of the instalment of "The Truth About Man," appearing in the November issue of THE LADY'S REALM, is November 30. No MS. must exceed five hundred words, and the Editor's decision in every case is final.

"LIFT WE NOW OUR HEARTS & VOICES,
JOIN WE ALL THE CHEERFUL CRY,
LEARNED BY SHEPHERDS FROM THE ANGELS:
GLORY BE TO GOD ON HIGH!"

A CHRISTMAS CAROL.

(From the original drawing by MISS A. L. BOWLEY.)

Photo by Henry Dixon & Son.

" ALLELUIA."

From the painting by Mr. T. C. Gotch.

A Painter of Womanhood.

BY MARION HEPWORTH DIXON.

IT is only a few months since Mr. Robert Fry, one of the ablest of our modern critics, was lamenting the death of symbolism in England. He raised the question, it is true, at the passing of that Colossus of the art world, Mr. Watts, but in doing so reverted to the old, old story of the maltreatment of our English Primitives of the 'fifties at the moment when Millais, Rossetti, and Holman Hunt founded their famous " Brotherhood." Now the hue and cry which greeted the exhibition of Millais' " Christ in the House of His Parents " (a picture familiarly known as " The Carpenter's Shop ") is difficult to conceive of in the twentieth century. Yet Charles Dickens, using his organ, *Household Words*, raised his voice in solemn protest against what he called the revolting ugliness of the canvas, and the philistine critics and the ignorant public were only too ready to join in

anathematising a school which was gradually and insidiously to regenerate the decorative arts of the modern world.

Not that this desirable consummation was accomplished in a day. The greatest of the Pre-Raphaelite brothers was destined to turn an apostate before the tenets of the school were either generally accepted or understood. Indeed, not only the original Pre-Raphaelites themselves, but their followers, William Morris and Burne-Jones, had grown to be considered in the light of insular eccentricities by the time that the Bavarian painter, Von Udhe, startled the Continent with his vast symbolic representations of Christ among the simple peasant folk of Southern Germany. But in the late 'eighties and early 'nineties the attitude of the general public had vastly changed. In forty years education had lifted the masses into some sort of appreciation of serious art. They no longer refused

Photo by Henry Dixon & Son.

" OLGA."

From the painting by Mr. T. C. Gotch.

to use their mental faculties in looking at a picture, while they began to appreciate the fact that the function of the painter is not exclusively to amuse. This in itself was a stride which made symbolic art possible in great public exhibitions, for art demands not only an audience, but a sympathetic audience.

It is necessary to state these somewhat bald facts in order to understand why Paris should have led the van of the new movement. For, as we have seen, it was not "La Ville Lumière" that invented symbolism. England and Germany had shown her the way. The superiority of the French lay in the fact that they had an educated public   Of that development his admirable canvases

ready to accept the new creed, and to welcome the astonishing can-vases which M. Henri Martin on the one hand, and M. Jean Béraud on the other, were already exhibiting in the rival ex-hibitions of the Champs Elysées and the Champs de Mars.

Now, I mention this precise moment in the history of symbolic art in France be-cause the subject of this article, Mr. T. C. Gotch, became a disciple of the new creed in the early 'nineties. Hitherto he had been an exponent of realism and *plein air*, a dweller at Newlyn, while he practised that shapely way of laying on paint which obtained in the Parisian *ateliers* when Bastien Lepage reigned supreme. We thus see that from "an out-and-out" realist Mr. Gotch received an impetus which, while keeping him closely in touch with Continental methods, proved to be peculiarly happy in assisting his artistic develop-ment.

Photo by Henry Dixon & Son.

"THE HEIR TO ALL THE AGES."

From the painting by Mr. T. C. Gotch.

Photo by Henry Dixon & Son.

" A PAGEANT OF CHILDHOOD."

From the painting by Mr. T. C. Gotch.

are the best exponent. His personal history can be told in a dozen lines. Born at Kettering on December 10, 1854, Thomas Cooper Gotch was educated at the Kettering Grammar School, and, like one of the most famous of our modern landscape painters, Mr. David Murray, was primarily intended for a business life. Thus we find both artists spending three or four of the most receptive years of their lives in uncongenial and unhelpful surroundings, when, flinging the routine of office life aside, they buckled to the strenuous task of educating themselves for an artistic career. Thus Mr. Gotch was fully twenty-one years of age when he set up an easel at Heatherly's art school ; but once having made up his mind to be a painter, the student's progress was phenomenal. Of work he was not afraid ; while in seeking to perfect himself in his medium he did not disdain to learn his lesson in many and divers lands. Baron Leys' well-known academy at Antwerp attracted Mr. Gotch first, as it had attracted both Mr. Napier Hemy and the late Onslow Ford. But with the future symbolist there were other and more potent voices calling. Returning to England, Mr. Gotch joined the Slade School ; but again wishing to widen his artistic horizon, he crossed over to France and enrolled himself among the

followers of the famous French painter, Jean Paul Laurens. Here the student remained close on three years, so that there is matter for small wonder that Mr. Gotch's technique became identified with the tradition in which he was trained. Clarity, directness, and sound drawing are tenets of the naturalistic creed, and to say that the English pupil subscribed to the articles of the faith goes without saying. Clean, dexterous, forceable, *bien observé*, there is much to recommend the French school which established its English offshoot at Newlyn, a spot at which Mr. and Mrs. Stanhope Forbes had already pitched their tent when Mr. Gotch returned to England. It was, then, in the nature of things that an artist trained under Jean Paul Laurens should gradually gravitate to Cornwall, and no less natural that his first canvases should deal with realistic representations of the life of the fisher-folk which surrounded him. Not that Newlyn satisfied the painter for long : a divine discontent, possibly necessary to the artistic equipment, drove Mr. Gotch on a voyage to Australia in 1883, while a few years later we find him planning a sketching tour in Denmark, and, again, in 1891 wintering in Italy.

It was before this date that Mr. Gotch gave the world the humorous canvas (a brilliant study in open-air effects) which he called "The Money Pig," and which depicts three children on the seashore, one of them holding her little playmates spellbound as she relates a whimsical story. The picture entitled "'Twixt Life and Death," a work which brought the artist prominently before the public, showed the sterner side of Newlyn life. For here, within the limit of four humble cottage walls, the tragic emphasis of a woman's love in the moment of crisis is conveyed in the uncompromising language of realism. From grave to gay, from comedy to tragedy, we see Mr. Gotch experimenting in many classes of subject before the moment of his final conversion came. For up to 1891, when the artist journeyed to Italy, he had occupied himself

Photo by Henry Dixon & Son.

" HOLY MOTHERHOOD."

From the painting by Mr. T. C. Gotch.

Photo by Henry Dixon & Son.

"THE DAWN OF WOMANHOOD.

From the painting by Mr. T. C. Gotch.

mainly with technical themes—with such problems, that is to say, as the lighting of his pictures and the exercise of rendering in pigment the actual atmosphere of life. Many of these characteristics remain in Mr. Gotch's symbolic work. The learned drawing, the loving rendering of surfaces, are there. But the change in the artist's outlook of necessity implies a change of venue, the manner becomes subordinate to the matter. In other words, Mr. Gotch is no longer concerned in giving us the mere copy in paint of the object seen, his purpose is to call forth and illuminate the inner and hidden meaning of visual things.

Now thus envisaged, the drastic change from such anecdotal realism as is conveyed in Mr. Gotch's early canvases to the decorative symbolism of "My Crown and Sceptre" and "The Child Enthroned" becomes easily understandable. Not that the influence of the Italian masters can be overlooked in even the briefest surmise of the artist's mental processes. From Newlyn to Italy seems a far cry, but Cornwall and Florence are not farther apart than are Mr. Gotch's early and later manners. For up to the present moment we have been con-

sidering the artist's change of subject only. But in crossing the Alps Mr. Gotch would seem to have changed his soul as well as his skies. What is evident is that he became a convert to the glowing colour of the Tuscan and Venetian schools, and from 1891 we find him clothing his allegorical figures in raiment of gorgeous textures, while he occupied his mind not only with symbols, but with colour schemes.

From this standpoint the picture already alluded to called "My Crown and Sceptre" may be looked upon as a revolt against what has been rather severely called "Newlyn colour-blindness." "A Golden Dream," at any rate, was Mr. Gotch's next venture—a picture which was exhibited with a portrait of Miss Hegan-Kennard in 1893. A portrait of his own daughter (if it is not an indiscretion to allude to an open secret) followed in 1894, and was instantly acclaimed under the significant title of "The Child Enthroned." Only twelve months later one of Mr. Gotch's most subtle and eerie canvases was exhibited at the Royal Academy, while a work entitled "The Child in the World" was seen at the New Gallery. The former picture is known to all art lovers as "Death the Bride," and depicts a wan, black-veiled, sybil-like woman, who, facing the spectator, lures him with her fatal and invincible smile. Wan poppies, the emblem of sleep, surround the beautiful seductress, whose beckoning movement is as haunting and enigmatic as any portrayed by Luini.

Not that the morbid and fantastic are Mr. Gotch's special prerogatives. Of the French degenerates' love of disease and death he would seem to have not the slightest trace. On the contrary, the serene and the virginal attract the artist to the exclusion of nearly every other quality, and it is to this love of purity and what for want of a better word I must call "detachment" in his allegorical figures that Mr. Gotch owes his hold on the public. What that hold is may be gauged by the painter's successes in America and on the other side of the Channel. For not only did Chicago honour the English artist, but two medals were awarded him by the Paris Salon of 1896, while, quickly following the example of Paris, Berlin equally singled out the new symbolist. That such distinctions had their effect in Mr. Gotch's native country goes without saying. It was impossible for England to lag behind in face

of this almost universal wave of approval. Thus in 1896 we find the large symbolic picture called "Alleluia" being secured for the nation out of the now much-disputed Chantrey Fund, and proving one of the few selections which have given entire satisfaction to the unbiassed public. For Mr. Gotch, it must be remembered, was an "outsider" and was practising a form of art that has seldom endeared itself to the more philistine of the older Academicians. More elastic and far-seeing, the provinces early

Photo by Henry Dixon & Son.

"DEATH THE BRIDE."

From the painting by Mr. T. C. Gotch.

recognised the merits of Mr. Gotch's work. Thus "A Golden Dream," a picture already alluded to, was purchased by the Corporation of Preston, while the important painting called "A Pageant of Childhood" was secured by the authorities of the Walker

contribution to Burlington House for 1897, the pictures called "Jubilate Deo," "Magnificat," and a portrait, "Edward, son of Professor Poulton," representing the symbolist at the New Gallery the same spring. In the same brief way, mention may be made of the

Photo by Henry Dixon & Son.

"A GOLDEN DREAM."

From the painting by Mr. T. C. Gotch.

Art Gallery at Liverpool. Actuated by the same laudable motive of acquiring a work by a rising artist, the Colonies joined hands with Preston and Liverpool. "The Story of a Money Pig" now hangs in the National Gallery of Cape Town, while not only the picture called "'Twixt Life and Death," but the symbolic work named "The Child Enthroned," was purchased by the Australian collector Mr. McCulloch, and is to be seen in the well-known collection at Queen's Gate.

Of more immediate efforts from the same hand little detailed description need be given. It will probably suffice to say that "The Heir to All the Ages" was Mr. Gotch's

canvas called "The Awakening," the portrait of Mrs. Thomas Buddicome, which followed three years later, and the circular picture called "The Message." This latter work was the artist's contribution to the Royal Academy of 1903, while as many as three paintings—namely, "Indecision," "Reading Aloud," and "The Portrait of a Lady "—were seen at the New Gallery. Always a staunch supporter of Mr. Hallé and Mr. Comyns Carr, Mr. Gotch sent the same number of pictures to the Regent Street exhibition last year. They were "The Sea Maiden," "Dear Lady Disdain," and the canvas called "Innocence."

THE CENTRAL HALL.

The Ladies' Automobile Club.

BY ANNESLEY KENEALY.

CLARIDGE'S HOTEL has been chosen as the happy and elegant meeting-place of the members of the Ladies' Auto-mobile Club of Great Britain and Ireland. Here is established a charming coterie of the car craft.

The writer of this article had the privilege of suggesting the formation of a Ladies' Automobile Club, to be kept sacred to the sisters of the sport. And the immense and immediate success of the scheme, and the rush for membership so soon as the club came into being, showed that there was room at least for one more woman's club.

The motor-car has long since passed the toy stage and settled down into working—and very hard-working—harness. And the fact that already there are in existence some three hundred of "Claridge's Chauffeuses," as we are euphemistically christened, shows that the woman motorist is in real earnest in the matter of horseless locomotion.

"But why do feminine motorists want a special club of their own? Why would not an ordinary social club-house suit their requirements?" is the question of many who are not motor initiates. These do not know that the Ladies' Automobile Club has not been formed for tea and chatter alone. We have these delightful accessories of life in a very pleasant form, to the accompaniment of Claridge's most excellent band, though some of our chatter may include the wisdom of the wise regarding carburetters or float feeds, and the sympathetic exchange of views as to the influence of ignition on explosive force.

But over and above such absorbingly interesting automobile confidences, the Ladies' Club is, and by its constitution must for ever remain, the central authority in the

MRS. E. MANVILLE WITH HER 14 H.P. DAIMLER, "THE TOMTIT."

woman motorist who pays her five-guinea annual subscription to the Ladies' Automobile Club of Great Britain and Ireland. As a matter of fact, the privileges are so many that it is worth while to become interested in motoring in order to join this very smart and sportsman-like club.

The Ladies' Club is said to possess a larger percentage of "titles" among its members than any other club in London. It most assuredly aims at representing the automobile aristocracy and remaining exclusive, although the club is markedly animated by a most friendly spirit of *camaraderie*.

feminine motor matters of Great Britain and Ireland. It is affiliated to its somewhat stern parent, the Automobile Club, on terms which allow practically all the privileges of masculine motorists to their less "scorching" sisters.

A member of the L.A.C. may take part in all races, sports, and runs held under the *ægis* of the Automobile Club. Does she contemplate taking her car abroad, she can command the privilege of the Automobile Club "open sesame," whereby many Customs formalities and some of the Continental red tape used in tying up the liberty of the foreigner may be avoided.

A large array of British hotels guarantee to house and feed Automobile Club members at a special discount; repairers throughout the country similarly contract to take a discount off club members' bills. The Motor Union fights the legal battles of the motorist who labours unjustly under the tyranny of an old-fashioned magistracy opposed to new methods of transport. A share in all these advantages accrues to the

The three vice-presidents—the Lady Cecil Scott Montagu, Mrs. Gerard Leigh, and the Lady Beatrice Rawson—are not only

Photo by Esmé Collings.

THE HON. MRS. CHARLES FORESTER,
Who is a member of the Committee of the Ladies' Automobile Club.

enthusiastic devotees of the motor, but are most skilful drivers.

The Lady Cecil Scott Montagu, a daughter of the late Marquis of Lothian and wife of the Hon. John Scott Montagu, M.P., who is interested in motor politics, drives a 22 h.p. Daimler, has toured throughout Great Britain and France, and took part in the 1902 thousand-mile trial runs. Lady Cecil condemns goggles and mask for car wear, and sets the fashion of dainty dressing on the motor.

open air, and devotes herself to her charming children.

The Lady Beatrice Rawson, also a Vice-President, owns two cars on which she has driven many thousands of miles without in any way lessening her love of horses. Lady Beatrice has recently been elected a member of the East Surrey Automoblile Club, this being the first occasion on which a lady has been admitted to membership in a masculine Automobile Club.

The club-house in Brook Street, W., is

THE DINING-ROOM.

Mrs. Gerard Leigh is Honorary Secretary and Vice-President of the club, and to her magic gifts of tact and sympathy, added to a rare talent for organisation, much of its conspicuous success and popularity are due. She drives a 15 h.p. Charron-Girardot & Voigt car on which she has covered some five thousand miles, and is an enthusiast on the "health, happiness, and wide horizon" resulting from the use of a motor-car. At her beautiful country home, Kidbrooke Park in Sussex, she interests herself in golf, gardening, and her motor-car, lives in the

small, but with the dimensions of Claridge's Hotel in reserve it has power to add indefinitely to its area. Its private entrance and its semi-detachment from the hotel proper make this motor-wing of Claridge's into a separate club-house, although easy communication exists within between the clubrooms and the central hall and restaurant of the hotel. The Ladies' Automobile is the first club to form its headquarters at an hotel, thus simplifying the problem of feminine life, " How to Cope with the Modern Servant."

A CLUB BEDROOM.

accounts for car repairs and the consumption of petrol —but they may not speak. Red striped silk tapestry adorns the walls, the pretty French windows are most charmingly draped, and the room breathes restfulness.

The White Drawing-room forms a lovely colour scheme in green and white. It is well stocked with palms and ferns and flowering shrubs, and is gay and lively of an afternoon with motoring members and their friends.

But the strains of the band in the adjoining central hall are apt, especially during the

While it is noticeable that the clubman simply revels in domestic detail, the mysteries of the *cuisine* and the supervision of the storeroom, these departments of her club are the *bête noire* of the average woman. After grappling with these problems at home she has had sufficient surfeit of cooks, butchers' orders, and the mathematics of the *menu*. Her club has no value if it do not give her a rest from this ceaseless routine.

Many men, on the other hand, with that love of domesticity inherent in the sex, a yearning sternly suppressed in her own interests by wise woman—for her value as a matrimonial asset is partly gone if she allow man to develop his latent genius for housekeeping—delight to probe and fuss in the kitchen regions of their club because that luxury is denied them at home. Hence the ideal woman's club of the future will doubtless form a branch of an hotel where servants will cease to trouble, and the weary women members of the committee will be at rest from the treadmill round of "ordering the dinner."

On the club ground floor is the Red Drawing or Silence Room, reserved for members only. Here they may pen their notes, take their tea, add up their

MRS. GERARD LEIGH,

Hon. Secretary of the Ladies' Automobile Club.

NANCYE, THE TWO AND A HALF YEAR OLD DAUGHTER OF MRS. GRANVILLE KENYON,
IN HER FAVOURITE MOTOR-CAR.

As soon as she is old enough Nancye intends to join the Ladies' Automobile Club

Should the club bedrooms be already occupied, country members may find accommodation in the hotel on easy terms of discount off the normal rates.

Claridge's possesses a large garage in which club members find a free shelter for their cars either when running up to town for a day's shopping or when stopping in the hotel.

Nobody can accuse the lady motorists of lack of practicality. Special reduced rates have been made with repair shops in the district, so that should my lady's car be "hung up" through something going wrong with the works, or if her supply of petrol run short, the fact that she belongs to the L.A.C. will enable her to get the wrong righted and her tank filled up at bargain rates.

A club badge of solid silver and enamel in Lincoln green or deep red has been most artistically designed by Mrs. Herbert Lloyd, a well-known motorist and one of the club

season, to tempt both hostesses and guests to desert the clubrooms and join this fashionable "five o'clock" function, which at Claridge's is well known to attract the most lovely frocks and frills of Society. Club members and their friends lunch and dine at a somewhat reduced tariff in the hotel restaurant, and many pleasant parties unload from electric and petrol brougham to take their supper after the play at the special little tables reserved in the restaurant for members and their friends, despite the fact that this latter-day feminine club has the distinction of being more expensive than any other club in London.

At present the club possesses only two bedrooms for the use of country members, but the scope of the club is already so widening out that the membership is out-running the confines of present accommodation

Copyright " Motoring Illustrated.

THE SILENCE ROOM AT THE LADIES' AUTOMOBILE CLUB.

MRS. A. RAWLINSON,
Who shares her husband's taste for motor-racing.

police and being summoned on a charge of speeding not wisely but too well.

Perhaps the immunity of women drivers from sur-veillance is due to police chivalry. We choose to ascribe it to a well-developed car conscience. It is certainly true that the motor woman so far is not a candidate for the "hurry heaven" which is the Mecca of many men motorists. A very high speed, unless the car be fitted with a glass screen, not only destroys a woman's every vestige of beauty and neatness, but it spoils her artistic appreciation of the

Committee. This badge is worn as a brooch, or on a larger scale is affixed to the members' cars, so that all who see these speed by may know that the owner belongs to the L.A.C.

So far the club has adopted no distinctive colours, though the matter is on the *tapis* as a sportsmanlike adjunct to the gymkhanas, club runs, and driving competitions many members intend to enter for.

The Ladies' Club run to Homburg was a distinctive and notable achievement of so youthful an organisation. Several mem-bers took part and drove their cars *via* Harwich and the Hook of Holland to Homburg on June 17 for the most notable and remarkable Gordon-Bennett race yet run. The route lay through the most picturesque country *via* Rotterdam, Utrecht, Dusseldorf, Cologne, Coblenz, and Frankfort, which led the motorists beside the most beautiful parts of the Rhine.

One striking point about the feminine motorist—or motorina—is that she has hardly ever figured before the law courts as a speeder. Her brother of the car is always falling victim to the traps and wiles of the

Copyright " The Car Illustrated."
THE LADY CECIL SCOTT MONTAGU,
Vice-President of the Ladies' Automobile Club.

points of the scenery and the many charms of roadside picturesqueness. For her own part the writer would as soon accept a position as engine-driver as speed a car at anything

over a road which in parts is in very bad going condition, arrived at 11.15 a.m., played two rounds of golf and motored back to Dupplin by 6.45, having thus covered sixty-

Copyright "Motoring Illustrated."

THE DRAWING-ROOM.

beyond twenty miles an hour. The mile or more a minute ambition evidently has no power to charm the feminine heart.

The man inoculated with the speed virus finds a more or less salutary anti-toxin in Court fines. But very few women want to urge their cars at the pace of a rifle bullet or convert a delightful means of locomotion into a source of rush and vibration.

The Countess of Kinnoull is one of the very beautiful members of the Automobile Club and an all-weather motorist. In her 14 h.p. Chenard & Walcker car which ranked among her wedding presents she recently motored from her charming Highland home —Dupplin Castle, Perth—to London.

Lady Kinnoull is an ardent and accomplished motorist, and often drives over on her car from Dupplin Castle to St. Andrews for a round on the Royal and Antient links. On one occasion she left the Castle at 9.45 a.m., ran the thirty-three miles to St. Andrews

six miles in about three hours without a single mechanical trouble.

Lady Kinnoull dresses simply and daintily on the car, preferring a three-quarter jackal fur coat for fine and a leather coat for wet weather, a small toque and motor veil, short skirt and thick shoes, which she regards as easier to use than boots for the foot work involved in driving.

The Hon. Mrs. Charles Forester, a member of the Ladies' Club Committee, is a further exponent of the fact that beauty and skill in motoring go so frequently hand in hand. On her 20 h.p. Wolseley car she drove some twenty-two thousand miles during last year, and she is opposed to the begoggled and bemasked kit of many women motorists.

The Lady Margaret Jenkins, also a member of the Committee, is well known for her enthusiasm for horses and for her marked skill as a whip. Nevertheless she has adopted automobilism *con amore*,

Photo by Alice Hughes.

THE LADY MARGARET JENKINS,
Who is a most enthusiastic motorist.

although she does not herself manipulate the levers, on the score that motor driving entails so much greater strain on one's attention than the driving of horses, and consequently is more tiring.

Mrs. A. Rawlinson shares with very keen zest and sympathy her husband's taste for the sport of motor-racing. She has frequently accompanied him on his racing Darracq when he has been rehearsing for a speed contest, but she confesses to a prejudice against more than sixty miles an hour. "It is too much like being suffocated when you get beyond a mile a minute," she says. Mrs. Rawlinson's true love of the motor-car and all its aggravating ways in the matter of tactless breakdown far from railways and repair shops is shown by the fact that she has stood by a car with a hopeless tyre puncture throughout an entire night on a deserted country road without regret or pity for the sorrows of a stranded woman. This shows the true courage of the heaven-born motorist. Most mortals under such circumstances feel a spice of malice against the motor mechanism. But Mrs. Rawlinson's love of and loyalty to her car are proof even against a summer's night spent sitting on a milestone waiting for a new tyre.

Her husband, Mr. A. Rawlinson, late of the 17th Lancers, is one of the most distinguished polo-players of the day, and he is well on the way to taking an equally high rank in the annals of the motor race-track. He is a magnificent motor-whip, and drives with a style and smartness entirely his own. On one of the three racing Darracqs specially built in Glasgow for the Gordon-Bennett race of 1904 he has given some admirable exhibitions of driving skill. For success in motor-racing depends quite as much—and some persons think more—on the man at the levers as the success of a horse in the Derby depends on the skill of his rider.

Mrs. Rawlinson is another exponent of the art and doctrine of daintiness and personal charm on the car; indeed, with so many types of feminine grace and beauty as appear in this article, nobody can ever again possess the courage to revive the tradition, which should have been dead and buried years ago, that motoring destroys feminine attractions. Perhaps it was a libel invented by the comic papers. Anyway, it has long ceased to have any point, since the earliest type of woman motorist who delighted to array herself as a species of automobile scarecrow has not survived to any extent. Woman's innate

Photo by Bassano.

Annesley Kenealy

love of the beautiful invariably reasserts itself.

Annual general meetings are not usually very decorative functions. But the annual general meeting of the Ladies' Automobile Club of Great Britain and Ireland brought together such a goodly company of graceful and beautiful womanhood that for the time being it seemed rather severe that the doors were sternly closed to the stronger and admiring sex. Which brings us to a very charming trait in the temperament of the feminine motorist.

Whereas it has long been notorious that no woman is permitted to cross the portals of the masculine Automobile Club, the Ladies' Club offers no reprisals. Husbands, fathers, brothers, and even masculinity in nowise related to the members are invited most hospitably to luncheon, tea, dinner, or an after-the-play supper. This attitude of a soft and hospitable answer to our brethren of the car may have the effect of turning

away the Automobile Club's wrath from women ! But it is only fair and just to remark that though they exclude us from their tea-parties and social functions, the attitude of the Automobile Club towards its young sister has been most kind and sportsmanlike. Indeed, the path of the L.A.C. would have been far more troublous and thorny had it not been for the helpful brotherhood accorded it by the older and more experienced Automobile Club of Great Britain and Ireland.

The first motor meet and parade was held on June 9, the procession, headed by the president, the Duchess of Sutherland, being witnessed by the King and Queen from a balcony of Buckingham Palace. A subsequent run to Ranelagh on the same afternoon, after a full-dress parade in Hyde Park, constituted the public *début* of the Ladies' Club, followed during the summer by a series of pleasant runs, meets, and garden parties.

Photo by E. Brooks.

LORD VIVIAN AND MRS. McCALMONT,
Who are both enthusiasts of the motor.

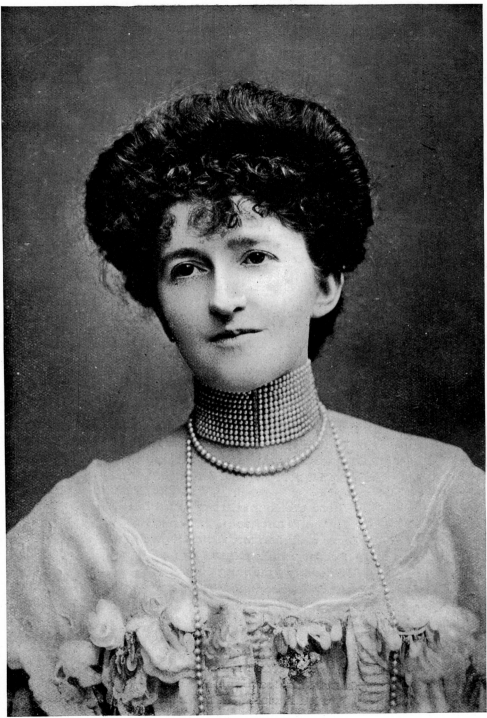

Photo by Langfier.

THE LADY ST. OSWALD,

Who has recently been entertaining considerably at Nostell Priory, Wakefield.

Photo by Langfier.

MISS GLADYS WILSON,

The talented daughter of Mr. Charles Wilson, of Warter Priory, Yorks.

Photo by Lallie Charles.

THE DUCHESS OF SUTHERLAND.

Photo by Langfier.

MISS VIOLET WOOD,

Whose engagement to Mr. Patrick de Bathe is announced.

MRS. RANDELL,

Who is a most enthusiastic motorist.

The Truth About Man

By a Spinster.

ILLUSTRATED BY FACTS FROM HER OWN PRIVATE HISTORY.

The author of " The Truth About Man" is a well-known novelist, who prefers not to reveal her identity. In her opening chapters she declares herself a free lance whose mission it is to show Man to himself, and warn him of sundry rocks in his path. She subdivides him into the Irresistible, the Admirable, and the Marriageable, and discourses on the unattractiveness of the Ideal Woman.

As he believes that the views of " A Spinster" may not be shared by all the readers of THE LADY'S REALM *the Editor has decided to offer prizes, month by month, for the best criticisms of " The Truth About Man." Particulars will be found on page 20 of the advertisements.*

CHAPTER III.

The Spinster hedges a little, and ends by quoting a Maiden Lady's letter in justification of her previous remarks.

AFTER making the somewhat sweeping assertion about Man the Inconsistent and the Ideal Woman, in my last chapter, I am seized with a dread lest my remarks may be construed into an attack, not only upon dear Man himself (who is certainly most estimable and delightful—till you know him !), but also upon well-established canons of perfection. Far be any such design from your humble spinster, whose standard of virtue is far beyond her own limited reach, but none

the less cherished. No; I did not intend to imply, for one moment, that the Ideal Woman is never to be found in the married state. On the contrary, at the risk of appearing paradoxical, I affirm that the majority of wives and mothers are of this admirable type.

The statement requires an explanation, and here it is. I contend that while Man really prefers the coquette to the modest human violet of his pretences, he has no power to keep her, when once married, a coquette. No more than, being a Lothario, he is able to maintain that character successfully under the yoke of matrimony. For the wedded couple, like a pair of skittish horses in harness, soon find that they must either pull together in harmony or hurt themselves. There can be little or no harmony between two persons who are each seeking excitement apart, and so the coquette often becomes, from necessity, an Ideal Woman ; the Lothario, for the same reason, a Good Fellow.

The fact of having several small imitators around them, with ears and eyes wide open, ready to reproduce all their faults, may have still more to do with this strange transformation. I have a theory—it may be quite wrong, but I hold it firmly—that even I, the most unideal of spinsters, might have become a model of the womanly virtues had I been haunted by miniatures of myself with round watchful eyes, copying all my ways and trying to grow up like " mummy " !

But the fact that marriage can have this wonderfully regenerating effect only goes to prove the excellence of its design, and to rebuke Man for his inconsistency. If he pretends to like ideal qualities in the maiden, he ought to cultivate them in her, to set the seal of his approval upon the third finger of her left hand. If he doesn't—if he prefers the society of the coquette, the unregenerate damsel who prinks, and powders, and wears Louis Quinze heels and straight-fronted corsets—let him be honest and say so. It isn't fair to make the innocent and unwary girl believe she must give up all her pretty gewgaws, her little natural vanities and bewitching, naughty ways in order that he may crown her with his royal love, and then turn his back upon her to run after a flirt in fashion-plate attire ! Such deception is mean and unworthy the Lord of Creation.

I was greatly impressed, a few years back, on reading in a weekly paper a pathetic letter from one of these simple dupes. It was such a moving epistle that I cut it out, and am thus able to quote it in support of my argument. Read it, O Man, and blush for yourself ! It is headed :

THE DECAY OF MAN.

I am a simple woman and very well brought up. My mother was a simple woman, and she taught me that if I did as I was told, and said my prayers, and learnt to sew, and cook, and knit, and keep house, and talk prettily, some day a man would come along and want to marry me. He has not come, and I am still waiting. I have never tried to find that special man, or to attract any other one who came my way, because that would be bold and unmaidenly. I have never learnt any manly games, because they are unwomanly and unbecoming. I have never cultivated my mind, because men dislike clever women. I have never done anything modern at all. My only amusements have been playing the piano and needlework. I am really domesticated, affectionate, meek, and even pretty ; qualified in every way to make any man a good all-round kind of wife, after the pattern we so often read about. But still he does not come. And now I am no longer a girl. I have reached that stage when one rather dreads sitting near the electric light, when one refrains from taking a walk in the sun without putting on a spotted veil. To tell the truth, I find existence very dull. There is so little to fill up my time : for my parents are well off, and there is no need for me to cook, or make beds, or darn clothes. I do a lot of fancy work and read a number of library books ; but even these delights are apt to cloy upon over-indulgence in them. Sometimes I am tempted to envy the girls I see going off on their bicycles to golf or hockey ; or the others who write books, lecture, and earn their livings in some way or another. At least they do not endure continually the half-contemptuous pity of their relatives ; they do not feel themselves to be hopeless failures. And by going out into the world the chance comes to them of meeting men who may be so good as to marry them.

But this is only the preface of what I started to say. I have been thinking over the subject lately, and I cannot help coming to the conclusion that there must be something wrong with man. He seems to be so different from the creature I have heard and read about. In the first place, my mother always told me that every man wanted to marry a nice girl, and have a home and children. So far as I can see, he does not want anything of the kind. In all the books

I have read, he falls in love violently, woos passionately, worships with chastity, and weds with devotion. I suppose there are, or have been, men who go on like that, but I have never met one. I have often seen them "spooney," but never passionate. And I want to know whose fault that is—the man's or my mother's? It is not mine, because I am the ideal woman of a system, just as I was made, and fit for nothing but to be a wife.

I have lived all my life in a moderately sized country town, and this town is full of spinsters and old bachelors. There are almost as many of the latter as the former. Most of them have dangled about me at one time or another, and they have also dangled about the other spinsters. But nothing has come of it—except gossip. We have all been engaged to one another by hearsay—no more. My two brothers, who are unmarried men, and live at home very comfortably (they are both getting rather fat and bald), might have married extremely nice girls, quite as domesticated as I am ; but, as they expressively phrase it, they "are not having any." "No fear," said one of them to me a few days back, when I was recommending a desirable sister-in-law : "what do I want to marry for? I have just enough money to live in comfort without saddling myself with a wife and children." In short, they fight shy of matrimony. Every few months they go up to London "on the spree," as they call it. They spend a good deal of time at the theatres and music-halls, and for a week after their return we hear of nothing but the various beauties of the stage they have seen. They must spend a good deal of money on those places of amusement, on dinners and suppers, and so on, according to their own accounts ; and certainly their appetites are spoiled for good plain fare and simple society when they get back. But, although they wax enthusiastic over the London ladies they have seen and met, neither of them brings home a wife.

At the same time, we are continually reading in the newspapers and magazines that the Earl of Tweedledum has married Miss Trotty Dimple of the Gaiety, or the Duke of Tweedledee has espoused Miss Pinky Pearl, whose high kicking has electri-

fied the halls. This seems strange to a simple, well-brought-up young woman, who has been taught that such persons are not to be mentioned in genteel circles, and that the place they illuminate are sinks of iniquity. Why does man, and not only mere man, but man with a grand British aristocratic title, cull these tarnished flowers to wear in his bosom? It is very perplexing and upsetting to all one's long-cherished ideas as to the rewards of virtue and vice.

I can but conclude that man must be growing less of a man than he used to be in the days of our simple mothers. He no longer falls in love with woman *as* woman, it appears, but only desires her when he sees other fellows running after her. Nothing else can stimulate his jaded fancy or his passion. Once upon a time he may have yearned for home, wife and offspring ; now he shirks the responsibility of fatherhood and fears the restraint of domesticity. He wants to avoid all trouble and enjoy himself ; he does not dare to plunge into the deeper waters of life. It is true that in escaping the cares he may miss the raptures, but that does not concern him, for he has ceased either to believe in or desire raptures. He wishes to be amused, not to *feel*. And if this is not the first sign of approaching decay, I should like to know what is? Before we die sensation grows weaker. As an artless feminine creature who would have liked to build a nest and rear a brood, I ask most humbly—what is to become of us if we are not sought by our natural mates? We are worse off than Adam before the miracle of Eve's creation, and even bridge will not console us.

I submit that the plainest sign of man's decadence is the fact that he is always grumbling at woman. In the good old days he just took her in hand and did what he would with her. Then he created : now he only criticises.

CHAPTER IV.

The Spinster continues to descant upon Love, and analyses its effect on mature Man.

WHEN a man of ripe years really falls in love—an occurrence of greater rarity than most people suppose, for what he calls love is usually about as strong a passion as a rabbit feels for parsley—he exhibits himself in such natural colours that one might take him for a boy. In fact he becomes a boy again, for the nonce, ardent, diffident, eager, nervous, modestly afraid and childishly violent. Sometimes he assumes all this and acts the part of a lovesick boy to gain certain ends that are as well calculated as his business projects ; but in many cases he is not acting—he simply follows an impulse and lets himself go.

I have known men of thirty and forty lose their heads as completely and absurdly as any lad of sixteen.

What things they say and do when this happens !

I wonder if a really beautiful and fascinating woman is ever able to maintain the least respect for Man ! She must so often see him in a condition of pitiable lunacy. As I said before, I am neither beautiful nor fascinating, and yet men have raved to me of my beauty until I have almost doubted the evidence of my own eyes and the truth of my looking-glass. They have called me ":goddess," "angel," "enchantress," "darling," " pet," " blessing," " treasure," etc., etc., over and over a thousand times ; have fallen at my feet and sworn to die without a moment's delay if I refused them ! Altogether it would be impossible to exaggerate the frenzy of their words or the wildness of their behaviour ; and perhaps it would be equally impossible to make any description believable to the reader who has not witnessed Man's amorous insanity. He gives himself right away, for the moment, to an extent we can never understand, and it is marvellous with what ease and rapidity he recovers himself afterwards. A woman who had lost self-control and commonsense like that would be so ashamed that she would probably go and bury herself in a convent !

Now if Man can make this exhibition before a woman of no special charm, one cannot help speculating upon his probable attitude towards the woman of great beauty and witchery. Surely she must see him as no other ever sees him : helpless, fatuous, unreasonable, almost imbecile. Of course the proportion of men who give way thus under the fire of passion is not large—perhaps one in ten—but there must be quite enough of them to lower a seductive woman's estimate of Man's general intelligence. One would like to know what Delilah, Cleopatra, Ninon L'Enclos, and other enticing beauties, ancient and modern, have thought of the Lord of Creation in their inmost hearts. I fear their private opinion would not be flattering to his strength of mind !

But is his passion sincere, asks the simple maiden in earnest inquiry—does he mean what he says when he vows devotion and all sorts of things ? Man himself will be the last to maintain that he is. In confidence he will declare that these paroxysms are but part of the game that men and women play, for the love of it ; that he has only been amusing himself and flattering her, because she loves to be flattered—this he will say when his fever is over. The rapture, the frenzy, the wild declarations have been but to please her and further his own designs.

Do not believe him.

There are, as I have already observed, cases where Man has simulated passion for ulterior ends ; but they are not common. When he makes a fool of himself at the feet of an attractive woman he knows, it is true, that his adoration will be sweet to her (as it always is, whatever she may pretend) ; but this is not the reason he shows himself so obsessed. He raves simply because a selfish, greedy passion has flown to his head and swamped his intellect, because he has lost control of himself and all the commonsense he ever possessed. He swears and vows and pours out streams of endearing names, just as the lion roars when he is hungry and smells a nice fresh kid. There is something delightfully primitive about it, something natural and vital and thrilling about this capability of falling head over ears in love, that appeals to most women. It does to me. The lion is an impressive brute, and the man in love is an impressive human animal. It is true we cannot exactly admire and esteem his mode of action, but we are carried away by it. And we certainly prefer to be wooed ravenously rather than coldly.

So it is not the passion itself that I have to bring up against Man the mature; it is the remarkable brevity of that passion.

Unlike the boy, whose adoration is founded upon idealism, a peculiar spiritual quality that preserves it from decay, the Man not only ceases, very soon and very abruptly, to express his sentiments and declare his aspirations, but, apparently, forgets all he has said and done! It is this that galls and annoys us. We never expect the sudden *volte-face*, the unwonted coolness and dignity, the rapid leap from the torrid to the frigid zone, that is one of Man's most extraordinary phenomena. He seems able, in an incredibly short space of time, to change his front completely, and obliterate, with one sweep of the mind, all memory of what has gone before. If a woman is ever so ill-advised as to remind a man of what he has once said or sworn, if she is ever so foolish as to reproach him with fickleness or to ask, "Do you remember?" he will turn upon her with an insolent stare, if not an insulting laugh, and forswear all his former words and actions. Either he does not remember, or it pleases him to pretend he does not.

I have sometimes, in pondering over the problem, wondered whether there may not be a simple enough reason for this mysterious change. May not a man in love be precisely the same as a man in liquor? We do not expect the drunkard to keep the promises he makes when inebriated; why, then, should we expect the intoxicated lover to mean anything he says? We cannot doubt that certain women have about their personality some weird, intoxicating atmosphere that flies to his head, and the old legends of Circe and the Sirens have had some foundation in fact. But when a man knows himself to have been intoxicated by strong drink he has usually the grace to feel ashamed of himself afterwards, and not to boast of his overthrow. When he has lost his senses over a woman the first thing he does on recovery is either to pretend he never did anything of the kind, or else just get up on a house-top and crow!

Well, we cannot alter his nature; we must take him as he is, "for better, for worse," and the only course we can pursue is to make ourselves as invulnerable as possible, to learn how to manage him, inebriated or sober, and to play the game with him in a sportsmanlike way, without hurting ourselves in the contest. In my next chapter I will venture to give a few suggestions for the use and management of Man when he is in love.

(To be continued.)

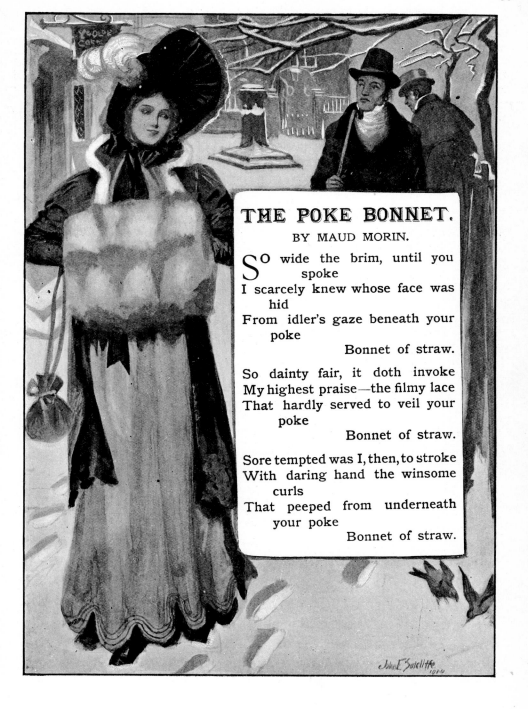

THE POKE BONNET.

BY MAUD MORIN.

So wide the brim, until you
       spoke
I scarcely knew whose face was
    hid
From idler's gaze beneath your
    poke
              Bonnet of straw.

So dainty fair, it doth invoke
My highest praise—the filmy lace
That hardly served to veil your
    poke
              Bonnet of straw.

Sore tempted was I, then, to stroke
With daring hand the winsome
    curls
That peeped from underneath
    your poke
              Bonnet of straw.

How to Defy the Cold.

BY "NARCISSA."

THERE is a saying, which probably originated among the roses and nightingales of Eden from the Mother of all Living, that a really beautiful woman is one who looks beautiful in every conceivable situation. Naturally, with perfect health, and a perfect climate, a purely vegetarian diet, without a worry, where dressmakers' bills had no terrors and a milliner did not exist, a woman would have no excuse for not being always beautiful.

But it would be hard indeed on lovely modernity if she was refused the palm of beauty merely because there were occasions when her eyes were not quite so bright as usual, her complexion not quite so clear, and her nose, perchance, slightly pink-tipped. Eve herself would have failed to look altogether lovely in a dentist's chair or a bathing-cap, and an east wind would most assuredly have deprived my lady of her delicate tinting. And it is on wintry winds and inclement weather, and their effects on one who would always be fair that I discourse to-day. A healthy girl in the late teens or early twenties may (?)—I write "may" with a big note of interrogation attached—look all the bonnier for her contact with the elements, and often comes in with sparkling eyes, rosy cheeks, and hair becomingly wind-tossed. But after twenty-five the effects of the winds and weather are not wholly lovely, the eyes are more likely to become reddened, the rosy cheeks purple, and the wind-tossed locks merely unbecomingly ruffled.

The knuckles rest lightly on the shoulders, and the arms are thrown back, while a deep breath is taken.

First and foremost, I am afraid it is necessary to inflict a little hygiene on my readers, not much, but just enough; for health and beauty, as I am for ever preaching, go hand-in-hand.

The people whose health—and beauty in consequence — suffers most in winter are those inclined to be thin and with proportionately delicate skins. Cod liver oil (it is not necessary to shudder and to put down the magazine in disgust, for there is a mitigatory " or " coming) or cream, for those who cannot digest the first-named remedy, should be taken regularly throughout the winter months. It is one of the very best safeguards against the sundry colds and winter ailments that the flesh is heir to.

Invariably throw a scarf across the face while going from the house to the carriage.

Heat-forming foods should be partaken of, and plenty of sugar, butter, and potatoes eaten, but not too much meat. The hot bath in the morning followed by a sponge down with cold, but not icy, water is bracing for those who can stand it, especially if followed by friction with warm, rough turkey towels, and a cup of cocoa made with milk sipped while dressing.

In order to ensure circulation being kept in a good condition, a few simple physical exercises should be done daily, the first and foremost of which is common or garden skipping.

The following breathing exercises, too, are invaluable for preventing colds in the head and quickening the circulation. Stand, with the heels together and the chest thrown well out, before an open window ; close the mouth and take a deep inspiration through the nose ; expire gently, *without holding the breath*, six times ; then, closing one nostril with the forefinger, breathe through the unclosed nostril three times, repeating the process by closing the other side. These two exercises have the advantage of keeping the passages of the nose and throat in excellent working order. Finally, during intervals of the day, do what, for want of a better name, I will call the yawn exercise, wherein the shoulders are thrown back and a deep breath taken meantime.

Many women suffer both in health and beauty because they will not dress warmly enough, having some mistaken idea that a warm garment means an increase of inches. Now most English women can, with advantage, stand a slight increase of bulk, but for those who have a rooted objection to this it

Liquid powder applied evenly all over the face with a large camel-hair brush forms a thin artificial skin.

avoided as much as possible. The bed-room should be of the same temperature as the living-rooms; but it is infinitely preferable to sleep in a cold room, rather than have it warmed by a gas fire or oil stove. The windows are shut up, the stove is lighted, the chill is certainly taken from the atmosphere, but so is the purity also.

Coming from the ballroom or theatre, it is often necessary to stand in the open doorway while waiting for a carriage. The cold air striking upon the face, often already flushed and dry by reason of the hot room, has a most injurious effect; therefore a scarf should always be thrown across the face while waiting. A long drive in the east wind brings out innumerable wrinkles, and gives the whole face a pinched

is possible now-a-days to obtain light, porous underclothing which is deliciously warm and yet fits so closely that it does not detract from the slenderness of the wearer. The feet, above all, must be kept warm and the foot-wear not tight; the stockings may be openwork, provided that they are of wool. Long-sleeved vests must be worn if any chilliness is experienced, those of Shetland wool being, in my opinion, quite the nicest.

Women who live where there are great extremes of heat or cold rarely or ever have good complexions. It is the daughters of temperate climates whose pink-and-white tints are usually so enviable. Coming from a hot to a cold room should therefore be

and aged appearance, reddens the nose, and roughens the skin permanently. Before going out on a cold day, therefore, it is necessary for the thin-skinned woman to protect her face with a layer of purest cold cream, which should be gently massaged into the face, not forgetting the tips of the ears and end of the nose. Wipe off any superfluity of grease, and lightly dust the face with powder; anoint the lips with lip salve before going out and on coming in: in this way they will not become cracked. If preferred, a liquid powder should be applied to the face with a large camel-hair brush, and wiped off with a soft handkerchief before it is quite dry. By-the-bye, liquid powder should never be washed off, but removed at night with cold cream. A gauze or lace veil is also a protection, but it should be left hanging, and not tucked under the chin; otherwise the breath is apt to condense upon the face, imparting a most unlovely appearance when the veil is lifted. The woman who hunts or takes violent exercise of any sort in winter will do well on coming in to bathe her face in buttermilk, and on all accounts should avoid the fireside for a couple of hours after exposure to the wind.

Next to the face the hands suffer most in winter. How rare a really beautiful hand is now, since the harp has gone out of fashion and gardening come in! Most of the troubles that afflict the hands in winter are owing to improper washing and drying. The water should be warm, neither hot nor cold; either soft or softened artificially. A pennyworth of oatmeal bought from the grocer's will keep the hands in condition for some time; and while on the subject of cosmetics I would impress upon my readers the desirability, if they would preserve their beauty, of never using any thing unless they know the ingredients of which it is composed. In the good old days every gentlewoman prepared her own powders and potions, and in consequence saved both her money and her appearance.

To return to the hands. Partially dry the hands and anoint them with glycerine and rose-water; then complete the drying process, treating each finger separately. It is perfectly astonishing the number of people who are under the delusion that glycerine does not suit them. If sufficiently *diluted* with rose-water, its healing properties are invaluable, and rarely indeed will it be found to redden the skin. *Never* sleep in gloves. If the treatment I have already described is rigidly adhered to, this is absolutely unnecessary. Where there is a tendency to chilblains the fingers should be massaged and each joint exercised. Finally, the thumb and finger of the one hand

Never allow the lips to become cracked. This may be prevented by anointing them with lip salve before going out.

should be slipped round the joints of the fingers of the other hand in a sort of corkscrew movement. Compound camphor liniment is excellent for chilblains as soon as they appear, but if they are obdurate, paint the places with colourless tincture of iodine, provided the skin be unbroken.

The hair often becomes rough and colourless in cold weather; the merest suspicion of brilliantine will give it colour and elasticity. Put a few drops on the palm of the hand, wipe it off with the brush, and lightly polish the hair with it.

Much to be pitied is the woman whose nose is habitually red. This is, alas! a very common trouble, arising from a variety of causes, among which anæmia and indigestion may be named, and restricted circulation caused by tight clothing. Some women are

under the delusion that as long as the garments round the waist are not unduly tight, nothing matters, totally ignoring the fact that any constriction whatever is a source of danger. The arm-holes especially should be roomy, while a tight glove or neckband is also liable to cause flushing. As to local treatment, a red nose is generally hot and dry. It is useless to powder, as powder refuses to remain on the shiny surface. The insides of the nostrils may be moistened with rose-water, and the nose itself anointed with the same; next anoint with the merest suspicion of cold cream, and powder fairly thickly. Some people advocate bathing the nose first in very hot water, followed immediately by cold, in which a few drops of lavender water have been added. Tea and stimulants should be avoided, especially before going out into the open air.

An article on How to Defy the Cold would be incomplete without a few words on how to avoid that most unsightly malady, an ordinary cold in the head. It is lamentably easy to catch cold, and proportionately difficult to get rid of the same. What a disfigurement a cold in the head is—with streaming eyes and nose, perpetual sneezing, and general misery! Tendency to cold can be greatly mitigated by attending to the laws of health and inhabiting a well-ventilated room. A cold once caught should be taken in time, and there is nothing better than the good old-fashioned remedy of going to bed early and drinking hot lemonade. Ammoniated quinine taken in the first stages often prevents

To prevent chilblains, slip the finger and thumb of one hand round the joints of the other, with a corkscrew movement.

further development of the evil, and a few drops of camphor or cinnamon on a lump of sugar are old-fashioned but valuable remedies for those who cannot take quinine. The cold once subdued, it is advisable to take a tonic, for anything that tends to lower the vitality of the system has a most injurious effect on the personal appearance.

Eyes, again, often become bloodshot and painful after exposure to the cold. They should be bathed daily with cold boracic lotion; and, by - the - bye, boracic lotion is a thing no woman should be without. Buy four ounces of boracic powder at the chemist's. To one tablespoonful of this add a quart of boiling water; bottle and keep for using as required, when it can

In the cold weather the hair needs special care. A few drops of brilliantine do all that is necessary.

either be used of the strength made or diluted with warm water. It is more agreeable to use if one-third rose-water is added to the composition. An old-fashioned remedy which is styled "A good medicine for eyes that are bloodshot and hot and red" is as follows: "Take a house leek and stamp it well; then take a new-laid egg, and make a hole into one end of it, and draw out all the meat of it, and put the juice of a house leek into it, and set it in the embers, and so distil it, and scum it clean with a feather, and at night, when you go to bed, let a drop thereof fall into your eye with a feather (lying upon your back): this will presently help you."

All the remedies given are extremely simple: they have all been, as an ancient book says, tried and proven. There is no reason, if carefully carried out, why they should not help my readers to successfully defy the disastrous effects of cold.

Cookery Notes.

SUGGESTIONS FOR A CHILDREN'S SUPPER.

Sandwiches.
Potted Meat.   Egg and Watercress.   Ham.
Strawberry and Raspberry Jam.

Sausage Rolls.   Chicken Patties.
Chicken in Jelly.

Pistachio Russe.   Blancmange Eggs.
Macedonie of Fruit.
Palmyra Cream.

Fancy Biscuits.   Cakes, various.
Grapes, Bananas, Oranges, Crystallised
and Preserved Fruits.
Chocolates.
Almonds and Raisins.

Lemonade.   Claret Cup.
Coffee.   Ices.

The sandwiches I have given are plain, as the more savoury ones would be too rich for children, and to make them attractive they should be cut into fancy shapes—crescents, stars, circles, and garnished with cress.

Chicken in Jelly.

Mince all the best parts of a cold chicken, seeing that the flesh is all free from skin and gristle ; add to this four hard-boiled eggs sliced, some capers, and salt and spices to taste ; make a jelly of gelatine boiled in water and flavoured with sherry, and as it solidifies place it in layers with the meat in a prettily shaped mould ; set in a cool place, and see that the jelly has quite hardened before attempting to turn out.

Pistachio Russe.

Soak $\frac{1}{4}$ lb. of gelatine in a half-cupful of cold water for half an hour ; whip one quart of cream, and turn it into a pan that can be arranged to stand in another of pounded ice or iced water ; add to the cream one cup of powdered sugar, ten drops of pistachio colouring, a teaspoonful of vanilla, and the grated rind of half an orange ; add half a cup of the cream to the gelatine, and, standing it over boiling water, stir until dissolved ; then strain this into the remaining cream, and continue stirring until it begins to thicken ; turn immediately into a mould that has been liberally sprinkled with chopped pistachio nuts ; stand in a cool place, and when set turn out on to a dish decorated with crystallised fruits.

Blancmange Eggs.

Make some ordinary blancmange, and half fill some tea-cups with the mixture ; when this is set, turn it out of the moulds, and place upon the top of each shape the half of a tinned apricot.

Macedonie of Fruit.

Melt one quart of lemon jelly ; pour a little into a wetted mould, and drop a few grapes and preserved cherries into it ; when this is set, pour a little more jelly in, and add some slices of apricots ; let this set ; then a layer of jelly and an orange peeled and divided into sections, and some more jelly and preserved pineapple cut into cubes ; fill the mould with the jelly, and when set turn out and surround with whipped cream.

Palmyra Cream.

Beat $\frac{1}{4}$ lb. of butter to a cream, and gradually beat in the yolks of four eggs, one by one ; then very slowly beat in three table-spoonfuls of strongly made coffee, $\frac{1}{4}$ lb. of castor sugar, and the whites of the eggs, which must have been previously beaten to a stiff froth ; continue beating for a quarter of an hour, until the ingredients are thoroughly mixed ; line a mould with sponge fingers stuck together with the white of an egg ; press in the mixture, and set in a cool place until required.

The table should be decorated with crackers and small dishes of bon-bons and chocolates.

I AM also giving this month some **SUGGESTIONS FOR MEALS FOR A DAY**, as it is sometimes difficult to think of anything fresh ; and especially at breakfast are grumbles heard of the everlasting " eggs and bacon."

BREAKFAST.

Baked Sardines.   Kidney Omelet.
Grilled Ham.

LUNCHEON.

Boiled Cod and Egg Sauce.
Steak Fingers and Ribbon Potatoes.
Brooklyn Pudding.
Cheese.

DINNER.

Tomato Soup.
Lobster Cutlets.
Roast Ribs of Beef, Browned Potatoes,
Beetroot, and White Sauce.
Woodcocks on Toast.
Pineapple Pudding.   Rice Cream.
Stilton Cheese.
Dessert : Oranges, Portugal Plums,
Nuts, Madeleine Cakes.

Baked Sardines.

Divide sufficient sardines into fillets, removing the backbone, and lay them on a dish with ½ oz. of butter ; pour half a wineglass of water over them ; beat two eggs and add to them 2 oz. of breadcrumbs, one-third tea-spoonful of finely chopped onions, ½ oz. of butter, pepper, salt, and a pinch of cayenne ; spread this mixture over the fish, and bake.

Kidney Omelet.

Skin the kidneys and cut into small pieces ; toss them over the fire in 1 oz. of butter for two or three minutes ; make an omelet in the usual way, and stir into it the kidneys ; cook as usual and serve very hot.

Steak Fingers.

Cut a steak into neat fingers ; sprinkle with pepper and salt, and boil ; knead 1 oz. of butter with some flour and a teaspoonful of minced capers, and place a small lump on each steak, arranged nicely on a hot dish ; serve with ribbon potatoes.

Brooklyn Pudding.

Lay a few macaroons in the bottom of a pie-dish ; cover with peaches and a little syrup from the tin of peaches ; make a custard with the yolks of two eggs and half a pint of milk, sweetened to taste, and when cold pour over the peaches ; whisk the whites of the eggs to a firm froth, and lightly brown the top ; serve either hot or cold.

Lobster Cutlets.

Preserved or fresh lobster can be used.   Make a sauce as follows : put 1 oz. of flour into a stewpan with half a gill of cold water, and stir over a slow fire until it forms a paste ; then add 1 oz. of butter, stirring until it is thoroughly mixed ; season with salt, pepper, and a teaspoonful of anchovy sauce ; take the pan off the fire, and stir in the yolk of an egg briskly ; pound the lobster and mix well with this sauce, moulding it into small cakes ; fry these in egg and bread-crumbs in a wire basket ; drain, and stick into each cutlet a sprig of parsley.

Woodcocks on Toast.

Pluck the birds, but do not draw them ; truss with the legs pressed close to the body ; skin the head and neck, and place the beak under the wing ; spit three or four birds on a skewer, and roast as many as may be required before a clear fire for fifteen minutes ; set some slices of buttered toast in the dripping-pan below the birds, and baste these well as they cook with butter ; serve each bird upon half a slice of toast, and let there be a little rich brown gravy in the dish.

Pineapple Pudding.

Put 6 oz. of castor sugar, ¼ lb. butter, and one pint of milk into an enamelled saucepan, and when they simmer remove from the fire and stir in 6 oz. flour gradually and smoothly ; stir over the fire for five minutes and again remove ; then add four eggs, one by one, and ½ lb. pineapple, which must be cut into small pieces.   The contents of the saucepan should then be turned into a well-buttered mould, covered with a piece of buttered paper, and steamed for an hour and a half.

The · Realm · of · Society ·

AMONG the well-known young people who have within the last three months taken upon themselves the responsibilities of married life were Lord Dunsany, an Irish peer and ex-Guardsman, and Lady Beatrice Villiers, youngest daughter of Lord and Lady Jersey, who are now settled at Rood Ashton, which they have taken from Mr. Walter Long for the winter. Lady

Photo by Esmé Collings.

LADY VIOLET POULETT, THE BEAUTIFUL SISTER OF LORD POULETT.

Lady Violet recently became engaged to Mr. Cecil Wingfield.

Hermione Grimston, the pretty daughter of Lord and Lady Verulam, who married Mr. Buxton, of the Royal Navy, early in October; Miss Marie Fitzwilliam and Mr. Walker; Lord Dalrymple, eldest son of Lord Stair, and Miss Harford; Colonel Baring and Lady Ulrica Duncombe, the last of the beautiful Duncombes to marry; Mr. Valentine Vivian and Lady

Photo by Langfier.

LORD GERARD

Came of age in November, when great rejoicings were held at Garswood, the family place in Lancashire.

Among the engagements which were announced about the same period, one of the most interesting was that of Lady Violet Poulett to Mr. Cecil Wingfield. Lady Violet is the sister of the youthful Lord Poulett, the owner of beautiful Hinton St. George, who quite recently established his claim to the earldom in opposition to the pretensions of a very well-known personage. Her mother was the late Lord Poulett's third wife, and a daughter of Mr. Hugh de Melville. Lady Violet and her sister, Lady Eleanor, have been going out in London this season with Lady Dallas, wife of Sir George Dallas, who was so long at the Foreign Office. Lady Violet is quite remarkably pretty, with beautiful eyes and hair, and was immensely admired at the various balls and parties.

Another engagement was that of Miss Marjory Nevill, the only daughter of Lord and Lady George Nevill, and granddaughter of Lord Abergavenny, to her cousin, Mr. Percy Nevill. Miss Marjory Nevill is just eighteen years of age, very pretty, with a charming face and figure, and a very good complexion. She has been out very little in London, as she is so extremely young, but those who know her unite in singing her praises. She usually lives at Dane Gate House, near Lord Abergavenny's beautiful Sussex estate of Eridge. Her *fiancé*, Mr. Percy Nevill, is the second son of Mr. Ralph Pelham Nevill, of Birling Manor, Kent, and nephew of the present Lord Abergavenny. The Nevills have the proud distinction of dating from the days of the Conquest, Gilbert de Nevil, the founder of the family, having been one of Norman William's companions-in-arms.

Miss Mary Dyke, one of the Queen's Maids-of-Honour, had been for some time engaged to Captain Bell of the Rifle Brigade, but the marriage was only officially announced in October. Miss Dyke's colleague, Miss Doris Vivian, also enters the bonds of matrimony with Mr. Sandys, thus creating two vacancies in her Majesty's household. Miss Dyke is very clever and charming, and like pretty Miss Doris Vivian,

Aline Dawson Damer; Mr. Harry Dillon and Miss Brenda Smith; Mr. Neil Arnott and Miss Hermione Cooper; and Captain Spender Clay and Miss Pauline Astor, were other brides and bridegrooms of the autumn.

is a great favourite at Court. The
dowry of £1,000 which used in old
days to be bestowed on the Maids
of Honour who married while still
holding the appointment, is dispensed
with in the new reign.

Other autumn engagements are
those of Lord Ennismore, Lord Lis-
towel's only son, to Miss Johnstone,
daughter of Mr. Francis Johnstone
and granddaughter of Lord Derwent ;
and of Miss Violet Wood, daughter
of Mrs. Nicholas Wood, to Mr. Patrick
de Bathe, younger son of Sir Henry
de Bathe.

A very noticeable feature of recent
years has been the number of Americans who are settling more or less
permanently in this country, and are
buying or renting large estates ; some,
as in the case of Mr. Waldorf Astor,
who purchased Cliveden from the
Duke of Westminster, becoming
naturalised Englishmen. One of the
most recent recruits to the ranks of
Anglo-American landowners is Mr.
James Van Alen, a millionaire celebrated for his sporting proclivities and
his princely hospitality, who, like his
kinsman, Mr. Astor, seems inclined
to settle down in the old country, as
he has purchased Rushton Manor,
Northamptonshire, in fulfilment of a
long-cherished intention of possessing
a place of his own in England. Mr.
Van Alen is likely to be very well
received in the county, as he is a well-
known personage, not only in New-
port, U.S.A., where he has built
himself a magnificent house and entertains continually, but in English
hunting centres like Leicestershire,
where "Jimmy" Van Alen is a
familiar figure at Melton and Market
Harborough, and in London. The
head of an old Knickerbocker family,
with his name writ large in the book
of the "Four Hundred," he hardly,
in one sense of the word, comes
under the head of new men in old
acres. Besides being an all-round
sportsman and a courtly and distin-

Photo by Thomson.

MISS MARJORY NEVILL.—The only daughter of Lord and Lady George Nevill,
whose engagement to her cousin, Mr. Percy Nevill, is announced.

guished gentleman, Mr. Van Alen has a special claim to the regard of English people, as during the South African war he furnished and equipped at immense expense a field hospital which he personally accompanied to the front, and which rendered great service in succouring the sick and wounded.

Lady Gainsborough is very fond of the country, and devoted to good works, as the poor round about Campden, especially those who are her co-religionists, have reason to know. Although there is a little private chapel in the house itself, Lord and Lady Gainsborough and their family usually attend the Roman Catholic church in the village, in which they are much interested. Lady Gainsborough is a very handsome woman, with a crown of soft waving grey hair, and her daughters have to a great extent inherited her good looks. Lady Nora Noel, the eldest, is passionately devoted to music and possesses a very fine voice. She is an excellent rider, and sometimes, though not very often, hunts with the North Cotswold. She and her sisters frequently follow on foot, however, when the hounds happen to be near and their brothers are at home to escort them.

Desirable as our millionaire aliens may be, it is pleasant, nevertheless, to turn our eyes to a young English peer who has just celebrated his twenty-first birthday in his own ancestral halls. Lord Gerard, who succeeded his father only a couple of years ago, came of age on the 10th of last month, when his majority was made the occasion of great rejoicings at Garswood, the family place in Lancashire, and at Eastwell Park, a more recently acquired property in Kent. He is the head of a branch of the ancient Italian race of Gherardi, who went over to Ireland with Strongbow, and of which the Dukes of Leinster are the chiefs. He is, like his forbears, a Roman Catholic, although his mother, who is a daughter of Mr. Henry Milner, is a Protestant. Lord Gerard was not sent to any public school, neither to Stoneyhurst, Edgbaston, or Beaumont, the three great English Catholic colleges, nor to Eton, where nowadays a certain number of the Catholic youth of England are educated.

The late Lord Gerard disapproved of the public-school system, and his only son was educated principally by private tutors at home. He has inherited some of the remarkable good looks of his mother, and of his grandfather, the first Baron Gerard, better remembered as Sir Robert Gerard, who was A.D.C. to Queen Victoria, and was elevated to the peerage in 1876. He bids fair to keep up the family traditions, and is as good a sportsman as were his father and grandfather before him. The late Lord Gerard was a first-rate shot, a very good rider, and a patron of the Turf, and Lady Gerard was, and is, a beautiful horsewoman, and was always in the "first flight" in Cheshire and Leicestershire. Although he has been accustomed to horses and has ridden all his life, the present Lord Gerard has, up to now, not shown any special taste for the Turf.

Lady Gerard is very fond of travelling, and it was during some of her wanderings in foreign lands that she and her daughter met with Baron de Forest, who inherited part of the fabulous wealth of the late Baron Hirsch, whose name as a benefactor to Jewish charities was a household word in Europe. The marriage of Miss Ethel Gerard to Baron de Forest took place in the private chapel at Garswood in the early part of this year, and the marvellous jewels of the bride, her costly furs, and priceless lace were quite a nine days' wonder. King Edward, who was a personal friend of the families of both bride and bridegroom, honoured Eastwell with a week-end visit in August last. The late Lord Gerard spent most of his time and much money turning Eastwell, which he had himself purchased, into an earthly paradise. It has been said that he rather overstepped the bounds of prudence in his expenditure over the place, which was at one time the residence of the late Duke of Edinburgh, and which is one of the finest estates in the "Garden of England." Garswood, the old family seat in Lancashire, is a huge house, set in a fine park; but although very comfortable and even luxurious, it contains no very famous pictures, except family portraits, nor bric-a-brac of any special value.

LONDON AND PARIS FASHIONS

BY MRS ERIC PRITCHARD.

ALTHOUGH the more fashionable among us have purchased our winter furs, many women are anxiously waiting for the sales to begin, while others are hopeful that Christmas presents may take the shape of fur in one form or another. The threequarter-length coat is certainly seen at its best in really good furs, but it is not every one who can afford such a luxury ; and I think that, except for motoring, to be successful the *Directoire* coat must be composed of a good soft skin. Therefore, in my opinion, the woman who wants a *Directoire* coat and cannot afford a costly fur, should turn her attention to cloths. The *Directoire* wrap in cloth appeared at the Paris race meetings in the autumn, and very smart it was worn over an attractive waistcoat of plain or embroidered kid, draped chamois leather or suède, with decorative buttons and cuffs. I have noticed that the majority of sartorial *modes* show a basque ; it is often very short, and the shortest are the smartest—in fact, the long threequarter length should only be worn by tall, slim women. The long, smart redingotes are distinctly quaint and successful wear.

Motoring *modes* have done a great deal for the economical woman who does *not* motor, for she can avail herself of the cosy fur coats in opossum, pony skin, musquash, and several of the lesser furs which have been revived with new and greatly improved dressings, and many of which are quite smart enough for ordinary occasions, as well as for travelling, motoring, driving, etc. A few years ago it was difficult to get sufficient warmth below the waist, but nowadays the woman with a limited income

can be comfortably clad in this respect, though I still think that nothing is smarter for town wear and calling than a thick zibeline skirt, with a fur bolero of the same colour, such as grey, black or white caracal, beaver, marmot, or musquash with a seal dressing. Many of these little boleros and coatees are beautifully cut, and can be purchased ready-made for four or five guineas.

I THINK a really good winter hat is a wise investment even for the woman of moderate means. I congratulate those of our country cousins who have put off the purchase of their best hat until this month, knowing they would come to town some time in December for their Christmas shopping. The winter fashions are now firmly established, and there are innumerable models to pick and choose from. As in other details of the wardrobe, *modes* in millinery are culled from almost every period, and it is indeed a matter of old friends with new faces. Here also are we truly historical in our choice. The Tudor toque is revived as well as the "Beefeater" hat of the same period, with its cluster of plumes at the side. But again the chief favourite of the *Directoire* era is made chiefly of old-fashioned Terry velvet, though to my mind it looks equally well in rough beaver or felt, adorned with big black velvet bobs.

Our artist has drawn in fig. 1 a charmingly becoming and novel model, which at the moment is all the rage in Paris. The brim is of whitey-brown cloth, while the crown is of white felt and folds of shot *miroir* velvet. The trimming consists of white and brown shaded ostrich plumes, one placed under the brim to fall on the *coiffure* at the right side, while the effect of greater width is obtained by a second plume coming from the crown over the brim.

There is a fancy for using *cabochons* of jet or velvet on many picture-hats of the Louis period. Worked chenille, too, is a very popular trimming, while very often some of the big black hats of velvet are lined with Chantilly lace, which gives a light finish to what might otherwise appear heavy. Nearly all the picture-hats have one long shaded plume or a delicious *pouf* of black or shaded tips at the side. Charming are the sailor-hats of *velours plissé*, with ruchings of shaded velvet round the crown, and one long coque's feather or ostrich plume resting on the *coiffure* beneath the brim. These small hats are raised by a high *bandeau*, and very

FIG. I.—A CLOTH AND FELT HAT TRIMMED WITH SHADED PLUMES.

of some of the smartest millinery. A lovely *plateau* of brown felt, for instance, is raised to a great height at the back, and is adorned with clusters of upstanding plumes. In Paris there is a perfect *furore* for very small, beautiful beavers, almost round, with a tiny crown and clusters of plumes at the back, a narrow band of velvet or a fantastic buckle being the only other trimming. There is certainly no prettier or lighter trimming than ostrich feathers; for the smaller shapes a cluster of plumes is preferable to the long, sweeping, single ostrich feather, though the latter is, of course, peculiarly effective on the big picture-hat.

Effective also are the *tricorne* shapes trimmed with plumes, though for more practical purposes these are made in felt with cockades of shaded ribbon, and a single quill or peacock's feather. Birds and wings are giving place to plumes, ribbons, and quills. Peacocks' feathers, breasts, and

smart and peculiarly French they are. Then the Breton sailor shapes are trimmed with two enormous shaded rosettes or cockades in the front, with loops of shaded ribbon in between.

As many as six different colours are used in one ribbon rosette, brown, bronze, and green being supplemented by various tones of red, bright blue, and wine colour. This gives a welcome note of cheerfulness to a sombre black or blue serge frock.

I think one is struck by the immense height

heads are a distinct feature of French millinery, at any rate, in spite of the fact that many people regard them as omens of ill-luck. For country wear and travelling, the Homburg shape, with the high, dented crown, adorned with folded scarves of ribbon or silk, is very useful, and is still much worn. It is also delightfully practical wear with tailor-made costumes, trimmed with a waving coque's feather.

Now let us consider the question of skating

FIG. 3.—A DELIGHTFUL VELVET COAT.
(*Sketched at Konski's, 49, Conduit Street, W.*)

garb, which should, of course, be built on sartorial lines. Americans are wearing a great deal of grey—cloth adorned with fur edgings and braidings being the favourite mixture. In fig. 2 our artist has sketched a frock seen last month at Prince's, and worn, I believe, by an American. It is in grey-faced cloth trimmed with chinchilla, fancy cord braiding, and buttons of embroidered kid. The waistcoat and collar are of fur, and any idea of hardness is dispelled by the addition of little pieces of embroidered kid in the corners and buttons of kid, while the undersleeves are composed of the same. Although trimmed, the skirt fits tightly at the hips, and comes out very full at the feet, which is a necessity for graceful skating. The chinchilla toque has a crown of velvet with a shaded grey plume right across the crown. The same idea would be charming carried out in brown cloth and mink, beaver or moleskin. The wearing of grey is extremely pretty for outdoor skating on clear frosty days, and is becoming to a good complexion. In the ordinary way, it should be remembered, the cold stone grey of chinchilla is very trying, and should only be attempted by the woman who is confident that grey suits her. Real scarlet looks charming on the ice, and so do reddy-brown tweeds and brilliant rose colour, the latter relieved with ermine or the blackest of caracal. Skating costumes nowadays are very *chic*, as the exercise is mostly taken in the presence of smart assemblies. It is here, I think, that we see some of the best examples of the short skirt and little coatee.

Do not let any one be foolish enough to adopt the threequarter-length coat, or even one with a long basque, with the short skirt that must be worn on the ice. I have

FIG. 4.—A BLACK VELVET EVENING GOWN TRIMMED WITH ROSETTES.

seen some terribly incongruous
specimens of this, and am convinced that the *Directoire* coat
can only be successfully worn
with a long flowing skirt. But
there is no doubt that every
form of *jaquette* has been worn
by Parisians during the autumn
season, and have been more or
less adopted in this country.
Our English tailors have proved
themselves extremely clever at
cutting these *jaquettes* the right
length to suit their individual
clients. They have also been
making the old-fashioned Newmarket coat in beautiful faced
cloths.

Braiding is much used on the
coats of half and threequarter
length. The short half-length
coat has become very popular in
Vienna, and it
lends itself admir-
ably to braiding.
A beautiful ex-
ample in puce
colour was braided
with silk braid in
a curious conven-
tional design. The
plain sleeve had
an insertion of
braiding let in,
and a neat turned-
back cuff treated in
the same way, with a
collar to match. This
coat was semi-fitting
and rather like a
riding habit, and the
skirt, which touched
the ground, was quite
plain except for the
braiding.

IN spite of the
utility of the *trotteuse*
skirt for practical and
country purposes,
there is no doubt that
it is not worn in town.
All the tailors are
making the smart
frocks with long skirts,
and they will con-
tinue to do so. I do

FIG. 2.—A CHARMING SKATING COSTUME IN GREY CLOTH, TRIMMED
WITH CHINCHILLA.

not say they trail on the ground, but they do not show much boot.

A delightful brown coat and skirt, where the coat was again semi-fitting and less than half-length, showed a design in white and gold passementerie, worked over with brown. This was softened by a jabot of lace, and accordion-pleated frills of taffeta were introduced in the sleeves. These were the only feminine touches about a rather severe style of coat, though the skirt was slightly gauged at the waist, and had rows of braiding round the feet.

Some of the short basque coats in cloth have a tiny frill of velvet just below the waist, which is very becoming to the thin woman who really requires a fluted basque to give her the necessary amount of hip.

Talking of tailor-mades reminds me that Konski, of 49, Conduit Street, W., is showing some delightful, original models. Our artist has sketched in fig. 3 a threequarter-length black velvet coat, trimmed with a new black silk braid and black accordion-pleated glacé frills. All idea of sombreness is dispelled by a dainty touch of white lace at the neck and frills of the same in the sleeves. The lining is of white silk, and down the front of the coat is the black silk braiding with the frills of accordion-pleated glacé. The rosettes trimming the coat are also of black accordion-pleated glacé, and the gaugings on the sleeves give a very becoming line. Konski is truly a master of sartorial art and braiding, and he is equally expert in his manipulation of furs. Even his most inexpensive fur boleros and coatees are so trimmed with kid and braid that they form the smartest of garments, while his collection of Russian sables is truly remarkable.

For morning wear Konski is making a great feature of braided cloths, and at 49, Conduit Street, you will find the coat of every length, the bolero ending above the waist, the smartly cut short basque coat, and the new *Directoire paletôt*. You are safe indeed if you place yourself, both for style and cut, unreservedly in the hands of Mr. Konski.

This is the month of country house parties and evening festivities for young and old alike, and the question of evening dress is an important one. An evening gown may be of the stiffest velvets and brocades of the Louis XVI. period, or the quaint, picturesque draperies culled from the simple Romney and Greuze ideals. There is one possession dear to the

heart of the woman who can afford it, and that is a velvet evening dress, while she who cannot afford velvet may well rest content with one of the excellent velveteens obtainable to-day at such moderate prices. It may console her to know that velveteen usually falls into more graceful folds than does the thicker velvet. Still, velvet or *chiffon-velours*, both in black and all kinds of glorious colours, commends itself to the woman who wants a dress for various parties, etc. The old pointed Court bodice has come in, and how becoming and dainty it is ! Our artist has sketched (fig. 4) an excellent model in black velvet for the matron. The Court bodice is draped in a becoming manner across the bust, caught with two rosettes having quaint old paste centres. Revers of family lace fall over the *décolletage*, and the old-world picture-skirt is arranged in pleats and gathers on the hips, leaving the front plain, so that it falls in graceful and becoming folds. The elbow-sleeves are caught up with a rosette. Such a gown would be beautiful in any colour, and its lines are becoming to young and old alike. It is observable that this frock does up at the back, which is a feature of the evening dress of the moment—a fashion beloved of the *couturière*, who has a firm belief that frocks so fastening are easier to fit.

This same model would be beautiful in some of the *vieux rose* and vivid blue stiff brocades of the Louis period. But I have not forgotten the girl, and the *débutante* on her own allowance must carefully consider the question of ways and means. There is no more profitable standby than a cream flannel-back satin gown, unlined or lined with soft muslin. As a rule the simple styles suit her best, and are generally easy to make with the assistance of a sewing-maid or working dressmaker. In fig. 5 our artist has drawn a charming dress for a young girl : it is made of satin, the skirt laid in pleats on the hips and finished with a thick ruche, which can be of cream silk or satin. The pretty fichu-like effect is arrived at by draperies of *Chine* ribbon, coming from a point in the front and crossing with sash ends at the back. The sleeves are composed of a *bandage* of ribbon tied in a bow at the elbow. The bodice is softened by a chemisette of tiny frills of Indian muslin or chiffon. I think that girls' frocks nowadays are extraordinarily pretty, and can be made up at very small cost. So many of the satins sold are washable, and the unlined skirt is not a difficult thing to make. Of course, when you wear an unlined skirt, it must be worn over a full petticoat of satin, brocade, or taffeta. Such a petticoat is not cheap, but it does duty

FIG 5.—A *DEBUTANTE'S* FROCK IN CREAM SATIN TRIMMED WITH *CHINE* RIBBON.

with various frocks for afternoon as well as for evening wear. It may perhaps appear somewhat strange when talking of economy to suggest brocade and satin petticoats, but I can assure you that in the end they will save you a considerable amount of money.

THERE is a revival of the old-world cashmere, and this month I am suggesting a house-frock of that attractive material, which *can* be purchased at 1*s.* 11*d.* per yard, though I advise you to give a little more. The sketch I am giving you in fig. 6 is of Quaker grey with a softening yoke of cream spotted net. You will observe that the shoulder is long and that velvet is threaded through. I find that this line is becoming to many of us, and is appropriate in a frock of this kind. If a sloping shoulder be unbecoming, the velvet may be arranged to give a certain amount of squareness. The shaped band finished with buttons is also of velvet, and a band of the same finishes the skirt, which is unlined, and worn over a silk, satin, or brocade slip. It is simply laid in pleats at the waist, with the front kept plain. The same model would be charming in white flannel, adorned with black pongée silk or Oriental satin, although for the moment I would suggest cashmere, which I always think lends itself admirably to soft folds. It also suggests itself to me that this *berthe* or yoke effect can be bought ready-made and placed over an ordinary cashmere blouse. But the house-frock offers so many possibilities to the amateur dressmaker that there is no reason why the girl on her own allowance or the woman with a very limited income should not look extremely nice at a small outlay. Of course, it is always a good plan to put a little piece of lining from the waist to about five inches below it, as this forms a firm foundation on which to sew your gathers or pleats. Cashmere is a washing fabric, just as flannel is, although the cleaners to-day are almost as cheap as the laundresses, and make such materials look almost like new.

I admit that it is difficult to get all we require on a small allowance, in spite of the cheapness of many really dainty garments. At this time of

J M PASH.

year we require a goodly number of blouses, warm undergarments, petticoats, dressing-jackets, and last, but not least, a cosy winter dressing-gown. The manufacturers produce delightful fabrics in pretty bright colourings, and when in search of warmth we are no longer obliged to resort to coarse scarlet flannel. The wise woman who invests in a dressing-gown will do well to have Viyella, which does not shrink, and is made in a variety of charming colours and designs and in various weights. Our artist has sketched in fig. 7 an attractive gown of that flannel in a bright shade of rose pink, with a big hemstitched collar and turned-back cuffs, and a fichu of inexpensive lace, forming a hood behind, which can be drawn over the hair in becoming fashion when so desired. A cheap pongée lining would make this dressing-gown a very handsome garment, or chilly people could have a flannel lining. There are reversible flannels which answer this purpose admirably, requiring no lining at all, made with a hood of net or lace. A flannel dressing-jacket is also a necessity in the winter. In choosing garments for bedroom wear it is advisable to select clear, clean colours, such as cream, rose pink, sky blue, or a pretty shade of mauve where it suits. Yellow is

FIG. 6.—A DAINTY HOUSE-FROCK IN UNLINED GREY CASHMERE AND CREAM SPOTTED NET.

FIG. 8.—SOME ACCESSORIES OF THE TOILET.

seldom becoming unless relieved with blue or mauve.

Cashmere-back satin is an admirable fabric **for** winter nightgowns, dressing-jackets, and the *saut-de-lit*.　It is so beautiful in itself that, with the exception of a little dainty hand-work or hemstitching, it requires no trimming, and it washes exceedingly well.

Great variety is obtainable in teagowns, and

I think I have before referred in these pages to the charms of velveteen, cashmere, and pale pastel cloth for five-o'clock teagowns.　Pastel cloth perhaps does not sound particularly attractive; but I have seen a model I must describe, which was cut *à l'Empire* and unlined, long and flowing, with an enormous cape of Irish crochet falling over the shoulders.　The high

FIG. 7.—A COSY DRESSING-GOWN OF VIYELLA.

the mixing of pale mauve and pastel blue is peculiarly French and successful. The gown was cut low, but the wearer had a separate chemisette made of tucked shaded chiffon and insertions of the Irish crochet finishing at the neck-line, and this she could put on at five o'clock, and on other occasions when she did not want a low teagown. It was a practical as well as a charmingly becoming garment.

I HAVE heard a good deal of discussion anent the blouse, and some people declare that only the tight-fitting garment of this class is *de rigueur*. But this is an erroneous statement arising from the fact that people *will* make the great mistake of confusing the shirt with the blouse. Of course, flannels, delaines, and similar practical fabrics should *not* be made up in fantastic style, but should be perfectly plain and shaped to the figure, worn with high linen collars and silk stocks, while the sleeves should be

waistband was composed of folds of palest mauve *miroir* velvet, caught up with a curious green, blue, and purple buckle. The sleeves were of mauve and blue chiffon, with insertions of Irish crochet. Any idea of hardness was dispelled by the addition of the chiffon, and of fairly small dimensions to wear under the smaller coat-sleeve. Some of these shirts are made with basque pieces below the waist ; but I think the most becoming are those finished at the waist with a well-shaped leather, kid, or suède band. These shirts may also be worn with little *plissé* muslin cravats and cuffs at the wrist to match.

A very good selection of shirts which are essentially French may now be seen at 28, New Bond Street, the home of the famous "La Samothrace" corset. The London Corset Company have added some delightful French *lingerie-de-luxe*, beautifully shaped belts, silk and muslin underskirts, and last, but not least, those really well-cut tailor shirts, as well as dainty blouses, to their excellent corsets. Particularly smart is a shirt of fine white flannel piped with a narrow edging of washing satin, made with a charmingly cut sleeve finished with a neat cuff. This shirt costs only 25s. 9d. But, of course, I went to 28, New Bond Street, in search of information regarding new *modes* in corsets. There is not much change in the dainty, comfortable garment we associate with the "Samothrace," and the craze for the "Tricot" still continues among leading Parisians. The delightful pliability of this corset and the manner in which it moulds the figure without compressing it are now well known, and no doubt give rise to the murmur that a change is about to be made in the length of the waist, and that we are to have a curve instead of an absolutely straight front. The great point about the London Corset Company's stays is not so much the fact that every pair is made in Paris, but that the variety offered is so enormous that every woman, be she young or old, stout or thin, tall or short, may find her ideal corset at 28, New Bond Street. She does well when she has found it to remain faithful to it, and so ensure for herself comfort, a graceful figure, and perfectly fitting frocks.

WE must not overlook the importance of furs as accessories. We have for some time past been wearing the daintiest little cravats of chinchilla or ermine, mixed with lace, and these will figure among the more acceptable Christmas gifts. Then long stoles of lace have edgings of ermine, one of which appears in the little group of accessories sketched in fig. 8, with a muff *en suite*. In Paris this is considered quite sufficient embellishment of an afternoon toilette of velvet, silk, or panne, except, of course, when the weather demands a warmer wrap. Irish crochet, edged with chinchilla, is a favourite cravat among Parisians. Very smart, too, for wearing with our tailor-made *Directoires* are broad bands of embroidery edged with narrow mink or sealskin. These fasten high and tightly round the neck, finished with little ends of fur, and so form a cravat.

FOR morning wear, even in Paris, linen collars are giving place to softer ones of muslin, with a stock of black or coloured ribbon beneath. But with real sporting garments the linen collar is high, like a man's, and worn over a soft, folded tie.

SOME of the belts are really beautiful specimens of tooled work and embroidery. The newest and best are rather plain, with the exception of a good many slides and buckles, of which I feel sure we shall tire ere long. With the basque coat, chamois leather, suède, and kid are all folded into a two-inch band held at intervals by slides and buckles back and front.

IN handbags we are still fond of white morocco, suède, and leather for morning use ; but those carried in the afternoon are of old-fashioned bead-work and dainty brocades, with chains of gold or gun-metal set with precious stones.

THIS reminds me that delightful novelties in the way of Christmas presents are to be found at 167, Regent Street, the home of the famous "Whitlock" pearls and diamonds, which are such perfect replicas that it is impossible to distinguish them from real stones. The new real tortoiseshell combs, set with "Whitlock" diamonds, are a pleasing addition to the *coiffure*, and these may be had from a guinea each. The jewellers of to-day show very good taste by copying old French designs, while the mixing of coloured stones has become as much a feature among our leading English jewellers as those of the Rue de la Paix.

There are some very beautiful copies of the old Spanish combs inlaid with gold and silver. Then some *débutantes* in Paris are wearing the floral wreath still : this dies hard, as it is very becoming to classical heads, just as a piece of pale blue ribbon run through dark hair surmounting a young face is suggestive of the Greuze-like type ; but these should be sternly avoided by the woman of maturer years. A big velvet bow or a lace cap is a pleasing addition to the teagown ; and very pretty, too, are old-fashioned lace lappets worn on the hair and caught up with some quaint jewel. Big wings of jet, flowers and odd enamels, are all worn in the hair, but I think it advisable to warn women not to overload the head. The simpler styles are generally the best.

WE THREE !

Concerning Chinchilla Cats.

BY FRANCES SIMPSON,
Author of the " Book of the Cat."

BEAUTY'S EYES.

IT is curious what an influence fashion exercises on all matters that concern woman, and this arbitrary power is extended even to the choice of her pets. Certainly in Catland at present Chinchillas and Persians are the *crème de la crème* of good society; they are to be met with in the smartest and most exclusive drawing-rooms, and are eagerly contested for in raffles at fashionable bazaars. Yet really there is very little general knowledge on the subject of these fascinating pets, and members of the different species are frequently mistaken for each other.

To the members of the cat fancy the term " chinchilla " at once suggests a pale silvery cat with soft grey shadings; but to the novice the title is very misleading, because the cats usually called " chinchilla " are, or ought to be, quite unlike the fur of that name, which is dark at the roots and lighter towards the tip. No breed of Persian cats has been so much discussed

THREE CANADIAN CREAM KITTENS.

shaded cats ; but whether darkly or lightly shaded, they still remain "silver." Then comes the question of what is nearest perfection in this variety of cat, which has only appeared of late years, evolved from the old silver tabby and the blue. The ideal silver should be the palest conceivable colour at the roots that is not white, shading up to a soft silvery grey. It is this slightly darker edging to the fur that constitutes the chief charm in these cats. When a cat is in full coat these tiny fleckings are almost lost.

The shaded silvers, so-called, have a dark spine line, which gradually shades off down the sides of the body ; the legs and head have tabby markings, more or less distinct. These cats have often been spoken of in the fancy as "spoilt tabbies," for they are neither one thing nor

by clubs, societies, and individual members of the fancy as these chinchilla or silver cats. They have puzzled judges and exhibitors alike, because when a separate classification was given for silvers and shaded silvers, the difficulty of knowing the amount of markings that constituted a shaded silver was very great. No two judges drew the line at the same animal, so that at one show a cat might win all the honours as a chinchilla or. silver, and a little later on would have the same prizes as a shaded silver. Many were the heart-burnings over fine specimens being labelled "Wrong Class."

So much has been said and written on this special variety of Persian cat, but as the fancy is ever on the increase I feel it will not be out of place to give some definition of the terms chinchilla or silver and shaded silver for the benefit of the novice. I have always strongly objected to these cats being called anything else than "silver": this title seems the most appropriate, and best describes the delicate colour of this most fascinating breed. They are all, so to speak,

A NOBLE BEAUTY.
(Bred by Miss Greatorex.)

A " DIMITY " KITTEN.
(Bred by Lady Marcus Beresford.)

another they are sadly disappointing, for a kitten may give great promise at six or eight months, and will slowly but surely develop into one of those nondescript cats that are neither silver nor silver tabby.

For some time it was considered that silvers might have green or yellow eyes; but the best authorities have now quite decided that green is the colour for this breed, and these seem to tone best with the pale silver of the coat. There is one rather peculiar feature in the eyes of some cats of this breed: this is the dark rim which often encircles the eyes, and which certainly enhances the beauty and throws up the colour.

Few Persian cats suffer so severely in appearance during the process of shedding their coats as silvers, and in the summer months they are really not fit to be seen, much less shown! The lovely, light, fluffy undercoat disappears, and even the delicate shadings seem to become dark streaks all over the body.

the other, yet their claim to beauty cannot be denied.

It is necessary to explain to the novice that these silver or chinchilla and shaded silver cats are almost invariably quite dark at birth, sometimes appearing almost black, and often covered with distinct tabby markings all over the body. It is seldom a silver kitten is born light; but gradually the markings and shadings will lessen, and perhaps just the one mite that was considered the dark, ugly duckling will turn into the palest beauty of the flock.

In this respect silver kittens may be considered most speculative, but in

There is a greater delicacy amongst silver cats and more difficulty in rearing the kittens than in any other breed of Persian, and this may be in some measure accounted for by the immense amount of inbreeding that was carried on indiscriminately at the

SILVER AND BLUE KITTENS.

" DON CARLOS."

time when silver cats became the fashion. Then, again, breeders have been so anxious to obtain light-coloured cats that they have given a second place to the very essential qualities of bone and stamina. However, a great improvement is taking place, and there are quite a number of good heads and strong limbs amongst the silvers of to-day.

And now I will take up the consideration of blue Persians, a breed in which I have always taken the greatest interest. It is more than twenty years ago since I exhibited the first pair of "blues" at the Crystal Palace. They created quite an excitement, as cats of this peculiar shade had not been seen before. They were called " London Smokes," and for some years no special classification was given to them. But as time went on several fanciers took up these cats, and a class for blue Persians was set apart at the Crystal Palace Cat Show of 1889. Since this date no breed of cats has made such rapid strides, either in improvement or popularity, as blues. In our present-day shows the blue classes are always the best filled, and there is a greater demand for blue kittens than for those of any other breed. Therefore it follows that for beginners in the fancy there is no better investment than a good blue-green of well-

MISS FRANCES SIMPSON'S "CAMBYSES."

known prize pedigree. Ten or fifteen years ago there used to be no difficulty in obtaining about £5 5s. each for blue kittens, but now, when so many blues are bred, the usual price may be fixed at about £3 3s. for a good all-round specimen.

The term "blue," as applied to a cat, sounds rather absurd, and, strictly speaking, the colour is really grey. It is, however, much the same in shade as the fur known as blue fox.

Blue Persians vary in tone ; but whether

So also as regards the colour of eyes. My famous old "Beauty Boy," a noted winner of bygone years, had bright green eyes, but now, in spite of his grand head, flowing coat, and splendid limbs, he would stand but a poor chance in the show-pen.

Judges may, however, be led into giving too much prominence to this one point of eye colour, for however desirable it may be, and assuredly is, to have deep orange eyes in this breed of cat, yet every other point ought not to be sacrificed. The eyes of all kittens

A LITTER OF BLUES.
(Bred by Miss Savery.)

dark or light, the fur should be the same colour throughout, so that when the coat is blown apart no light or white should be seen at the roots. The highest number of points are awarded for soundness of colour in blue Persians. As tiny kittens, blues often exhibit tabby markings, but these quickly disappear as the coat grows. A white spot on the throat of a blue cat is now considered a great blemish, whereas formerly this defect was not much taken into account by fancier or judge.

when first opened are blue, but at about six weeks old these gradually change colour, and the experienced breeder can tell whether the dreaded green or the hoped-for orange is making itself shown. There are many blue cats with what may be called indefinite-coloured eyes, neither yellow nor green, certainly not orange : these are yellow on the outer circle and have a green rim round the pupil, which, according to the time of day, will be wide or narrow. The perfect eye in a blue should be abso-

MISS SAVERY'S "MOSES."

of lovely kittens left recently for New Zealand, where their arrival was anxiously awaited.

There are specialist societies for silver cats and for blue. In the former club, "smokes" and silver tabbies are included. The Blue Persian Cat Society numbers about two hundred members. Amongst silver breeders the

lutely of one uniform colour. There are, however, two distinct types which are correct, namely, the bright golden eye and the deep orange eye.

Blue Persians may be considered a fairly hardy breed, and they are certainly suitable cats to keep as pets in London, as their colour does not show the dirt.

It is not only in the English cat fancy that blues are so popular; our American cousins are great admirers of this variety. I saw several fine specimens sent to fanciers over the water. A short time ago two handsome blues were despatched to Natal, and a pair

Photo by Mrs. H. E. Adams.

POSING FOR THEIR PORTRAIT.

name of Lady Decies is inseparably connected as the owner of the wonderfully pale silver female " Zaida," who has won more prizes than any other cat.

Lady Marcus Beresford has practically retired from the cat fancy, but still retains a lovely silver, called " Dimity," as a pet puss. Lady Maitland had quite a number of blue Persians at one time. Lady Rachel Byng and Lady Evelyn Guinness are new to the fancy, and have taken up this breed. Miss Gertrude Jay has the proud distinction of having possessed the best blue female ever exhibited, for " The Mighty Atom " was second to none.

Mrs. Slingsby has recently held her own at all the leading shows with her splendid blue males. Sir Hubert Jerningham has the finest blue neuter cat I have ever seen, which will probably make his *début* in the show-pen during the coming season.

The pictures illustrating this article are taken from cats and kittens either prize-winners or from noted prize stock. The paleness of the chinchillas and the soundness of colour of the blues not being reproduced by photography, these points of excellency must be left to the imagination of my readers. The portraits, however, I feel sure, cannot fail to call forth the admiration of cat fanciers and cat lovers, whether they understand or are ignorant of those points in the chinchilla and blue Persian cat that must commend themselves to the critical eye of the expert and the judge.

WHEN TIME HAS CHANGED.

By GEORGETTE AGNEW.

YOU will not love us any more, you say,
     When Time has laid his hand upon our hair,
Robbing its raven-black or golden-fair,
Has dimmed the fervour or the tender play
That alternates within our eyes to-day,
And drawn a line of suffering or care
About our winsome lips,—you'll cease to wear
The badge of love for us then, so you say !
Dear Friend, is Friendship's love so slight a thing
That it should end where ends the bloom of flowers—
When winds of destiny on Autumn's wing
Break down the beauty of bright summer bowers ?
If this be so, how faint the comforting
In all the glad to-day's love-laden hours !

BY E. KEBLE CHATTERTON.

IF a wife should show herself unwilling to honour and obey her husband, and insist instead on her own impetuosity, what is the recipe for a husband who has given her once and for all time his affection and respect? There are two methods, and two only, applicable to the two types of womanhood. For, speaking generally, it is not inaccurate to divide femininity into two classes, according as each is characterised by its endowment of heart or mind. In the one the mind is dominated by the heart, in the other the heart is obedient to the mind. Through the whole realm of literature and the drama this will be found to be an exact definition; and since history is for ever repeating itself, and types recur again and again, it is not surprising to find different people in different ages under different names performing the same deeds under similar conditions. Shakespeare understood the working of feminine character in his age. In the twentieth century Mr. Cosmo Gordon Lennox possesses a similar knowledge of the other sex, though with an insight less philosophical than that of Mr. Pinero.

Human nature in the reign of Queen Elizabeth was the same as in the time of King Edward VII., and the two separate types just indicated prevail. In Mr. Gordon Lennox's *Freedom of Suzanne* he has selected for his heroine and the pivot of his play the woman endowed with more heart than mind. In *The Taming of the Shrew* Shakespeare chose Katharina as the woman with more will than affection. The motif of both plays is identical. Both Katharina and Suzanne are

Photo by R. W. Thomas.

MR. LOUIS N. PARKER AT HOME.

Mr. Parker, who is the author of a number of charming plays, collaborated with Mr. W. W. Jacobs in writing *Beauty and the Barge*, in which Mr. Cyril Maude has made so great a success.

Photo by Johnston & Hoffmann.

MISS CLARITA VIDAL,
Who looked so charming as one of the Ladies-in-Waiting to Queen Sonia in *His Highness my Husband.*

impetuous and therefore rebellious. The climax of either play is that point at which the husband is most widely separated from his wife, owing to her own foolishness and obstinacy. The end is the same in both instances, for these rebellious people are both women. The methods of attaining this end are different, since Suzanne and Katharina were of dissimilar natures. The former sought the stool of repentance because she was wearied of that which she had asked to be granted; the latter became submissive because what she demanded was denied to her. Suzanne raved for freedom and the liberty to use her own life. She obtained her divorce, and did as she pleased. But the paint came

Photo by Langfier.

MISS JUNE VAN BUSKIRK,
Who is taking the part of Miss Wyatt in *The Walls of Jericho.*

off the new toys, and their charm soon went, and so to find happiness she set out in a motor-car and evening dress to regain her husband. Katharina's affection was never born until her mind was subdued to the will of Petruchio. Happiness came to husband and wife only because the former persistently refused to give way to her mad impulses.

It is one of the paradoxes of life that desire and gratification are ever at variance, and Suzanne Trevor found this to her cost. In the opening scene of Mr. Gordon Lennox's comedy Charles Trevor is awaiting the return of his wife. If the title had not been appropriated some years ago by Mr. Henry Arthur Jones, one

Photo by Ellis & Walery.

MR. ARTHUR BOURCHIER
In his latest production *The Walls of Jericho.*

Photo by Ellis & Walery.

AN INCIDENT IN THE WALLS OF JERICHO, NOW BEING PLAYED AT THE GARRICK THEATRE.

Photo by Ellis & Walery.

MR. GEORGE EDWARDES,
Who, although he is the busiest theatrical manager in London,
finds time to devote himself to golf.

might have fittingly called this play *The Case of Rebellious Susan*. Suzanne has not yet returned to dinner, and it is already after midnight. Among Charles Trevor's guests are his mother, Lady Charlotte, Fitzroy Harding, Sir Horace Hatton, the family solicitor, Miss Fanny Minching, Suzanne's plain but worthy companion, and Lady Isobel Bury. True to life, Lady Charlotte is more vehement than charitable in criticising the conduct of her daughter-in-law. Harding is a *roué* and Suzanne's uncle, so that the desire to dissipate was evidently a family failing. Into the battle of words which is waging Mrs. Trevor, the prodigal wife and daughter-in-law, bursts. There is nothing of the penitent

about her. She comes in impudent and callous. What will follow is obvious. She will, of course, resent the sarcasm of her mother-in-law, and will seek sympathy from her friend in the company, who happens to be Lady Isobel. "Well, and where have you been?" every one is asking, although no one is speaking. Suzanne ignores the silent suspense, and expresses a cold desire that the others may have all enjoyed their evening as much as she has enjoyed hers. "I cannot congratulate you on your extreme sociability, and so I'm going to bed," says Suzanne.

But Mrs. Trevor was reckoning without her lord and master. Charles Trevor not unnaturally insists on first knowing where she has been spending the evening, and in whose company. She therefore tells her story in her off-hand, irresponsible manner, and mentions that she has paid a visit to a music hall, had supper at a certain hotel not far from the Haymarket, that there had been some disturbance in Piccadilly, and that in the midst of this Captain Harry Cecil, a handsome but undesirable personage, had come forward, rescued her, and driven her home. The account is

Photo by Bassano.

MISS PHYLLIS DARE AND MISS ZENA DARE.
Miss Zena Dare has been playing with marked success at the Vaudeville.
Her sister is appearing in pantomime.

not unnaturally punctuated by ejaculations of surprise on the part of Trevor's guests. When the latter depart, Suzanne, foreseeing that a severe scolding is awaiting her, takes the precaution of fetching Fanny, her companion, from her bedroom in a scarlet dressing-gown, to be a witness, if the incident should be brought up again. Suzanne, of course, guesses correctly. Trevor takes her to task, and mildly shakes the little rebel. Suzanne calls on Fanny to witness this technical cruelty, and between the first and

which in this case is marital. For staying in the same hotel is Suzanne's divorced husband, and the surprise and uneasiness occasioned by his arrival are compensated for by the opportunity thus given of her temporarily avoiding the society of her admirers. Of the two principal lovers, one had proved himself to be a fool and the other a brute.

The change in Suzanne's plans is most interesting in its development. It is a wonderfully true picture of feminine character. First she finds persistent attention

THE SECOND SCENE IN *THE FREEDOM OF SUZANNE.*
Suzanne (Miss Marie Tempest), staying at Maverly-on-Sea, is surprised by the arrival of her husband (Mr. Allan Aynesworth).

second act obtains from the Court her decree nisi.

The second scene is in an hotel at Maverly-on-Sea. Suzanne has been to Dieppe, and her admirers have followed her to the English watering-place. Gradually she begins to tire of their attentions and to find that even her freedom has its fetters. The situation suggests conclusions, and had this been an old English play or a modern melodrama, we should have had a strong speech and the centre of the stage reserved for the hero to declare that the only liberty attainable is by obedience to lawful authority,

monotonous. Then she is not slow to realise the worthlessness of her admirers. These being pushed aside, she is assailed by her loneliness. This would be considerable in the case of any woman of Suzanne's nature — with an endowment of great affection — but in the case of a woman who has for a time at least revelled in the protection and society of her husband the feeling of loneliness would be nearly unbearable. But, besides, there is the news that Trevor has left the hotel and been persuaded to go up to town with a certain Mrs. Tunstall, whose beauty and powers of fascination were obvious even to Suzanne. Suzanne hated Mrs. Tunstall at any time. When it was discovered that she was seeking to occupy the position formerly held by herself, Suzanne loathed her with all the vehemence of a distorted

comedy after so long an absence is most welcome. Mr. Aynesworth played the part of the husband with distinction and in the best possible taste.

It has so often been said that the play-

Photo by the Biograph Studio.

THE COMMENCEMENT OF THE DANCE IN THE LAST SCENE OF *THE TAMING OF THE SHREW* AT THE ADELPHI THEATRE.

affection. And so, just as in *The Wife without a Smile* and in many another drama in the theatre or human experience, Suzanne sets forth to win back her husband, borrows a motor-car, throws a coat over her evening dress, and rushes up to town to Trevor's flat.

When she reaches the flat she is surprised to find that her rival is not there. Trevor treats her with the utmost consideration, but Suzanne's spirit is even now rebellious. The remark from Trevor, " I knew you would come back," was hardly tactful when made to an impulsive being like Suzanne. Finally, however, Trevor insists on removing her wet stockings, places her near the fire, and brings her food, and by proving that he had put a man from the King's Proctor's Office to watch outside, he shows that her decree nisi cannot be made absolute. She is not sorry. She has had her freedom, and is content to come back. The play is excellent in the first act, good in the second, and passable in the last. Miss Marie Tempest as Suzanne is inimitable, and her return to

going public will not pay to see Shakespearian plays that it is interesting to see the success of *The Tempest* at His Majesty's followed by another victory at the Adelphi. In *The Taming of the Shrew* Mr. Oscar Asche has won a triumph over prejudice by his own clever acting and that of his company. Here and there are weak places, sometimes in the direction of being too farcical; but the acting as a whole is thoroughly strong. Miss Lily Brayton's interpretation of Katharina is exceedingly impressive. It is so natural and real, and yet artistic, that it will probably rank as one of the best efforts she has hitherto made. It is not overdone, but yet powerfully appealing. All the obstinacy of the wayward wife is brought out to the smallest detail. Mr. Hampden, who made so successful a *début* in *The Prayer of the Sword*, scarcely adds to his reputation in the present play, and he has still to learn the value of gesture. There are comparatively few " cuts " in the version of the play presented, and the Induction is not omitted, as it has been on certain other occasions. The scenery and dresses are beautiful, and precautions have been taken that the play should be thoroughly well rehearsed before being presented to audiences which are nowadays never more critical than when seeing a Shakespearian production.

The revival of *Lady Windermere's Fan* after so long a lapse is justifiable. The in, so to speak, against their will. A situation is forced, the dialogue is unnaturally turned in a direction so as to give occasion to introduce a smart epigram. When *Lady Windermere's Fan* was written it was in the correct fashion; but since then a reversion has been made to strong situations rather than to witty remarks. In places the dialogue of the play is weak and dull. But

Photo by Ellis & Walery.
SUZANNE HAS ARRIVED AT HER HUSBAND'S FLAT WET AND HUNGRY, AFTER A HURRIED DRIVE
IN A BORROWED MOTOR-CAR.
The Last Act in *The Freedom of Suzanne.*

author of *The Importance of Being Earnest* was not a born dramatist, but there is a delicacy of touch and an amount of wit and clever cynicism in his plays which is not always observable elsewhere. One feels in *Lady Windermere's Fan* as one does in *A Woman of No Importance*—that the play has been written for the display of epigrams, not the epigrams written for the play. Sometimes, indeed, they are dragged the play as a whole is solidly constructed, although, to continue the metaphor, there is little dramatic ornamentation. The second and third scenes, difficult in this case to arrange effectively, were cleverly handled by an author who was brilliant by nature. There is no playwright among us who can quite take his place in giving to us so much originality of ideas and, in places, dialogue so rich in wit. Those who have already seen *Lady Windermere's Fan* will be glad of an opportunity of seeing it again at the St. James's Theatre. Those who did not see it on its first production will find Mr. Ben Webster and Miss Lilian Braithwaite interesting in the characters of Lord and Lady Windermere, and Miss Marion Terry delightful in her original part.

In support of a special appeal for the Samaritan Hospital for Women, Mrs. George Alexander, assisted by Mrs. Kendal, Mrs. Beerbohm Tree, Miss Winifred Emery, and others, held a reception during one of the wintry afternoons of November in the St. James's Theatre. Her Majesty the Queen had been pleased to purchase ten of the guinea tickets. Tea was served on the stage, which, by an ingenious scenic arrangement, had been transformed into "The Garden Beautiful." All the stalls had been removed from the auditorium, with the advantage of allowing considerable space to the large number of guests. Miss Alice Nielson and several members of the San Carlo Opera Company from Covent Garden contributed to the musical programme.

Photo by Johnston & Hoffmann.

MR. LYALL SWETE AND MR. CHARLES ROCK
In *The Taming of the Shrew* at the Adelphi Theatre.

The unfortunate fiasco connected with the production of *The Flute of Pan* by "John Oliver Hobbes" at the Shaftesbury has caused the question to be raised again, "May a playgoer exhibit his disapproval of a play if he wishes?" During the last year or two disorderly scenes have been witnessed in some of the West End theatres on the production of a new play. It is equitable, surely, that if one has a right to applaud a good play, one should not be denied also the opportunity of exhibiting one's displeasure if the play or the acting deserve it. But it were more courteous to perform this unpleasant task by a persistent silence. The desired end would still be obtained, and there would be no possibility of such unseemly booing as takes place now so frequently in the gallery.

Even with the worst plays, acted by the least imaginative artistes, it is quite unreasonable to "boo." On a first night there is always electricity in the air. Every one, from the author to the call-boy, is suffering from a bad attack of nerves. The least excitement will upset the balance of any actor who has any feelings at all at a *première*. There has been the terrible strain of long and weary rehearsals for weeks past, frequently lasting till the small hours of the morning. At the last moment something always goes wrong. A whole act has to be reconstructed, pages of dialogue have to be "cut," new "business" inserted to make the play less uninteresting.

And yet, when every member of the company is feeling at his very worst, he has to face the dramatic critics, the regular first-nighters, and a spoiled public clamouring in the gallery for something better than the best that has been hitherto given them. Can one wonder that actor-managers occasionally find the strain too much, become inadvisedly irritable, and lose command over their temper and their tongue? Many an actor has prayed for the time when criticism will be suspended until the play has been running for a week. There are certain obvious drawbacks to such a suggestion, but at least it would render the opinions of the critics, the stalls, and the cynics in the gallery far more valuable and representative.

Photo by Johnston & Hoffmann.

MRS. BROWN POTTER

As Julie in *A Man's Shadow*, recently played by Royal Command at Windsor.

"THE HESPERIDES," A SYMBOLICAL OVERMANTEL MADE FOR THE RIGHT HON. A. J. BALFOUR.

The Poetry of Metal Work.

BY LILIAN JOY.

ILLUSTRATED BY EXAMPLES OF MR. ALEXANDER FISHER'S WORK.

THERE was a time when every article of household use had a voice of its own, and spoke, to those who had ears to hear, the message of the maker. In those days no line was drawn between the artist and the craftsman. He who designed a thing with his brain made, or helped to make it, with his hands. The commonest objects became thus emblematic of some phase of a man's very soul. All true art must give witness to a truth, and as the worker learnt truth through experience of life as he toiled, so he expressed it in his work.

Then came a sterile period, from the close of the eighteenth century, when design and workmanship began to be disassociated, and the metal worker, among others, instead of following the magic path of his imagination, servilely copied published design. It was, of course, William Morris, that true friend of the applied Arts, who instigated their restoration.

Among the first to claim metals for his good use was Mr. Alexander Fisher. Simultaneously he revived that beautiful lost art

of enamelling. It came about in the simplest fashion. He was asked by a friend to mend a small enamel box, and was seized with a desire to make such things. He became a member of the first class in enamelling at the Kensington Art Schools in 1885, consisting of ten pupils. Since then he has turned out many successful and promising pupils from the Finsbury and Regent Street Art Schools and from his own studio. Among them will be found the best-known enamellers of the day.

Such a career as his must have been perforce one of discovery. His field of enterprise lay in ancient examples of the art, in a few old French books on the subject, and in perpetual, painstaking experiment. To say that a man is a metal worker and enameller is to call him among the most patient of his kind. It is perhaps because a good enamel is a standing witness to this quality that there is something so singularly restful about it. Yet one wonders that in this age of "nerves" there can be found any one with the necessary evenness of temperament to carry out all the tedious

A PORTRAIT IN ENAMEL, PURCHASED BY HIS MAJESTY KING
EDWARD VII. AND PRESENTED BY HIM TO THE DOWAGER
EMPRESS FREDERICK IN 1896.

metals. This has to be crushed to powder in a mortar, mixed with water, and laid on the prepared surface with a knife. After the application of each colour the object has to be consigned to the furnace, and finally must undergo a lengthy and tedious process of washing and polishing.

There are several different methods of enamelling. The *Bassetaille* is that in which a bed is made for the enamel by carving the design in relief on the metal, as in the King's Cup to be referred to later. For *Champlevé* enamels the designs are "scorped" out, and then filled by the enamel to make them flush with the metal surface. *Cloissonné* enamels, as is pretty well known, are outlined and contained by fine gold wires, which are bent to the desired shapes by forceps and pliers, and then soldered to the background. *Plique à jour*

operations; and when these operations were rendered yet more delicate and uncertain by a lack of positive knowledge the wonder is increased.

In its simplest form the process—which is that of fusing a coloured glass on a ground of metal or pottery—was in use among all the ancient races—the Egyptians, Phœnicians, Assyrians, Greeks, Romans, and Etruscans.

Mr. Fisher began with some knowledge of pottery enamelling; but with metal as a background an added difficulty was presented on account of its tendency to turn the colour of the enamels, besides which the smooth surface does not lend itself to the purpose. Endless experiment eventually overcame these two obstacles. It is possible now to buy excellent enamel; but when Mr. Fisher first began he had to make it himself. It is in appearance like lumps of coloured glass, of which the colour is obtained by staining with oxide of various

PORTRAIT OF THE LATE EARL OF WARWICK
IN ENAMEL SET IN SILVER GILT.

PRAYER-BOOK COVER IN ENAMEL AND SILVER GILT, SET WITH RUBIES AND EMERALDS.
MADE FOR THE HON. MRS. PERCY WYNDHAM.

enamels are those which allow the light to pass through them, and are secured in position by cloisons. The improved and latest development, generally called Limoges after that home of the Renaissance form of the art in the fifteenth and sixteenth centuries, is in reality more accurately described as "painted enamel." The term is not only descriptive of part of the process, but also acknowledges modern differences and improvements on the original Limoges methods.

A celebrated example of this mediæval work is the King's Cup in the Gold Room at the British Museum. It was bought, chiefly by subscription, for £8,000 some few years ago. Its historic interest, in having been the property of the kings of England from Henry VI. to James I., is as great as its intrinsic beauty. Scenes from the life of St. Agnes are represented on it in colours of ruby and sapphire.

Yet Limoges enamels, although attaining to a very high degree of technical excellence, fail to exemplify the chief and peculiar possibilities of the material. These appear to have awaited modern discovery, and in this way it seems that from the artistic, if not from the executive point of view, the modern revival in enamelling has produced results better than anything that has gone before. There is at any rate in present-day work a striving for feeling and "colour," which is characteristic of and in sympathy with the age, rather than for the exquisitely fine

A BEAUTIFUL CHALICE MADE IN SILVER GILT FOR ST. PAUL'S, EALING.

A MAGNIFICENT JEWEL CASKET WITH ENAMELLED MEDALLIONS.

detail which was considered of paramount importance in earlier times.

It is these qualities of feeling and colour that give the great charm to Mr. Fisher's work. He is a reader and thinker who believes, as he himself says that every artist should believe, in his material. He thinks, too, in such a manner that one is tempted to call him a poet, rather than an artist, in metals and enamel. This definition will be better understood after an examination of the over-mantel in our illustration designed for Mr. [...]our. Let us leave aside the question of [...]hnical merits, which show a develop-[...] the combined arts of metal work [...]el so new and so original as to be [...]thout the pale of comparison. [...]aginative standpoint, from which [...]ks can be judged, it must be [...] a creation of a high order. [...] once a desire to fathom its

meaning, to follow out the maze of the maker's mind in delicious anticipation of the discovery of some precious truth or some delightful fancy that has inspired this speaking imagery.

It is called the "Garden of the Hesperides": the ancient myth being taken as a parable of the life of the worker, the life of all those who would attain great ends. In the central design can be traced the form of an inverted heart, surmounting a dragon. This heart encloses three figures, of Love, Truth, and Power in robes of red, yellow, and orange, seeming to merge in one flame, the flame of desire. So if a man greatly desire to reach the goal of his ambition, he must bear in his heart, first, love of his work; next he must be ever true to it; finally he must possess the power to do. But before he begins at all he will have to slay the dragon of Ignorance. And the fruit of his labour, the apples of the Hesperides, which he shall win in the end will be Success. In the panel on the left there is a figure symbolic of the Inspiration, and on the right the name of the worker is being recorded on the scroll of Fame.

The faces and hands of the figures are exquisitely carved in ivory. The accomplishment of this, perhaps the finest of Mr. Alexander Fisher's works, occupied a year and a half, and it was exhibited in the New Gallery in 1900.

It was not until Mr. Fisher had been employed some time on his art that it was suggested to him to exhibit at Burlington House. "But," he said, "they would not take work in enamels. They never have anything of the kind." He nevertheless did send in

five examples that year, 1893, and every one was accepted.

Much of the beauty of ecclesiastical metal work is due to the fact that it is bound to be symbolic, and therefore imaginative. Yet the Crucifixion is a subject in which so many artists have seen only the pain and agony, and forgotten that these symbolised the death of sin, and the triumph of love and forgiveness. In the beautiful, peaceful crucifix here illustrated, the dove, messenger of victory, hovers over the Sacred Head. The very wood branches forth into that tree of which the Divine Sufferer Himself had said, "All the birds of the air shall dwell therein."

The little silver statuette, a part of an electric lamp, in one of our illustrations,

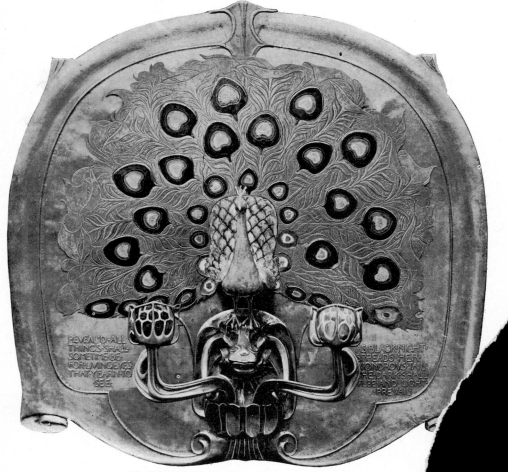

AN OVERMANTEL IN SILVER, STEEL, AND ENAMEL.

needs a word of explanation. It represents that angel Israfel, "whose heart strings are a lute, and who has the sweetest voice of all God's creatures," as recorded in the Koran— a solitary mention that inspired the lovely poem of Edgar Allan Poe. A thing to dwell upon is the exquisite sweep of the wings as the figure throws itself backward in the ecstasy of song, with arms and eyes upraised to the light above him. The light in the finished work is held in a dome supported by pillars. Its rays concentrate in the crystal ball on which the angel's feet are placed, making him look as though he stands upon a star.

A like grace of pose was noticeable in the figure of Aphrodite, that formed the motive of an electric-light fitting on view in Mr. Fisher's exhibition last summer. In the other combined electric-light fitting and overmantel, illustrated here, the eyes of the peacock feathers are represented in green and blue enamel. The jewel

casket cannot be passed without a brief description. It is in silver gilt, and the enamels on each side represent the ruby, pearl, emerald, and sapphire. On the top is a very simple and fine design with bosses at the corners. In the central medallion, representing the opal, the subject lends itself to the peculiar genius of the material, with a result that recalls all the elusive beauty of the real stone.

One of the most fascinating characteristics of this metal work is the way in which the various treasures of the sea and earth are seized upon and used, either to harmonise with the subject of the design, or as an actual type of some thought. For instance, an inverted shell, gracefully mounted, canopies the head of the figure in the Aphrodite electric over-mantel; and pearl blisters are a further and equally appropriate ornament used. In an inkstand, exhibited at the same time, a winged figure is shown leaning over between the receptacles

MANY ARTISTS HAVE SEEN IN THE CRUCIFIXION ONLY THE PAIN AND THE AGONY. IN THE BEAUTIFUL AND PEACEFUL SYMBOLISM ABOVE, THE ARTIST HAS SOUGHT TO EMPHASISE RATHER THE TRIUMPH OF LOVE.

for ink and gazing into the sea of thought of which the shining surface is typified by a piece of changeful green opal matrix.

In conclusion come a few words on a very interesting and distinct branch of enamel work — that of portraiture. Cursory criticism condemns the attempt. To stray from the accustomed media of oil and water colours appears at first sight an unauthorised step likely to lead beyond the realms of true art. Yet, be it remembered, an enamelled portrait is not a mere reproduction of an oil painting, but an original creation : it might, indeed, be termed a painting in durable glass. Then, again, enamel has in itself that translucent quality appertaining to human flesh, but so singularly wanting in the composition of oil paint. Beyond all this there is the fact that an enamelled portrait can last for all time. The cele-brated King's Cup is as brilliant as on the day it left the furnace. It is possible that when other civilisations have swept over and across the earth, the owners of the far future may find the most vivid presentments of the people of our age, not on canvases blackened by centuries, but in the imperishable beauties of enamel portraits.

The last decade has seen the rise of a number of craftsmen in England who have both originality and taste in them. Originality and sincerity are qualities bound to make themselves felt in the long run, and a public weary of the obvious and of lifeless classicisms has not been slow to appreciate a movement which seems to have been well founded.

At the same time, it is not to

THE ANGEL ISRAFEL, A STATUETTE DELICATELY WROUGHT IN SILVER FOR AN ELECTRIC LAMP.

be supposed that the new school was permitted to rear its head without a protest. The craftsman's path is not altogether one of roses, and even Mr. Fisher's career was not without those incidents which speak of the thorny path which lies before the innovator.

Nor is an art rightly acquired in any other way. The short cuts to success— such successes as sometimes emanate from the forcing-house of some particular Parisian studio—it is easy to see, have the seeds of decay in them at birth. For the cramming system, the system of most schools, is obviously of little use to the craftsman, who must have, not only intuition and imagination, but a subtle and delicate understanding of the very life which he wishes to portray. Of a certain bravura in technique, a manner often mistaken for style, these things the schools give in abundance, and of these things our current exhibitions are notoriously full. But, as will be seen from the accompanying beautiful illustrations, such a criticism could not be made in regard to the delicate metal work of Mr. Fisher. It is strong without being clumsy. It is poetic without striving to be weak ; it is not cramped, and yet it happily avoids the grotesque which is the curse of most modern art-work. For art consists not in sensationalism, but in the creation of the beautiful, whether in form or colour, or in both.

HER EXCELLENCY
THE AMBASSADRESS

Photo by Stuart.

THE BRITISH EMBASSY, PARIS.

BY MARY SPENCER WARREN.

[So important a part has recently been played in European affairs by diplomatists that the following article, which shows what it is to be the wife of a British minister, will be read with more than usual interest. ED. L.R.]

IT has been said that it is the diplomatist, not the government, who causes or averts war ; and it must be generally conceded that every foreign representative of His Britannic Majesty treads a more or less thorny path, and that only the possession of an abundance of dignified tact can safely steer him successfully through the complex difficulties of his position. That a British minister may be much helped or hindered by his wife goes without saying; but much more depends upon her than is generally understood, especially when her husband is accredited to a court whose relations with us are rather strained—when an unwise word might lead to decided unpleasantness in the chancelleries, and when a smile or a tactful remark in the right direction might prove highly conciliatory.

It was Lord Beaconsfield who said, " Man conceives fortune, but woman executes it. It is the spirit of man who says, ' I will be great,' but it is the sympathy of woman that usually makes him so." There are few

diplomatists but would be willing to concede that much of their popularity is due to their wives, for the latter, indeed, have a very large share of duties in the direction of entertaining, and in organising and assisting philanthropic work, not only for the resident English community, but often for the native born themselves. Also, it is a recognised fact that woman's power in personal influence can do an enormous amount, without in any way infringing upon the prerogative of the man's position.

The first diplomatic appointment to a foreign court must cause many anxious moments to a minister's wife, for it not only brings such a complete change to previous experiences—opening up an entirely new circle of acquaintance and separating from the old—but it also brings many and great responsibilities to which she has hitherto been quite unaccustomed, as well as a host of duties entirely new and unfamiliar. The ambassador practically plays the *rôle* of king ; he is the direct representative of

Photo by Miss Spencer Warren.

THE THRONE-ROOM IN DUBLIN CASTLE.

majesty, and must worthily uphold the dignity of his country ; hence his Excellency's wife must of necessity play the same exalted part.

Modern-day customs have somewhat modified some of the former stately ceremonies of receiving an ambassador and his wife on their arrival to take up new duties ; and whereas they formerly journeyed by sea on a man-of-war, and on land by state coaches and horses sent up by the royal court to which his excellency was accredited, they now occupy state cabins and railway saloons as do other travellers of importance, and drive to their destination in the carriages of the embassy.

Photo by Thompson.

LADY MACDONALD,

The wife of Sir Claude Maxwell Macdonald, British Minister at Tokio. Lady Macdonald was, together with the other inmates of the British Legation, besieged for two months in Pekin in the year 1900.

Of course there is an official reception at the landing-place or station, and in some cases quite a popular demonstration in their honour. In Dublin or India, where the British diplomat goes to take up the position of viceroy, there is a formal state entrance, the military and civic display, together with the presence of vast numbers of people, making up a very brilliant scene. In India especially, where everything is done on a scale of gorgeous magnificence, such a reception is given the British minister and his wife as, in the words of a former vicereine, they "certainly never before witnessed," not the least impressive part being the vast crowds of Europeans and natives of every caste and size which lined the streets to give them greeting; some in gorgeous uniforms with flashing jewels, some in all the colours of the rainbow, and others in nearly nothing at all.

The official residence in Calcutta—as also at Simla—is grand and stately, and in addition to the European staff which the viceregal family take out, there are literally

many as eight Indian men in one's bed-room, all gravely performing their different duties."

But apart from the oriental surroundings and the lesser or greater responsibility, vice-regal life in India or Dublin does not greatly differ. Each has its own court, issuing its Court Circular recording the movements of the viceregal family, and particularising all dinners, balls, attendances at various functions,

Photo by Stuart.

THE DINING-ROOM OF THE BRITISH EMBASSY, PARIS.

swarms of native servants in gorgeous uniforms of scarlet and gold and white turbans. But, as her excellency continues, "They are all men for every possible duty, and all of them strictly mindful of caste. He who puts water into your jug would not deign to pour it out; one who cleans your shoes would consider it derogatory to pass a cup of tea; and one puts a candle in a candlestick, while another sets light to it. It is not at all surprising to find as

etc., of both their excellencies. Military escorts attend when their excellencies ride out in state, and even for the private drives of the vicereine there are mounted men in attendance. Naturally, there are large numbers of state officials attached to these viceregal courts, and guards of honour are mounted and bands in attendance as in the case of Royalty itself. At either place a goodly portion of her excellency's time is taken up with entertaining. There is one succession of dinner-parties, large or small, interspersed with receptions, drawing-rooms, balls or garden-parties, in accordance with the season. Often two or three thousand guests are invited for one function, and though mercifully the vicereine does not have any catering responsibility as an ordinary hostess might do, yet she must go through the lists, and these large functions are an undeniable tax upon the tact, forbearance, and strength of any lady.

The philanthropic work connected with either country is something prodigious. In

a very exalted and extensive social circle. It is a busy life, with very little time for other than public duties, which by the nature of things are onerous and continuous.

This state of things also applies to the wife of an ambassador, who, from almost the date of her arrival at the official residence, finds herself all but overwhelmed with demands upon her time. At the earliest possible moment the ambassador lays his credentials before the sovereign of the court, and then visits are at once exchanged between the various embassies and the

Photo by Miss Spencer Warren.

AN ORIGINAL SKETCH BY THE GERMAN EMPEROR, PRESENTED TO THE BRITISH AMBASSADOR IN BERLIN.

The picture now hangs on the walls of the embassy.

this her excellency is expected to take the lead. In India, Lady Dufferin's scheme for bringing medical aid to women monopolises very much of the vicereine's time, the present "first lady" in the country having inaugurated a special branch of this work; while in Ireland, the promotion of the "native industries" is the foremost benevolent work in which her excellency of that country is interested. But apart from this, there are bazaars, prize-givings at schools, visits to hospitals and various charitable institutions, as well as a voluminous correspondence, and all the incidentals peculiar to the head of

leaders of society in the city. A diplomatic dinner is given at court in honour of the new minister and his wife; after this, dinner-parties all round are very soon the order of the day. In addition, her excellency — if it be during the season — holds a weekly reception, always numerously attended.

The wife of the British ambassador in either of the great continental cities is of necessity one of *the* leaders of society. Her salons are amongst the most brilliant, and are attended by all the *élite* as well as by the diplomatic staff of every embassy. Her excellency assists to receive all persons

Photo by Miss Spencer Warren.

THEIR EXCELLENCIES' CORRIDOR, DUBLIN CASTLE.

bassy by being present at a dinner or other function.

Every British embassy is expected to be the centre of much good work in the capital in which it is situated, and it must be said that this expectation is universally fulfilled ; such is really more particularly within the province of her excellency, and her works in this respect are multifarious. It is then one of her first duties to make herself acquainted with the various societies and organisations in vogue, by paying personal visits, or receiving the officials. Of course, there is now an English church in each of the continental cities, the chaplain of which is also chaplain to

of importance of her own nationality who may be passing through or making a short stay in the city; at any time she may be called upon to receive Royalty itself, for the King and princes and princesses of our own Royal Family, when visiting the capital, repair to the embassy either to luncheon or dinner, and in certain instances actually make it their headquarters. Also, the sovereign of the court to which the ambassador is accredited will often honour the em-

the embassy. There is an ambassadorial pew, always regularly occupied by their

Photo by Miss Spencer Warren.

THE THRONE-ROOM OF THE BRITISH EMBASSY, BERLIN.

Photo by Lafayette.

THE COUNTESS OF DUDLEY.

Both Calcutta and Dublin have their own court, issuing their own
Court Circular recording the movements of the vice-regal family.

have the knack of becoming familiar with detail. The multitude of appeals for assistance in all manner of difficulties which she will receive in her correspondence can scarcely be computed. Much of this properly comes within the scope of the societies above named, but probably the writers of the letters deem that they shall receive more favourable replies if such come directly under her excellency's notice. But it is all a tax upon time, and as one lady, wife of a prominent minister, said, her "duties lasted practically from seven o'clock in the morning until midnight or probably later." A portion of the day might be spent, certainly, in paying visits or receiving callers, but such were a part of the duties of the position, and often tiring in the extreme. Should there be a bazaar or sale of work, her excellency is expected to take the lead in organising and in general preparations, and on the opening day she more often than not performs the ceremony, and of course is expected to make purchases at each stall. She must visit hospitals, orphanages, give prizes at schools, attend the summer and winter entertainments of such, and take part in a hundred and one things inseparable from her position.

Some of the entertainments given at the various embassies are on a very lavish scale, and costly in the extreme. At Paris—which is of course the premier diplomatic centre—dinner-parties and receptions are very large, while the garden-parties are often attended by as many as three thousand persons. Each embassy has its own service of plate, that at Paris including a fine collection once the property of Jerome Napoleon. It may be mentioned that the embassy was formerly the residence of Pauline, the beautiful sister of the great Napoleon.

Sir Edmund and Lady Monson—who are retiring from office almost immediately—will be succeeded by Sir Francis Leveson Bertie and Lady Bertie. Lady Bertie has had a perhaps somewhat exceptional opportunity

excellencies, who, together with the chaplain and his wife, are the leaders of all church work. Her Excellency makes herself acquainted with the schools, the Girls' Friendly Society, the institutes for governesses and artists which exist in nearly every city, the British Institute, where established, the Dorcas Society, the British Charitable Fund, and a host of other things too numerous to mention, but all under the jurisdiction of the embassy and the church. Each of these societies does very useful work; some of them owe their existence entirely to the initiative of the embassies, and some from even higher sources. The annual meetings of these various societies, of which her excellency is often the president, are more often than not held at the British embassy, and presided over by the ambassador.

In order to successfully undertake all this work, the wife of an ambassador should be essentially practical and business-like, and

of early acquiring a complete insight into the duties which will presently devolve upon her, for she is a daughter of the first Earl Cowley, who was ambassador in Paris when King Edward paid his first visit to that city as a young man. Lady Bertie, who was one of Queen Alexandra's bridesmaids, is looking forward with particular interest to taking up her abode in the residence where she spent a great part of the days of her girlhood.

Another imminent change is at Rome, where Sir Edward and Lady Egerton will take up residence, in place of Sir Francis and Lady Bertie.

In all, Great Britain is represented at thirty-six different courts, but eight only of the ministers are ambassadors, these being severally appointed to France, Germany, Russia, Austria, Italy, Spain, Turkey, and the United States. It will be remembered that the Kaiser was recently present at the wedding of Miss Lascelles, daughter of the Ambassador at Berlin, this being only a typical instance of the way in which our representatives abroad are honoured. It may be said that the wife of

an ambassador enjoys the same privileges as does the minister himself, one being perfect immunity from the laws of the country in which she is residing, and certain important privileges are granted. Every embassy is of spacious proportions, and luxuriously furnished; semi-state carriages are provided, and the minister and his wife are entitled to full military honours and salutes.

Of course, her excellency must not have any political opinions. She must hold the difficult position of absolute neutrality and friendship with all with whom she comes in contact; in short, hers is a position which, though of great honour, is beset with difficulties. It is not often, though, that danger is added to the list, as was notably the case with Lady Macdonald when at Pekin in 1900. Together with all the inmates of the British Legation, she was besieged in their residence from June 20 to the night of August 13. Lady Macdonald— who adds to her other accomplishments the art of a clever and forcible writer—has herself described the terrible sufferings the

Photo by Stuart.

THE DRAWING ROOM OF THE BRITISH EMBASSY IN PARIS.

Photo by Stuart.

THE BALLROOM OF THE BRITISH EMBASSY IN PARIS.

At the extreme end will be noticed the throne-room.

little garrison had to undergo in those few weeks, her excellency herself helping to nurse the large number of wounded people, filling in her time by preparing necessities for the hospital, and making sand-bags used for barricading—all of which was carried on on meagre diet, and under the constant firing and whiz and scream of bullets. Fortunately, Lady Macdonald's was a rare experience, but still, it is one that the wife of any British minister *may* perchance have to encounter.

The Minstrel.

BY HUGH PARR.

SINCE ever now from Love's embrace apart,
　　Like some pure hermit in his holy cell,
　　In lonely splendour doth my lady dwell,
All the glad notes she woke within my heart
Must from the music of my verse depart;
　　Fled is their charm; nor can I longer tell
　　How sweet the magic of her tender spell
Whose haunting echo mocks the singer's art.

But let her deign to hearken to my prayer,
　　And my poor verses shall such glory take
That lovers I must listen and despair,
　　The while my songs for her delight I make.
So men shall praise her beauties rich and rare,
　　Till sun and stars their wonted course forsake.

When Youth Begins to Go.

BY "NARCISSA."

The lady saw her youth
Depart, . . .
And wondered who the woman was
Fronting her silent in the glass.
BROWNING.

"AND WONDERED WHO THE WOMAN WAS
FRONTING HER SILENT IN THE GLASS."

THE mere idea of growing old is terribly repellent to some women; nevertheless, it need not be so, for the loss of youth does not necessarily mean the loss of beauty. Max O'Rell declared that the secret of a woman's looks lies in resplendent health and a cheerful mind. This statement may have seemed ironical to those who are delicate and therefore liable to depression, but mind and body act and react on each other in such a marvellous degree that the cultivation of a calm and contented spirit is one of the surest ways to preserve a youthful appearance. Now, though it is possible by various artifices for a woman to look at least ten years younger than she really is, this deception is one that only lasts for a few years; and I would impress upon every woman not to be afraid of looking her real age, provided that she looks as beautiful as possible, and my reason for this advice is as follows.

Just as each successive season of the year has its own special charm, so has each stage in a woman's life, and therefore, if she tries artificially to prolong a youthful appearance, she pays for it sooner or later by looking at least ten years older than she should do later on. The freshness and brilliancy of colouring of extreme youth are delicious in the extreme, though they cannot be expected to last; but the expression of face and development of figure which take their place more than make up for the loss of pristine freshness in late life; so, from girlhood to womanhood, from womanhood to middle age, and onwards through the various gradations to old age, each period has its own especial charm, provided nature, aided with a little care, is allowed to work her will.

The art of how to be for ever becomingly garbed is discussed elsewhere in these pages; but the woman whose youth is, well, just thinking about going, must remember that the setting is by no means the least important part of the picture, and that a still appropriate frame enhances, and one that is inappropriate detracts from, the beauty of form and face. The woman who goes to nature for her tints and colourings will not go far wrong. During the spring of life pure, delicate colourings and light fabrics will best become her; at midsummer nature is stronger hued, but makes up in richness what she lacks in delicacy; and in the early autumn of life it again becomes possible to wear the most delicate hues and fabrics. Still, transition periods are trying, and perhaps the most trying is when the complexion is inclined to become somewhat indefinite and the hair neither one thing nor the other. It is at this period, usually, that a woman turns her attention to the subject of make-up. This is a difficult question. My first piece of advice is, "Don't begin." Nevertheless, a few judicious touches here and there are perfectly permissible, provided the paint is not obvious; still, all arts and aids must be used with extreme caution, or the latter stage of the unwary woman will be infinitely worse than the first. The chief difficulty lies in the fact that, unless the woman is at heart an artist, she usually chooses the wrong shade of rouge and powder, and the wrong tints for her hair—her eye, being untrained, overdoes the effect; therefore, unless born with the artistic sense, it is well to take a few lessons in the gentle art of making up from an expert. The most harmless and perfect rouge is composed of cold cream as a basis, tinted with rose petals; if this is applied in infinitesimal quantities and dusted with pure powder afterwards, the colour is extremely natural, and little,

TO PREVENT A WRINKLED THROAT, MASSAGE WITH COLD CREAM.

if any, harm is done to the skin itself. All make-up should be removed with cold cream when the face is washed before going to bed at night. But without doubt, the women who are most beautiful at all stages of life are those who have lived healthy lives and never used other cosmetics than soap and water. The ladies of St. James's of

TAP COLD CREAM INTO THE CROWS'-FEET.

were, the line from throat to chin becoming either wrinkled or blurred in outline, according as to whether the possessor is thin or stout. Before twenty - five the layer of sub - cutaneous fat beneath the skin prevents the formation of lines, and little or no artificial nourishment is needed; but after twenty - five this same layer of adipose

whom Austin Dobson sings so charmingly, who "painted to the eyes," were exquisitely lovely for a few short years, but developed into what can only be described as hags in middle age, unless they first died from the effects of red and white which they so freely used; while the early Victorian ladies, who considered the slightest touch of paint or powder immoral, are now reaping their reward in rose-leaf complexions and silvery hair.

I have wandered far away from the lady "fronting herself silent in the glass." I would advise every woman over twenty-five to sit before a good mirror in the very strongest light and mercilessly criticise herself. The result is often depressing, but it is only by really facing a situation that the best can be made of it, and the little onslaughts of time can be checked. This critical survey will probably reveal the fact that tiny lines are forming round the eyes and mouth, that the cheeks are not quite so full as they once

tissue decreases, and then it is that cream and facial massage come in. But once facial massage is commenced, it must at all costs be continued, long experience teaching that should the habit be suddenly discontinued the face will fall into ten times more lines that it would have had if left alone.

Let me not alarm my readers, however, for this does not mean that it is necessary always to be within reach of a toilet specialist; a few simple movements, such as each woman can do for herself daily, will be all that is required to keep the skin in a healthy condition and comparatively free from wrinkles. To begin with that terrible enemy, a wrinkled throat and flabby chin, the following exercise, if persisted in, will work wonders. Wash the throat and chin in hot water; then, lubricating the fingers with cold cream, start with the left hand under the right ear, and draw it briskly but firmly from ear to chin; then take the right hand

and do the same from the left side ; the hands should follow one another as rapidly as possible, and while the "movement from chin to ear should be light, a considerable amount of pressure should be brought to bear under the chin itself. This should be done daily for ten minutes at a time, and the process completed by bathing the neck and throat plentifully with cold water, to which has been added a little of the oft-quoted lavender water. Regarding the facial lines, the cheeks should be kneaded with a circular movement upwards and inwards. Great care must be taken while treating the delicate tissues round the eyes, or the skin will become stretched and the trouble increased instead of decreased. There is much controversy on the different methods of massaging the face, but the following treatment will be found most successful. For lines beneath the eyes, anoint the finger-tips with cold cream and *gently stroke from the nose to the temple.* For the crows'-feet at the corners, tap in cold cream with the fleshy part of the fingers. For the lines on the forehead, anoint two fingers of each hand with cold cream, and draw them to and fro across the forehead; then, taking three fingers, press the horizontal lines which appear between the eyes.

DRAW THE FINGERS TO AND FRO WITH FIRM BUT GENTLE PRESSURE.

I have in previous articles given minute directions as to the treatment of the hair and complexion, and I will not further enlarge on these, but will merely remark that, when the proper time comes for the hair to grow grey, it is wise to let it go, though during the time of transition period the roots must be kept well nourished. The scalp at this time is liable to be unduly dry ; the very best hair-wash, therefore, is one composed of two parts of bay rum to which one part of castor oil is added —the spirit neutralises the unpleasant odour of the oil. This must be sprinkled into every parting and well rubbed into the roots with the finger-tips ; a little of the same wash may be applied with advantage to the eyebrows, a tiny brush being used for the purpose. Fair hair that is losing its colour may be innocently brightened by the application of a decoction of strong tea, used after shampooing.

It is needless to say that the teeth should receive the most regular care from a skilful dentist, for however perfect a false set are, they never suit the mouth as well as one's own. The front teeth should be crowned as soon as decayed, and made to match exactly those that they replace.

Nothing conveys the impression of youth

so much as supple figure, and exercise and diet will prevent that middle-aged spread which so many women justly dread. It is impossible to remain lithe and graceful if the body is cased in too stiff or tight corsets; long may smart looseness of apparel continue in fashion. The woman who keeps up the childish habit of daily touching her toes without bending her knees need never fear stiffness, and agility and lightness of movement are preserved by the daily habit of skipping with or without a rope.

Finally, when youth begins to go, avoid fatigues and worries as you would deadly poison: the women who are always rushing are not the women who accomplish the most; the very busiest woman has always time to snatch a few minutes of indolence during the day, to put her feet up and close her eyes. Kingsley says, "Every time a woman catches cold she insensibly shortens her life." It is perfectly true a chill of any form does lower the vitality and so tend to shorten life—therefore take any small ailment in time. In conclusion, I would remind my readers of the beautiful words of A. H. Clough:

And not by Eastern windows only
When daylight comes, comes in the light:
In front the sun shines slow, how slowly;
But Westward, look! the land is bright.

As I have laid stress throughout these articles on the necessity of only using the very purest cosmetics, I append a list of homely but efficacious remedies, and give one or two recipes for the preparation of creams and washes such as can easily be prepared at home at a small cost.

The following should be in every toilet cupboard:

Benzoated lard, for chapped hands.
Cocoa butter, to strengthen the eyebrows.
Oil of sweet almonds, for brittle nails.
Fine oatmeal, $2\frac{1}{2}d.$ per pound, for softening water.
Precipitated chalk, as a dentifrice.
Prepared fuller's earth, as a toilet powder.
White wine, as an astringent wash.

RUB THE LOTION INTO THE ROOTS OF THE HAIR.

ANOINT THE EYEBROWS, USING A SOFT BRUSH.

Let the first two ingredients stand in a warm place, then strain. Melt the wax and spermaceti together, and add the oil of almonds and alkanet. Stir the mixture till it is thick, and perfume with a few drops of otto of roses. The salve can be coloured if desired with a little pure carmine or a few drops of cochineal.

A cooling and healing face wash is prepared as follows :

> Elder-flower water, ½ pint.
> Friar's balsam, 3 drams.

Mix these, put them in a well-stoppered bottle, and shake very vigorously till they are thoroughly mixed.

A good cream for the hands is prepared as follows :

> White wax, 1 oz.
> Cocoa butter, 1 oz.
> Oil of almonds, 1 oz.

Melt them together, and stir till the mixture becomes thick and white, and perfume with a few drops of otto of roses.

The following is an excellent wash for hair that is falling and inclined to be greasy :

> Rum, ½ pint.
> Spirit of wine, 3 oz.
> Rose water, ½ pint.
> Tincture of cantharides, 2 drams.
> Carbonate of ammonia, 2 drams.

While for dry hair or excessive dandruff I can recommend the following pomade to be applied to the roots of the hair :

> Glycerine, 5 oz.
> Oil of sweet almonds, 5 oz.
> Lime water, 5 oz.
> Tincture of cantharides, 5 drams.

Lavender water, a little to be added to the washing water.
Elder-flower water, for bathing a flushed face.

The following recipes are prepared according to the formulas advised by two well-known doctors. The first is for a very reliable lip salve :

> Oil of almonds, 3 oz.
> Alkanet, ½ oz.
> White wax, 1½ oz.
> Spermaceti, ½ oz.

THE TRUTH ABOUT MAN.

By a Spinster.

ILLUSTRATED BY FACTS FROM HER OWN PRIVATE HISTORY.

The author of " The Truth About Man" is a well-known novelist, who prefers not to reveal her identity. In her opening chapters she subdivides Man into the Irresistitle, the Admirable, and the Marriageable, discourses on the unattractiveness of the Ideal Woman, and analyses the effect of Love upon mature Man. As he believes that the views of "A Spinster" may not be shared by all the readers of THE LADY'S REALM *the Editor has decided to offer prizes, month by month, for the best criticisms of " The Truth About Man." Particulars will be found on page* 20 *of the advertisements.*

CHAPTER V.

The Spinster gives advice gratis to other spinsters on the use and management of Man the Lover.

NOW it needs no very brilliant discernment to perceive that when once the woman has a man in love with her, she holds in her hands a tremendous power for her own advantage. In the first place, whether rich or poor, young or old, handsome or plain, a devoted admirer is always useful to a woman. She can, by means of him, bring others to her feet : for one of Man's most noticeable weaknesses is the impulse to follow a leader ; and we women have an unspoken proverb :— "Lovers never come singly." When one man sees another courting a girl, his attention is instantly arrested. He begins to wonder what there is in her to attract so-and-so, and from being interested in her it is ten to one that he ends by wanting to cut the other fellow out !

It is, therefore, a most important thing for a woman to have a hanger-on, "a fetch-and-carry—get-out-of-the-way-kind of-neuter " (as O. W. Holmes expresses it) if possible, for such are harmless and interfere very little in the game ; but a willing slave, anyhow, whose affection is marked enough to strike attention. Thus equipped, she is well armed for conquest, and if the lover be also rich, she can maintain quite a superior attitude for a long

time, whether she announce an engagement or not.

To the Ideal Woman this gross worldliness will be, of course, distasteful. " Rather let me remain neglected by my hearthside," she will say, with virtuous disdain, " than attract men by such disgraceful means. If I do not intend to marry a certain man, I will tell him so plainly and refuse to see him again. I will not keep him hanging on to play him off against his inferiors and traffic with his honest love. Such conduct seems to me despicable and unworthy of my womanhood."

Ah, my dear girl, your sentiments are very beautiful, and I, for one, thoroughly appreciate them. But alas ! Man does not. The honest-hearted lover you would scorn to make use of so meanly would never adore you as he adores that laughing, scheming, clever little coquette with tippity-healed shoes and eighteen-inch waist. For the more she plays with him and makes him a decoy for others, the more he grovels before her and lends himself to assist her further conquests. Man is built that way, and *don't you forget it.* Once let the coquette show a sign of compunction, a glimpse of her heart, and—hey presto ! her slave vanishes. She holds him by her vagaries, her real indifference and pretended liking, her uncertain smiles and fluctuating humours. In fact, she holds him by the fascination of insecurity and peril, the fear of losing her altogether, the rivalry of others ; and she can do this only so long as she cares nothing whatever about him, suffers no regret at hurting him.

It will thus be seen that the most important rule of the game for a woman is to avoid falling in love. Under no circumstances must she ever allow a man to believe he has won her entire affection, for that knowledge is absolutely fatal. It is not always easy to keep a serene and indifferent heart under the siege of an ardent lover, for Man is, when all is said, a vastly lovable being, and even his faults—indeed, chiefly his faults—have a most unholy attraction for us. But it is positively necessary to keep guard of the citadel against his batteries, for when once surrendered the game is up. Man the Conquered is a very different creature from Man the Conqueror. The first is always ready, and longing, to afford us everything in the world we desire, ready to sell his immortal soul for our pleasure. The second grudges us a kind word. That is all, but I think it is eloquent.

There was a time, many years ago, when my heart being young and my eyes obscured by a rosy film, I refused to believe the cynical doctrine that man desires woman only so long as he cannot get her. Man, himself, will always indignantly repudiate this doctrine ; he has sworn to me, over and over again, that love begets love, and that if I would but return his, he would become doubly and trebly my slave. Unfortunately I have never found this to be true. While I held him in uncertainty my lover has been faithful, devout and kind ; but whenever I have allowed him to see that I cared for him, given him the long-entreated right to kiss my lips—from that hour he has slid away from me as surely as a snowflake melts into the earth ! And the man whom I have loved most, to whom I have granted most, and from whom I expected most, has been the one who has callously inflicted upon me the most bitter pain and humiliation of my life.

But you say, " These are exceptional cases, and your individual experience counts for little."

I am quite willing to admit that there are men who devote their lives to making some fortunate woman happy. My point is that such instances are so rare that they do not affect man in the abstract. My experience has been that of ninety women in every hundred, and I have always found that a yielding on my part has been followed by a recoil on the part of my admirer, sooner or later. Let man but think he has you, safe and sound, in his power, give him one glimpse of your affection for him, allow the least privilege he craves, and, unless he happens, by a lucky accident, to be of the rare type to which I have alluded—the good fellow with a tenderness for all hapless creatures under heaven—you will speedily become an object of absolute indifference to him.

Remember this then, maiden reader, and resolve that, if you ever detect yourself returning a man's love, your only policy is to disguise the fact from him. Don't let him enchain your interest, if you can possibly help it, for the Little Blind God is your most dangerous enemy, as poets have warned you through the ages. Who does not know the lines :

> Sigh no more, ladies,
> Ladies, sigh no more,
> Men were deceivers ever.
> One foot on sea and one on shore,
> To one thing constant never.
>   Then sigh not so,
>   But let them go,
> And be ye blithe and bonnie ;
> Converting all your sounds of woe
> To hey nonny, nonny ?

This was written by a man who knew his own sex uncommonly well. He was quite aware that what man likes is the damsel " blithe and bonnie," and he doesn't care a rap whether she has any other qualification.

So " be ye blithe and bonnie," maidens, remembering that " men were deceivers ever," and when they pretend to want your love, it is only because they have some doubt about getting it. So long as that doubt exists they will continue to adore you —and *no longer*. You may keep the liking, the friendship, of a man after you have given him your heart, if you are clever enough to dissemble a little.

(*To be continued.*)

BEING ABLE TO PASS WELL IS THE STRONGEST FEATURE OF A HOCKEY TEAM.

HOCKEY FOR WOMEN.

BY M. V. WYNTER.

DESPITE some adverse criticisms which we hear anent the absolute un-suitability of hockey as a woman's pursuit, there is no getting over the fact that the game has come to stay. Whereas fifteen or twenty years ago hockey was played only by schoolgirls and schoolboys in a very amateurish fashion with few recognised rules, at the present time there is scarcely a town or large village in England which does not possess a flourishing club of its own, whose ambition it is to produce a member capable of upholding the honour of the team in a Ladies International Match.

However strongly—and perhaps truly—its detractors may inveigh against the in-elegance of hockey, the roughness of mixed games, the unnecessary objects some players delight to make of themselves, there is one potent reason in favour of the game which must outweigh any argument that can be urged against it, namely, the exceedingly economical lines on which it is pursued. There is no winter game which combines all the elements of excitement, skill, and, last but not least, as vast an amount of exercise

in so short a space of time—no inconsider-able attraction this to many girls—for so small an expenditure as hockey.

The subscription to even the best-known hockey clubs rarely exceeds ten shillings per member, and in many villages and some private clubs is as low as five shillings or even half a crown. This sum covers all expenses of rent of ground and up-keep, new balls, flags, etc. And all that is left for the player to provide is her own stick, for which an expenditure of ten shillings will provide as good a one as can be desired.

Although we have stated the monetary aspect of hockey to be one of the most influential points in its favour, there are many other reasons which conduce to render-ing it one of the most desirable games for girls.

First and foremost it is almost the only unselfish game—if we may use the word—open to women. By unselfish we mean a game in which the player thinks not only of her own personal chance of losing or winning—as in golf or tennis—but learns to sink her own glorification in the good of her side. Girls are taught in hockey, as their brothers are in cricket and football, that "Unity is strength," and the hard-working, unselfish player who thinks only of the good of her team is infinitely more valued by the captain than the more dashing, brilliant one whose one aim is to secure "all the fat" for herself.

Another and not the smallest element in favour of hockey is the fact that it is devoid of all pot-hunting and gambling interest. Those who play play for the sport alone, not to make money or to win prizes ; and in this strictly practical age, when few people care to expend their best energies on a game unless they have something on the result, it speaks volumes for the interest of hockey that it should continue to be played so enthusiastically and keenly by both sexes, solely for love and the joy of victory.

There is no more important point to instil into a young team than the necessity of playing into each other's hands. "Combination," says Mr. Creswell, "is at the present time the one great road leading to success, and the team which does not thoroughly understand and put into practice the art of passing cannot have much chance

of winning matches. So true is this that we frequently see a team composed of fine individual players beaten by far inferior elevens, simply because the latter understand and act up to the maxim, "United we stand, divided we fall."

One of the hardest rules for the beginner to recognise is the necessity of keeping in her proper position. This proceeds partly from a desire to be perpetually in the fore-front of the battle, partly from an erroneous idea that to keep still for a few moments must necessarily imply idleness. Where places are not strictly kept, however, combination becomes an impossibility. For instance, a left wing forward, seeing another hard pressed, leaves her own place and rushes off to assist her. Not only will she in all probability collide with a third, whose work it is to assist the second player, but before she can return to her own place, the opposing side, taking advantage of her absence, will have made a determined rush and dribbled the ball half-way down the field. The principle of not keeping to the allotted place is wrong, and although it is hard to say that circumstances never occur in which a player should leave his or her appointed place, yet such circumstances are not very frequent,

A FOUL.

and should then only be made when there is a complete understanding between another player who will at once take the vacated position.

We sometimes hear the "danger" of hockey urged as another reason for tabooing the game for women, and of course an element of danger can be found in almost every pursuit in life if we stop to think about it. At the same time, although accidents do occasionally occur in the hockey field, they are very few in comparison with the number of players, added to which the greater portion of them are caused by carelessness, not from

—upon whom devolves the whole responsibility of defending the goal—a sure defence is an absolute necessity, in addition to which these are not as a rule so hurried in their stroke as are the halves and forwards, so that in their case it is better to stop the ball with feet or hands and thus make certain of hitting. With the halves, and more especially the forwards, however, quickness in passing is an essential, and even the few seconds of delay caused by stooping to stop the ball with the hand may make a considerable difference to the game. In stopping with the hands and feet there is also the danger of in- advertently carry- ing or kicking the ball forward a few

HITTING A GOAL.

any inherent danger in the game. "When a player strikes at the ball, his stick must not during any portion of the stroke rise above his shoulder," says rule No. 14, and the captains of teams cannot impress too strongly upon all beginners that by disregarding this rule they not only give a free hit to their adversaries, but run the risk of inflicting very serious damage upon their fellow players.

Opinions vary somewhat as to the best methods of stopping the ball, some players almost invariably stopping with either hands or feet before hitting, whilst others are able to rely on taking passes with their stick alone. With the goal-keeper and full backs

paces and thus giving a free hit to the opposing side. Given a good eye, taking passes on the stick alone is simply a question of practice, and one which every player should cultivate assiduously.

Most young players are inclined to be too slow in "passing," also in making up their minds to tackle an adversary. They must remember, however, that although by running in at once they may miss the ball themselves, they at any rate muddle their opponent, and prevent her from getting a clean hit. When a leader sees her forward in a good position ready to make use of the ball, she must pass to her at once, instead of

A CENTRE "BULLY."

pottering along with the ball herself until her forward be surrounded and the opportunity gone.

In hockey, as in most games which are worth playing, there is plenty of exercise for the brains as well as the body. We often see many dashing, energetic players who, from over-excitability and a tendency to lose their heads at the critical moment, are not half the service which they ought to be to their side, and *vice versa* ; there are some players who, though they may have a thorough grasp of the technique of the game, yet do not possess sufficient skill to make the best use of their knowledge. When once the rudiments of the game have been

A THROW IN FROM THE BOUNDARY.

"STICKS."

"When a player strikes at the ball, his stick must not . . . rise above his shoulder."

mastered, reading what has been written by the best authorities on the subject will be found of assistance—watching really first-class matches still more of a help—towards learning *what* to do. *How* to do it can only be acquired by constant practice and a determination not to be above accepting hints and criticism from other players.

One of the most difficult tasks which falls to the lot of the captain of an eleven is the selection of the team for the various matches: enjoyable as the practices may be, they are not, of course, equal to the excitement and interest of playing in a match, in addition to which there is the honour of being selected to represent the club; so that unless the members are an unusually large-minded set, there is generally some amount of heart-burning amongst those who are not chosen. As the success of the club is the first consideration, the captain will have to harden her heart to complaints, and select the team she considers best, whether the selection is popular or not.

A PENALTY CORNER.

Careers For Women.

VI.—SECRETARYSHIPS.

BY "FIVE YEARS A PRIVATE SECRETARY."

IT is not of secretaryships in general, but of private secretaryships in particular, that I wish to write. Good secretaryships are undoubtedly among the best positions open to educated gentlewomen : I am, of course, considering no others. There is a steady demand for trained women secretaries, a demand that is, I think, tending to increase, though the extent to which it will increase is clearly a matter which women have in their own hands.

Women so frequently overlook the " possibilities " of a position. Before engaging in any career, before accepting any position, one should ask one's self, " What possibilities, what opportunities does it offer ? If I stay in that position three years, to what extent am I likely to have added to my knowledge and general capacity ? Could I reasonably expect to work out of that position into a better and more responsible one ? " If the answer is " No," then strain every nerve not to be forced into accepting it.

A Suitable Career for Women.

It is more because of the possibilities frequently offered by a secretary's work than because of the actual work itself, that I consider a secretaryship as one of the careers most to be recommended to women. Certain kinds of secretaryships are undoubtedly more suited to women—capable, energetic, and business-like—than to men.

When I speak of a secretaryship, I mean a secretaryship, and not a clerkship under another name. I know that every girl with a modicum of knowledge of shorthand and typewriting, and no experience whatever, wants straightway to become " a secretary." It sounds so much better ! She does not realise that a real secretary's post always requires far more, and not far less, knowledge

and training than an ordinary shorthand clerk's. I have had many more or less likely aspirants to secretarial work come to me for advice, and I have invariably told them that they cannot hope to become really good secretaries unless they go through a first-class office, either commercial or legal. Commercial offices are certainly far the easiest to get into, and the experience gained in them is the most generally useful. You cannot reasonably expect to gain your experience of ordinary office routine, of good methods of filing letters and papers, keeping letter-books, etc., at your employer's expense. Every one will have certain "fads" as to how he likes his work done and his papers kept ; but when once you have seen the working of an orderly, well-managed office, you should have little trouble in adapting yourself even to the most exacting individual.

The Training Necessary.

Broadly speaking, therefore, the first part of the training for a secretaryship should be the same as for a shorthand typist. Persistent " slogging " at shorthand and persistent practice in typewriting, using a well-known make of machine—there is no other way to begin. I should advise any one wishing to be as economical and speedy as possible to live in one of the residential hostel-clubs for working gentlewomen, and where it is possible to live at from a pound to twenty-five shillings a week—that is, supposing you live in the country. Much the quickest plan will be to come to town, where in the way of schools, polytechnics, and typewriting offices there is every facility for learning.

As to the actual cost of training in shorthand and typewriting, I think it should be covered by about £10, probably less, though it is possible to spend very much more, but with doubtful advantage. Another extra £10, however, may with the greatest advantage be spent on the desirable accomplishment of book-keeping, though it is not always necessary, and on acquiring a good corresponding, reading, and if possible conversational, knowledge of French and German—the most necessary languages. Spanish and Italian might be very useful, but are not likely to be often asked for. I strongly recommend one of the large schools, employing foreign teachers, unless a really first-rate private native tutor can be secured. Certainly a large institution costs much less, and my experience is that they often have admirable teachers of foreign languages, under whom if you do not learn it is your own fault. French I consider an absolute essential for any one wishing to qualify for a good private secretaryship.

French and German Shorthand.

There is the question also of French and German shorthand. They are not often asked for, but when they are, the pay is usually good. The acquiring of them is a question which every one must decide for herself. It is an investment of personal capital which may prove highly remunerative, and may bring in nothing. One friend of mine has somehow managed to teach herself French and German shorthand, by modifying Pitman's system; but every one is not clever enough for that.

Learn typewriting only in a good office, never in a school, and never by yourself, as you will infallibly get into all kinds of bad ways. While learning it, you will have the evenings in which to practise shorthand and work at anything else in which you may be weak. I should begin by studying shorthand and either bookkeeping or a foreign language; and when my shorthand was at the speed practice stage, then I should enter a good typewriting office. There are excellent, old-established offices which charge only two guineas for teaching typewriting, and in which you will be allowed to earn directly you are fit to do so. In six weeks you should be earning something.

You may find it advisable to stay some time in such an office, especially if it is one from which you are sent out to take shorthand notes; or you may find it better, when sufficiently experienced, at the end of perhaps six months, to set about entering a good commercial or legal office. The latter is the better plan, I consider. The recommendation of the typewriting office should now stand you in good stead. Still, you have now arrived at a trying stage. All beginnings are difficult, and it is often far more than the first step which costs. One piece of advice I cannot too often or too emphatically repeat: avoid all agencies as you would ten thousand plagues. An employment agency usually takes your money, it may be at a time when you can very ill afford it, and it does not do, probably does not intend to do, possibly could not do, anything for you. By far the best way to get a position, especially for any one without useful, i.e. influential, connections in London, is to watch the advertisements in the daily papers, and answer at once, first thing every morning, those that are for positions such as you can fill, always enclosing a stamped, addressed envelope.

How long will you hunt about? That will depend on the state of trade, the time of year, wisely worded letters of application, and chance good fortune. I should say about two months was a fair average time in London, for any one seeking a first post. What may you expect to get? From twenty-five to thirty shillings or possibly thirty-five shillings, if one language is really usable, and you are quick and capable—hardly more at first.

A Confidential Position.

Now there are such things as commercial private secretaryships, but they are really more confidential shorthand-clerkships. Still, I have known girls who held them, and were very well paid. But the kind of private secretaryship which I take it you will have in view would be to an editor, to a literary, political, or other public character, to a society, philanthropic or otherwise, usually for older women with experience, or to a woman's club. In filling such positions private influence is usually an important factor. Nevertheless, I had none, and I have had what was, when I held it, certainly one of the best private secretaryships open to a woman. Always bear in mind that a secretaryship worth holding must be a more or less, and is often an exceedingly, confidential and responsible position. In a private secretaryship, also, you are generally brought into contact with your employer's family, who may or may not be agreeable, but who will certainly be human. In other words, much more tact, forbearance, and patience are usually demanded of a private secretary, especially if resident, than of a secretary to a commercial man or of an ordinary shorthand clerk. The duties also are far more varied, at times even multifarious. Any one wishing to be a journalist's, editor's, or literary man's private secretary cannot read too much good literature, and in the first two cases, at any rate, she must keenly follow the daily papers, and she will be all the better for reading the principal articles every month in the leading magazines.

Besides the ordinary duties of any secretary's position, I included among mine at various times (1) attending public meetings, and taking a verbatim note; (2) transcribing that note, crossheading, editing, and generally putting it in shape for the printers; (3) translating from French and German; (4) hunting through files of newspapers for some special fact, or cuttings bearing on some question of the day; (5) sorting bundles of newspapers under subjects—a very tiring and by no means easy task; (6) calling upon ambassadors and diplomats, French being sometimes our only common language; (7) reading proofs; and, lastly, doing the still more thankless work of tidying haystacks of papers and letters, and generally creating some kind of order out of chaos.

Many of these duties I do not think the average private secretary need fear. Nor do I think the excessively long hours I often worked are common, though a private secretary's hours, as those of most persons in a responsible position, are somewhat inclined to be variable and irregular. And yet, knowing what I know of the difficulties frequent in such positions, I still say that a private secretaryship is one of the most suitable careers now open to educated women.

IN PARTING.

BY ANTONY CLARE.

I DO not say to you " Remember me,"
  If to remember me be pain.
Since we must part, then let our parting be
  Filled with the haunting of no sad refrain.

I would not have the thought of me in spring
  Rob any fragrance from the flowers,
Nor make the summer seem a sadder thing,
  Nor dim the brightness of the autumn hours;

But if, in years to come, you should recall
  This hour, and me, who love you, dear,
I only pray, "Think kindly"—that is all;
  I would not have you grieve or shed one tear.

LIFE AND TRAVEL

IN BURMA.

BY V. C. SCOTT O'CONNOR,
Author of "The Silken East."

TWENTY years ago the house of Alompra still ruled at Mandalay; the Burmese were still a nation; and although oppression and the leanness of the northern soil drove many of the King's subjects to the British province in the south, the people took pride in the existence of a Burmese sovereignty. That sovereignty has ceased to exist. Mandalay, the royal capital, has declined to a provincial town, surpassed by the strenuous growth of British and commercial

THE SHWAY DAGÔN PAGODA.

Rangoon. The King is growing old in exile; his Court has vanished; the traditions of a dynasty are fast sinking into oblivion. All over the last surviving territories of the Alompra a great change is taking place. The jungle is become the haunt of punctual trains, the great rivers echo to the scream of the passing steamer; settlements that stood, and in truth still stand, upon the edge of savagery, the happy hunting grounds of raiding Chin, Kachin, and head-

SURATI MOSQUE, RANGOON.

Indian Empire has broken through another barrier, and Burma, so long hidden, so long remote, is becoming the highway of a yet vaster expansion.

In the midst of such change and activity, in a country peopled by one of the most charming and attractive races of the world, in a land watered by superb rivers, of which the Irrawaddy, navigable for nine hundred miles, is chief, and rich with the splendid hues of the tropics, it would be strange if the travellers found no interest. As a matter of fact he finds much, once he can sufficiently escape from the magnetic pull of India to come to Burma at all. He begins, let us say, at Rangoon, the capital, noticeable for its Shway Dagôn, its cosmopolitan life, its abounding vigour, and its desperate fall into

MOGUL STREET, RANGOON.

hunting Wa, are become the commonplaces of the world traveller, hurrying with blind eyes on his way. The British frontier that only twenty years ago was a line (drawn along the ruler of Lord Dalhousie) through the heart of Burma is already an international factor reaching over to France and China ; and the sentries of these nations traffic with our own. The expanding force of the

architectural ugliness; and proceeds then by train and steamer to the northernmost frontier, which it is unsafe to be curious about without an escort of armed men. Nearly all the centres of life in Burma lie along the banks of the Irrawaddy; and the the ocean-like edge of the river reaching away into misty space. He will of nights see the blue dome of heaven lit with a thousand stars, the Great Bear and brilliant Orion, while his ship at anchor rocks idly in the mid-flow of the river, and the whole world about him is asleep. He will wonder about his own identity, and shiver under the spell of a mystery, as he recalls the roar of Whitehall and the voice of his own people.

ON THE RIVER.

steamer traveller, as he progresses amidst the luxury of his own civilisation, has the opportunity of seeing a whole country, with nearly all the relics of its past, defile before his eye. Sitting in his long-arm chair, an invention of the East, with an obliging skipper at hand as cicerone, with, it may be, a French *savant*, a German baron, and an American beauty for his companions, servants to wait upon him, and a butcher, a baker, and a cook in the galley, he can reflect upon the transitoriness of life, the irony of cities named immortal less than a hundred years ago and already in the toils of a swift decay. Fresh it may be from the quiet colouring, the gentle harmonies of Northern Europe, he will be confronted with colours of dazzling extravagance and beauty; he will see the full-orbed moon rise up and face the sun already upon the horizon, and setting in a passionate ecstasy of colour behind the dark outlines of palm-trees, and

The illusion of which he has been hearing of late will grow into a new reality in his brain, and he will wonder with a kindlier wonder at the withered monks seated in contemplation in their monastery courts, turning the beads within their fingers, and muttering their half-heard litanies—*Aneitsa, Dukha, Anata*, the transitoriness of all that is in the world. He will begin to get faint glimmerings of understanding of the people he has come to look upon, bared to the criticism of his foreign eyes. And so the river will bear him, as he floats past the wide plains and the waving grasses of the Delta; past Donabyu, where the fields are ripening in the entrenchments of Bandula, the Burmese general who made his little ineffectual stand here against the might of England; past the orchard Rhine-like hills of Prome with its golden spire and its history of two thousand years; through the Fourth, and southernmost, Defile, where the hills draw near the river in

IN THE ARACAN PAGODA.

Zigon, and for eight miles in line the tapering forms of the ten thousand churches of old Pagan. He will never believe, as he looks upon this opulent spectacle, as of a city in its glorious prime, that he is coming to a city of the dead; to a city that reached its climax a thousand years ago.

In the midst of Pagan itself he will see strange things: the people of the country-side, still faithful to the shrines of the long-abandoned city; monasteries that have been rebuilt generation after generation upon the traditional sites; and perhaps, most curious of all, a population of religious slaves, the descendants of distant ancestors vowed to the temples and monasteries of Pagan by the kings of her prime. He will see the tablets of stone upon which the names of those ancestors are recorded, and he will read the terrible anathemas levelled upon all such as may dare to break the conditions

its course and narrow its waters; to Thayet-myo, a cantonment of yesterday; to the oil wells of Yenan-Gyaung and the mud volcanoes of Minbu; and to the old capital city of Pagan, the greatest output of the Burmese race. Across the sea of heliotrope water, still as a sheet of satin, unruffled, he will see the white spires of the Ananda, the Thap-yinnyu and the Gadawpalin, the famous Pagan trinity, cleave the air and throw their growing image on the mirror before him. He will see the golden bulb of the Shway

of this perpetual gift. In the midst of this city, which rose to its full height upon the conquest of its neighbour Thaton (in the year A.D. 1060), he will meet an old man travelling with a certain pomp, a red um-brella held over his head by an attendant, and he will learn that this is the King of the Pagoda Slaves, the lineal descendant of the captive King of Thaton. In all these eight hundred years this family has neither ad-vanced nor retreated. Its head is still a prince, and still a slave. But of the blood of Anawrata, the conqueror, there is no living representative. Pagan was destroyed by the invading horde of the Tartar, Kublai Khan, and the palace wall is almost the only surviving relic of its secular past. It lies in the midland of Burma, in the dry zone of country that is flanked on either hand by the moist and tropical territories of the north and south: it is to this dry air and lack of rain that the continued existence of Pagan is due.

Far overlooking Pagan, across the great waste of waters ten miles in width, that here in its flood season constitutes the Irrawaddy, stands the Tangyi Swai-Daw Pagoda, lifted up on the summit of the Tangyi hills, one thousand feet above the world. Standing here the Buddha is believed by his people to have foretold the greatness of Pagan; and, if some may doubt the authenticity of his tale, no one who stands here can doubt its poetic fitness. Across the blue sea of the Irrawaddy the city lies spread out in all its vast extent; and one appreciates the instinct of grandeur in a people who selected such a site for a capital city. Think of London, or Paris— "Roaring London— Raving Paris"—displayed in this manner before the eyes of a spectator! In spite of its remoteness, and the steep ascent, many people climb up to worship at the Tangyi Pagoda; and may the traveller as he makes his way there come upon such

a spectacle as greeted me, when I first visited it. The flagged platform of the pagoda was void of all worshippers save one; and she was an aged woman, white of hair, too old, you would think, to have ever come so far. She knelt on the edge of the platform, where the last flagstone, unbounded by any wall, hangs sheer over the precipitous fall to Pagan. Her hands were clasped before her in prayer, and a spiritual ecstasy was upon her, as she fixed her eyes upon the city.

NEW TAZOUNGS AT THE SHWAY DAGÔN PAGODA.

[Mr. V. C. Scott O'Connor, the author of this article, is the present Comptroller of Assam, and has recently written a most interesting and authoritative work on Burma, which has been published by Messrs. Hutchinson & Co.—Ed. L.R.]

The Realm of Society

IT is a noticeable fact that, since the beginning of this reign, the whole Royal Family have been more closely in touch with English society than they were previously, especially in the matter of paying visits to country houses. Scarcely a week-end passes without the King staying with one or other of his subjects, and here and there, on special occasions, he is accompanied by the Queen. During the past year His Majesty has been the guest of the Duke and Duchess of Devonshire, of Lord and Lady Ormonde, of Lord and Lady Savile, of Lord Gerard and of Lady Gerard, of Lord Burton, of Lord and Lady Cadogan, of Mr. George Cavendish Bentinck, of Mr. and Mrs. William James, and several others. King Edward is gradually making acquaintance with his dominions and with the country homes of his loyal subjects.

January has always been rather a favourite time for these Royal visits, and this month, if all goes well, Lord and Lady Alington, at Crichel, will be among the first hosts to entertain His Majesty in the year of grace 1905. Lord Alington has but lately come into his kingdom, and death duties notwithstanding, possesses a very large fortune, which is by no means the case with most great landed proprietors in these

Photo by Langfier.

THE HON. CLARICE NAPIER,
Daughter of Lord Belhaven and Stenton, and who is married to the Master of Napier.

days. The sale of Alington House, in South Audley Street, was effected chiefly because Lord and Lady Alington are quite satisfied with their fine house in Portman Square. In his capacity of a county magnate, the world in general has not, as yet, had time to judge of him, as he has not been settled long in his Dorsetshire domain. As Mr. Humphrey Sturt, he had the reputation of being the best-dressed man in London— not of the "masher" type, as he is too big and broad to come into that category—but as always wearing the right thing at the right moment. With Lord Ribblesdale, he was one of the pioneers of the clean-shaving movement, and if knee breeches and silk stockings ever become general as evening attire for men, Lord Alington will probably be among the first to adopt that becoming costume. As well as being something of a dandy, he is a thorough good sportsman, a capital shot, and a straight rider to hounds. 'though

Photo by Lafayette.

EARL SPENCER,
The leader of the Liberal Party in the House of Lords, has led a particularly active life, and has been on different occasions Viceroy of Ireland and First Lord of the Admiralty.

not such a tremendous supporter of the turf as his father was, he is very often to be seen at Newmarket and Sandown.

Lady Alington is a daughter of the late Lord Hardwicke, popularly known as the "Glossy Peer," in consequence of the immaculateness of his attire, and the wonderful sheen of his curly brimmed hats. As Lady Féodorowna Yorke, she was a remarkably beautiful girl, and although her own daughter, Miss Diana Sturt, has already been out two seasons, she is still a remarkably beautiful woman. Lady Alington is very fond of society and of London, and already ranked as a notable hostess before her husband succeeded to the family honours. She likes a little originality in her manner of entertaining, and the "head" dance which she gave a season or two ago at her house in Portman Square was one of the social events of the year. She is a great frequenter of the opera, is very fond of music, is always exquisitely dressed, and is a clever and witty conversationalist. Lord and Lady Alington's only daughter is tall and handsome, and was one of the notable *débutantes* of her year. She is the fortunate possessor of a very beautiful voice, which is being carefully trained.

Crichel, the family place in Dorsetshire, used to be the cheeriest of country houses to stay in, when the late Lord Alington's

Photo by Langfier.

THE HON. MRS. GOLDMANN,

Received the Royal Red Cross in 1901 for her services in connection with the Boer War. She is the daughter of the first Viscount Peel, and is greatly interested in the Female Emigration scheme to South Africa.

coming Royal visit. It is understood that Lady Alington intends to continue the famous "White Farm," in which Evelyn Lady Alington took so much interest. The White Farm has been so often described that it would be superfluous to enlarge on it here; but unless one has seen it, it is impossible to realise how delightfully the scheme is carried out in all its details. Every

beautiful daughters and their father, himself the most genial of hosts, held sway; but for some years before his death, and not long after his second marriage, to Miss Evelyn Leigh, who nursed him with such untiring devotion, his health prevented him from doing more than seeing his immediate family and very intimate friends. The present Lord and Lady Alington bid fair to revive the glories of Crichel, as their first great party there is to be honoured by the presence of the Sovereign. The house itself is a very good one, and the King's hostess is an adept in all appertaining to house decoration. Considerable improvements have been made in view of the

gate, every fence, every utensil is pure white, and white also are the cows, the farm horses, the snowy hens, the fluffy geese, the peacocks, and the pigeons. This month the little white snowdrops poke their heads through the ground, and the white crocuses and the lilies follow in due season. In the summer white roses shed their delicate perfume over the dairy door, and in the mild Dorsetshire air the white chrysanthemums are blooming right up to Christmas.

During his stay at Crichel His Majesty, as at present arranged, intends to pay a visit to Lord Portman, whose splendid place, Bryanston, is well within a motor drive of Lord Alington's country seat.

LONDON & PARIS FASHIONS

BY MRS. ERIC PRITCHARD.

THIS is a month of sales, and so appeals to the well-to-do community as well as to those who are less fortunately placed. At the same time new fashions, which are indications of those to come a little later on, are daily making their appearance on the Riviera. The majority of English women do not migrate there until February, which is the Riviera month as far as we are concerned ; but even in the midst of January sales in London, it is interesting to hear rumours of the fashions of the future, bringing, as they do, a promise of spring and of brighter days.

I always look upon January as a difficult month in which to renovate and add to a wardrobe with discretion, and before enlarging on the entrancing subject of sales, let us consider the wants of the *débutante* and those who are still rejoicing in holiday time and New Year festivities. In spite of the yearly grumbles about "Christmas ills and Christmas bills" and worries in general, there are mercifully a large number of young people who thoroughly enjoy the old-fashioned festivities and simple amusements.

DURING the last few years there have been many impromptu fancy-dress dances, and it is well for the individual who can put together, at short notice, a really amusing or effective fancy dress, making use of garments and various odds and ends she has by her. The statuesque woman can look charming in a hastily devised drapery of sheets and Indian shawls. A deep velvet belt, a fichu of muslin, and a short, striped skirt, make an effective "Swiss peasant's" costume. A Spanish mantilla and a black lace frock form a very becoming and quickly arranged fancy dress, as indeed does a Japanese kimono, with some fancy pins and chrysanthemums stuck in the hair.

Of course, if we be invited to several smart fancy-dress balls, it is well worth while investing in a pretty costume which need not necessarily be a costly one, and which can be used afterwards. Our artist has sketched in fig. 1 a pretty idea for a "Bacchante" in mauve accordion-pleated chiffon, the bodice prettily draped and trimmed with grapes and vine leaves. The fruit, by the way, can afterwards be utilised to trim a hat. The skin of a lynx arranged on the front of the dress gives a wild and fantastic touch. This gown would be equally effective in shaded green or vivid rose. The new wine colour would also be appropriate. This costume has the advantage of being easy to dance in, and its brilliancy would be becoming to many women. But I think it is a foolish woman who allows her love of the eccentric to have the dominion over the idea of becomingness in the choosing of a fancy dress. Then, many of us have to consider to what use a fancy dress can afterwards be turned. It is not original by any means, but the woman who looks well in black can have no prettier style of fancy dress than that which represents "Night," carried out in black gauze or chiffon, studded with silver moons or stars. There are many women who may look quite their worst in a regulation ball-frock, but quite beautiful when garbed in a gown copied from the fashion of a bygone period, or in some peculiar garment which is beautiful in itself, but not fashionable at the moment. But I think the real fun of fancy-dress dances is at a big, country-house party, when we have to turn over the wardrobes of a good natured hostess and her guests, and devise impromptu costumes, with very often the most excellent results.

WHILE on the subject of ball dresses, we must not forget the first appearance of the maiden of seventeen who is not really "out," but who makes her *début* at a Christmas party, wearing a long skirt for, perhaps, the first time. Always charming is a frock of net, accordion-pleated chiffon, or some airy-fairy, gauzy material which we associate with youth and pleasure. On the other hand, we must bear in mind that the girl who is just about to come "out" is shortly going to be put on her own allowance,

and when having a frock given her, will naturally wish to choose one which will be useful in the future as well as in the present. For this purpose taffeta or Oriental satin is an admirable fabric, both being adapted to subsequent renovation and cleaning.

In fig. 2 our artist has given us a charming design in ivory-coloured taffeta, simply trimmed with quaint ruches and a prettily shaped gold or silver band, which could occasionally be replaced by a white or coloured sash. The skirt is slightly full on the hips, but is otherwise plain, the necessary *frou-frou* at the feet being secured by broad flounces trimmed with pleated ruches. These ruches are

FIG. I.—DESIGN FOR DRESS IN MAUVE
A PRETTY "BACCHANTE" FANCY ACCORDION-PLEATED CHIFFON,
THE BODICE BEING TRIMMED WITH GRAPES AND VINE LEAVES.

FIG 2.—A CHARMING FROCK FOR THE *DÉBUTANTE* IN IVORY-COLOURED TAFFETA.

arranged in festoons, which is a good idea for a dancing-skirt, as if it be too plain at the feet it is apt to look skimpy. The bodice is also arranged with taffeta ruchings, a certain amount of fulness being necessary in the case of a first ball-dress to conceal the angles of girlhood. Three or four extra yards of material will go a long way towards making a *débutante's* gown a success.

And here sales are so useful. You can buy robe-lengths of silk, gauze, net, or lace, beautifully cut and shaped, the skirt pleated, gauged, and inserted, and ample material for the bodice. In some cases it is only necessary to put these ready-made and charmingly effective robes over a well-cut, trained petticoat or underslip of washing silk or satin. Ready-made

boned sashes and waist-bands can also be bought at sale prices this month. In these matters sales prove a blessing to girls on their own allowances, as well as to women who can buy beautiful Parisian and Viennese models at reduced prices. But let me here remark that it is foolish to buy a thing *because* it is cheap : the woman who gets value for her money at the sales is she who has waited, perhaps a couple of months, to get the particular garment or fabric she requires. A use can always be found for good pieces of lace and dainty coloured chiffons, and remnants of brocade, silk, and satin come in admirably for afternoon and evening petticoats.

AN absolutely indispensable garment at this time of year is the teagown. The teagown *de luxe*, bought ready made, must always be expensive, and even when

FIG. 3.—A DELIGHTFUL TEAGOWN OF BLONDE LACE, VELVET, AND CHIFFON.

soiled it fetches a fair price. A graceful teagown is always difficult to make,
and to fall well it must be of a good
fabric. The foundation may be of soft
satin or silk, veiled with chiffon or lace,
with individual touches in the way of
trimmings. Sale remnants are very
often suitable for turning into a pretty
teagown, while they are admirable for
the construction of the lounge-gown,
the *saut-de-lit*, the bed-jacket, etc.

In fig. 3 our artist has given us a
charming example of a teagown in
one of the new light makes of blonde lace, a
flounce width and a wide piece-lace being
used together. It is in *écru* colour over a
foundation of white Oriental satin. The quaint
ruchings are finished with touches of *vieux
rose* velvet, and the cream satin revers are
embroidered with shaded pink old-world ribbon
work. This same model could be effectively
carried out in *point d'esprit* or some of the
inexpensive nets that now abound. It would
be charming, too, in all-black chiffon, with a
touch of jet.

In Paris they have been wearing, both for five
o'clock and quiet "at homes," regular *paletôts*
of flowered silk or taffeta, somewhat resembling
the Louis XVI. coat, with a soft under-dress of
pleated muslin or lace. These are very pretty
in pale shades of green, tomato red, *vieux rose*,
and fancy silks over a contrasting colour. In
England we are remaining faithful to the lace
coat as well as to the coat of net. Many of
these are semi-fitting, and of Louis XVI. outline,
but, in my opinion, the prettiest are long,
flowing, and altogether classical.

For bridge the short, smart lace coat has
somewhat taken the place of the lace coat,
though one is really as useful as the other,
and here again do we see various uses
for sale remnants. A coat of whatever
length the remnant permits, with an under-
dress of chiffon and a few smart velvet
rosettes, makes a really charming garment.
A *paletôt* of lace cut in three pieces and
ruched to the knees had a fitting slip of
soft satin beneath. At the waist was a
girdle of gold, and a suggestion of gold
braid appeared in the epaulettes out-lining
the plain, flat shoulder. Gold and silver
braid used as a trimming, but sparingly,
is rather a feature, at the moment, of
fanciful styles of dress.

FIG. 4.—AN
EARLY RIVIERA
MODEL. THE DESIGN
IS SUITABLE FOR THICK
WHITE ZIBELINE OR FOR A MIXTURE OF VELVET AND CLOTH.

teagowns, loose or fitting, simply finished with a *berthe* or fichu of old lace, real for preference, though good imitations are often very effective, particularly the finer guipures. But in Paris some of the pea-green effects have been distinctly *bizarre*. An extremely effective demi-toilette in shot blue-green taffeta had peacock's feathers embroidered thereon in shaded silks. This design was also worked on either side of the bolero bodice, and the vest was of accordion-pleated chiffon with a *jabot* of old lace.

I HEAR that corsets are slowly but surely changing their shape, and there is more indication of a waist than we have lately been accustomed to. But not for a moment do I imagine that we shall take to tight lacing, for, despite all we hear about the follies of the smart set and the fashionable woman, I doubt if we would ever again put up with such obvious discomfort. We are surely wiser than our grandmothers were, and the day of tight lacing is over. The leading *corsetières* are really skilful, and are able to devise means by which they conceal the bad points of a figure and bring out the good ones ; thus we can all possess good figures if we take the right step. Just now is rather a happy time to visit 28, New Bond Street, the home of "La Samothrace" corsets, for the London Corset Company are selling off a few of their charming corsets at exceptionally low prices. And here one grasps the idea of the corset of to-day and to-morrow at its best, for all the corsets sold here come from Paris. The corset is the most important garment of all, and the wise woman will give it her best attention.

FIG. 5.—A *CHIC* TRAVELLING COSTUME IN A GREY FRIEZE MIXTURE.

AT this time of year one must not ignore the charms of velveteen, and I think I have before spoken of the craze there is for peacock blue. This colour is charming in velveteen, and admirable for simple house-frocks and

THEN the corselet belt requires almost as much fitting as the corset itself. At sale time we may pick up bargains in this way at some of the best West-end shops, and to get a thoroughly well-made band is a great advantage to the economical dresser, for it forms a wonderful finish even to her oldest skirts and blouses. Other accessories which call for attention are the cravat, the collar, and under-sleeves of lace and em-broidered muslin, which we can now pick up ready made. Indeed, I think all these things are cheaper and better when so bought. There is rather a tendency to edge some of these cravats with beads and pearls.

QUITE beautiful are some of the enamels in vogue just now. Some women are twisting pearls and beads in the hair, while others are wearing the coronet plait in the front—always a charming idea where there is a quantity of hair, as it shows it to the best advantage Tortoiseshell combs of every sort and kind are worn; in fact, tor-toiseshell work has been brought to great perfection. French-women are even wearing tor-toiseshell hatpins. But let me implore all women, and especi-ally girls on small allowances, to be cautious in the matter of accessories. Hatpins can be quite inexpensive and very pretty, for charming enamel flowers may be had for a few shillings; while the designs in Art Nou-veau are always in good style.

WITH the tailor-made frock there is a return to the use of handkerchiefs with coloured borders or wide hems, like a man's; checked lawns in faint colours are also used. For evening use we have lace handkerchiefs and pretty, dainty little squares of lawn with a narrow edging of Valenciennes. With a sporting dress I have seen some very good specimens of silk and lawn mixtures more or less resembling the homely duster!

IT is early yet for the average English-woman to contem-plate clothes for the Riviera; but for those who are lucky enough to get away this month, our artist has drawn in fig. 4 a charming and cosy white costume, show-ing a Louis XVI. coat. The chief trimming consists of a border of stitching and some kid buttons, and the waistcoat is of old brocade and lace. The skirt may be lined or not, as the wearer pleases. This is a good design for thick white or fawn zibeline, or for a mix-ture of velvet and cloth. With this is worn a smart morning hat of white felt simply trimmed with two enor-mous white birds.

THERE is no doubt that the *Directoire* coat will run through the early spring, and there is

FIG. 8.—A SMART SABLE COAT OVER A *CRÊPE-DE-CHINE* DRESS.

much to be said in its favour. It is a useful length for walking, and it is also cosy in wintry weather. One sees some really very pretty examples of these coats in velvet with taffeta skirts when lunching at the various London restaurants. At the present moment I think a restaurant is the only cheery place, and here one always sees a goodly number of pretty women and pretty frocks and hats. Of course one also sees here a few *bizarre* costumes; indeed, there is perhaps a greater variety in *toilettes* at lunch than at any other time of the day Those who have to motor or travel by train to town are garbed in the neatest coats and skirts, for the best tailor costumes are cut rather plainly with a plentiful amount of hand-braiding; for this purpose blue serge and black, dark brown, green, and smoke-grey cloths are most in favour. With these sombre garments a brighter note is struck in the headgear. For instance, a dull fawn, neat, cut-away coat, braided in the same shade, and a skirt made with graduated tucks, also braided with heavy silk braid, were worn with a three-

corner hat of brightest rose-coloured, long-haired beaver, with large silk and velvet rose covering the crown, and further adorned with a high cockade of taffeta. Then a dark blue serge braided in black, worn with a bright green beaver *Directoire* toque, trimmed with black braid cockades, was distinctly smart.

SARTORIAL art has indeed reached perfection, and even when motoring we wish to look smart, while we make a special point of wearing our best tailor-mades when travelling. In fig. 5 our artist shows a very smart travelling-costume in a grey frieze mixture. The skirt just clears the ground, which renders it extremely practical for walking purposes as well: it is cut in pleats and held in place by tiny straps. Fig. 5 shows a beautifully cut waistcoat of white leather with the bolero coat turned back with revers of green and gold embroidery, fitting tightly into the waist with a short basque over the hips. There is a certain studied simplicity about this garment, in spite of the elaboration of trimming and the difficulties of cut, which renders it particularly striking. It could be

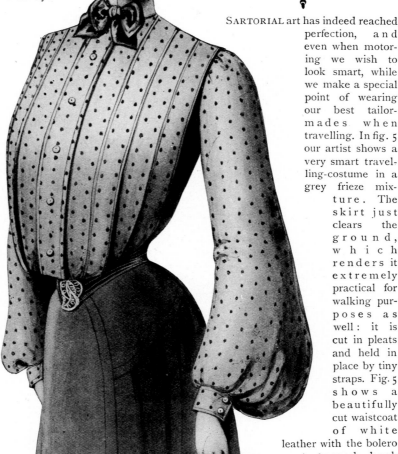

FIG. 7.—A BOX-PLEATED SHIRT IN SPOTTED FLANNEL.

charmingly carried out in dark green cloth with a waistcoat of pale tan suède ; or it might be made without a waistcoat, and worn with a plain fitting shirt.

There are two distinct classes of tailor - mades that have to be considered. One is the smart *toilette* which we require on so very many occasions, and the other is the essentially sporting and athletic costume. Therefore we require two tailor - mades, one for town wear and one for the country, and one is as difficult of construction as the other. Where the country garment is concerned, one has to take into consideration the various exercises for which it will be required. Leather is still a favourite

FIG. 6.—A USEFUL COAT AND SKIRT WITH CUFFS AND COLLAR OF LEATHER, SUITABLE FOR WALKING AND GOLFING.

think, would look its best in a dull buff-coloured linen. This skirt is cut plain with a slight fulness round the feet, the only trimming being a piece of stitched cloth. A rather smart shoulder is arrived at by the squaring of the same with a piece of stitched cloth. This squaring of the shoulder is rather in vogue among our sporting tailors just now, and a very becoming fashion it is.

I think those who cannot go to a leading tailor should endeavour to get a ready - made coat and skirt. They are often beautifully cut and extraordinarily inexpensive, and some of the West-end drapers sell the smartest little tweed and serge coats and skirts at four or five guineas. How they do it I do not pretend to know; there can be but little profit made over these garments,

trimming for sporting costumes. Fig. 6 shows a very useful coat and skirt with cuffs and collar of leather. It is in a red-brown mixture and dark brown leather. The waistcoat, I for they are, as I have said, really well cut, and have a smartness and a *cachet* which can seldom be achieved by a mediocre tailor or dressmaker.

The cult of the ready-made has become quite a feature of the fashions of to-day—coats and skirts, dresses and blouses, not to speak of the hundred and one bargains we can obtain just now in the way of evening wraps, beautiful ulsters, and travelling-coats, as well as in furs.

I HAVE seen some lovely examples in the homely and inexpensive grey squirrel. A neat grey cloth costume was completed by a bolero of squirrel cut just above the waist-line and laced up with silver cord; the big cape sleeves were lined with accordion-pleated grey chiffon. A large grey beaver hat with silver cockades completed this costume, the whole effect of which was charming.

THERE can be no doubt that grey is gaining favour, and will be more or less a feature in the early spring. I have noticed some lovely afternoon blouses in accordion-pleated grey *crêpe-de-Chine*, very simply made, with an introduction of old-world embroidery in the shape of a box-pleat down the front, and also on the collar and perhaps across the shoulders. Pretty, too, are the evening blouses with lace *jabots* and very high collars of muslin. The old-fashioned sailor-collar of lace and muslin with an inner chemisette is fast coming into vogue, but I think the general tendency is for the rather severe type of blouse, made of linen, box-pleated, or of embroidered flannel and delaine.

FIG. 7 shows a shirt of spotted flannel, finished with a linen collar and a black satin bow, with some pretty little fancy buttons down the front. Such a shirt is always in good style, and is admirable for such fabrics as delaine, flannel, *linon*, and silk. We nearly all require a goodly number of shirts and blouses, and it is not much use laying down hard-and-fast rules about them. Washing *linon* blouses seem to be as much worn in the winter as they were in the summer. The box-pleated shirts have to be beautifully cut and fitted.

THE high linen collars are still holding their own with the essentially country shirts; but I think most of us prefer a high collar with a turnover piece of white muslin and a dainty stock or cravat. A softening touch at the neck is nearly always becoming to women. There is a puritanical simplicity about the frock for morning wear, and, indeed, about many of the evening gowns as well. Grey cashmere is rather a favourite material for the evening, and grey silk, with a dainty fichu or old-world tucker of net, lace, or muslin simply drawn up with a piece of black velvet ribbon, is also *chic*. In fact, the tucker of bygone days is as much in vogue as the Marie Antoinette fichu. Quaintly pretty is a little quilling of muslin or lace at the neck and wrists of our day-gowns.

BUT I do not think we are simple in the matter of furs and wraps, and this is the month in which we may hope to pick up bargains in this respect. The furrier of to-day is an ingenious person, and there is no skin of which he cannot make use. He dresses and dyes the skins in various ways; but I doubt if furs dyed to match velvet will ever become popular. For instance, caracal has been dyed all sorts of curious dahlia shades, turned into a toque, and trimmed with velvet flowers of the same tone. Surely this is too *bizarre* a mode to remain long in vogue among the well-dressed community!

IT is always rather difficult to deal with fur for modistic purposes, and even sable and mink require some relief in the way of lace and bright plumes or flowers. Gold fringe is rather pretty, especially on moleskin. Then I think a lace *capote*, with edging of fur and great clusters of gardenias or fruit, and a touch of some brilliant colour at the side, can be very effective where a neat style of headgear is becoming. We shall see more of this kind of millinery next month: it is a fitting accompaniment for the scarves of lace edged with mink or sable which are now in vogue.

EMBROIDERED leather, embroidered cloth and fur, are used to-day on travelling-toques as well as on the smarter millinery; but I think that for travelling plainer things look best. A perfectly round turban of white caracal was trimmed with a scarf of beautiful lace, and had a cluster of shaded brown plumes on a *bandeau* of golden brown velvet. Then to be worn with a smart black caracal bolero with a plain white kid waistcoat was a very pretty turban of black, trimmed with *rouleaux* of white kid, embroidered with silver, and caught up with a silver cockade.

THE first meal of the day is difficult to vary sufficiently to tempt capricious appetites, unless one possesses a first-class cook. The continental custom of rolls and coffee early in the morning, followed by a substantial meal between eleven and twelve, appeals to many; but, except for people of leisure, it is impossible to carry out. The ordinary household of three or four, which is conducted by two or three servants, generally contents itself with bacon and eggs varied with fish or sausages.

With a little thought a number of tasty and appetising dishes can be quickly and easily prepared, as will be seen from the following recipes.

Risotto.

This needs 1 teacupful of rice, $\frac{3}{4}$ oz. of butter, $\frac{1}{2}$ onion, $1\frac{1}{2}$ oz. of grated Parmesan cheese, 1 teacupful of milk, and salt and pepper to season. The milk must be boiled, when the rice and onion (chopped very fine) is thrown into it; cover, and boil for twenty minutes, shaking the pan occasionally to keep the rice from burning; then stir in the butter, pepper, and salt, and leave on the side of the fire for a few minutes. Serve very hot.

Baked Eggs.

Take 1 egg for each person, 1 teaspoonful of minced parsley and onion, 1 cupful of gravy, and a handful of fine breadcrumbs; pour sufficient gravy into a baking-dish to cover the bottom, and place in the oven until it begins to boil; then break the eggs carefully into it, and sprinkle thickly with breadcrumbs and season with pepper and salt; put these into the oven for 3 minutes, and then pour over the remainder of the gravy (which should be hot and have the parsley and onion mixed with it) and sprinkle with breadcrumbs. When the eggs are set, serve in the same dish.

Kedgeree.

Take the remains of any cold fish, and separate the flesh from the bones, skin, etc.; boil some rice until each grain is separate, about the same quantity as there is fish; melt a lump of butter in the frying-pan, and throw in the rice and fish and stir until quite hot, flavouring with cayenne pepper and salt; take two eggs, well beaten, and stir them into the kedgeree at the last moment, serving very hot. This dish is very nice eaten with bacon.

Kidneys on Toast.

Mince 3 or 4 kidneys very finely with a little lemon peel, salt, and cayenne; fry in butter; and when done, beat up 1 egg and add it to the kidneys. Serve on buttered toast.

Potato and Bacon Rolls.

Mix some cold boiled potatoes into a crust with the addition of a little flour, milk, and butter; roll out about $\frac{1}{2}$ inch thick, and cut into squares (about 4 inches); put a thin slice of bacon on each, roll neatly, and bake in the oven until brown.

Mushrooms Baked.

Take $\frac{1}{2}$ lb. of mushrooms, 1 oz. of breadcrumbs, $\frac{1}{4}$ teaspoonful of finely chopped parsley, 3 tablespoonfuls of oil, cayenne, lemon juice, salt, and pepper; put half the oil on a baking-dish, and sprinkle with half the breadcrumbs, half the parsley, and a squeeze of lemon juice; lay half the mushrooms on this, then a second layer, beginning with the oil as before; bake for $\frac{1}{2}$ hour, and before serving dust with cayenne. The same dish should be used.

Flaked Haddock.

Pour boiling water over a dried haddock, cover, and let it soak for 10 minutes; then remove the bone, and flake the fish free from the skin; put the fish into a saucepan with $\frac{1}{2}$ pint of milk and a seasoning of cayenne, and bring it slowly to boiling point, and let it simmer for 10 minutes; thicken with a little flour and butter, and serve on a flat dish.

Savoury Mould.

Line a mould with uncooked bacon; put 3 oz. of butter in a saucepan on the fire, and add any cold meat finely minced, then 3 tablespoonfuls of grated Parmesan cheese, and break 3 eggs into it; soak $\frac{1}{2}$ lb. of bread in water for 10 minutes, cut off the crust, and squeeze the water out; add the soaked crumb to the other ingredients in the saucepan, pepper and salt—as much as would lie on the point of a knife—and some cold thick stock; stir over the fire until soft; place in the mould and cover with slices of bacon, and then bake in a hot oven.

THE · EDITOR'S · PAGE

IN the next number of THE LADY'S REALM will be made known the first awards in "The Truth About Man" Competition.

Considerable interest has been roused by the outspoken criticisms of "A Spinster," and at the moment of going to press MSS. written in defence of Man are arriving in numbers. Many of these authors, taking up cudgels to protect Man's fame and character from the onslaught of a mere spinster, ask how can "A Spinster" possibly be in a position to speak "The Truth About Man" since she is herself still unmarried? But in her first chapter the "Spinster" pointed out her knowledge of the inner nature of Man by remarking that fifty-seven different men, on different occasions, had made love to her.

One competitor, however, belonging to the same sex as "A Spinster," suggests that if there is one period of a man's existence when he may be expected to be unnatural and excused, even if he seem abnormal, it is when he is under the influence of a tender passion which is unrequited—as in the fifty-seven cases cited as types by the "Spinster."

Another defender of Man—this time a man himself—remarks: "Even were it not so stated, there could be little doubt as to the writer being a Spinster. To use an Irishism, no spinster can know 'The Truth About Man' until she has been married to one for a year or more, and often not then."

In spite of the interesting opinions of some of his readers, the Editor is convinced that the best defence of Man has not yet been forwarded, and he will be delighted to receive any criticisms for "The Truth About Man" Competition month by month, provided attention is paid to the rules of the competition given on page 20 of the Advertisements.

177

Photo by Henry Dixon & Son.

ON A FINE DAY.

From the painting by Mrs. Stanhope Forbes.

BY E. KEBLE CHATTERTON.

THE one play of the month which stands out conspicuously above the other productions, whether written for children or grown-up children, is the most fantastic work that the most fantastic of our playwrights has hitherto attempted. *Peter Pan ; or, The Boy who wouldn't Grow Up*, at the Duke of York's, possesses the double claim of appealing both to young boys and maidens, old men and matrons, and to all who have not yet lost either their sense of humour or that child-like half-belief in fairies and creatures born of a pure imagination. It is not so easy a thing nowadays to write a play that will be applauded by an average London audience. It is still more difficult to do so when the audience is composed of men and women of the world and clever wide-awake children

home for the holidays, and therefore expecting much : but Mr. J. M. Barrie has succeeded twice over. Pantomimes are now old-fashioned, and gradually but surely the parodied fairy-tale of the music-hall is giving way to that class of drama which has every right to be called a Christmas play.

Peter Pan is charming because it is original as well as fantastic, and because there is a humorous and happy blend of the mystical and the real. On the programme, Miss Ela Q. May, a very small child, is named as the author. The curtain is still down when she walks on to the stage and stamps her small foot at the conductor as a signal to begin. It is the same little girl who, at the end of each of the first two acts, walks across the deserted stage with a smile that signifies mild ridicule and con-

THE CHORUS IN THE SECOND ACT OF *LADY MADCAP*.
The new musical comedy at The Prince of Wales's Theatre.

Photo by Bassano.

MISS MAIE ASH,

Who has been appearing in Miss Zena Dare's *rôle* in *The Catch of the Season.*

we're only pretending." It is just this spirit which makes grandparents laugh, and which kills at one blow the remark which the very modern matter-of-fact schoolboy is waiting to utter. He cannot say, "What awful rot! No one ever believes in fairy-tales nowadays," because that is precisely the utterance Mr. Barrie anticipates.

Mr. and Mrs. Darling have three delightful, typical English children. Wendy is the motherly unselfish, little daughter of the family, and the eldest, John Napoleon Darling, is the impetuous, manly boy of the " What rot ! " species, the kind of being who has been brought up on G. A. Henty, R. M. Ballantyne, and *The Iron Pirate.* Michael Nicholas Darling will probably grow up to be the more sentimental of the two brothers. Whilst they are asleep in their beds Peter Pan comes in through the window. Wendy awakes and asks him who he is. He has

tempt for all the make-believe that is going on. It is a clever touch of Mr. Barrie to have designed this trivial incident. After he has soared to the tip-top point of the mount of " Once upon a Time," and taken his audience there with him, he suddenly stops, turns round and tells his followers, " This is awful humbug. It isn't really real ; we're only pretending. Let us be wildly fantastic, but, remember,

LONDON'S LATEST PLAYHOUSE.

The Coliseum is now one of the sights of London. The height is enormous, and the illustration shows the proscenium, looking down from the roof, and the arrangement of the boxes.

Photo by Bassano.

THE VILLAGE SCENE IN THE SECOND ACT OF *LADYLAND*, PRODUCED AT THE AVENUE THEATRE.

come from the Never, Never, Never Land, peopled by those children who have been so unhappy as to fall out of their perambulators. He has come to fetch away his shadow, which he had left behind on a previous visit. So they proceed to look for it, find it in a drawer, and Wendy eventually stitches it on for him. By this time John and Michael are awake. When they see that Peter Pan can fly, they of course want to fly too. The " What Rot !" boy is still scoffing at the idea when he finds himself with his brother and sister flying out in the air through the nursery window, piloted by Peter Pan.

The next scene is the Never, Never, Never Land, where the members of Peter's band are awaiting his return. Seeing a white figure coming through the clouds, they shoot at it, and an arrow wounds Wendy as she comes flitting down to earth in her night attire. Gradually she recovers, and as an

Photo by Stage Pictorial

MR. G. P. HUNTLEY AND MISS ADRIENNE ANGARDE IN *LADY MADCAP*.

Mr. G. P. Huntley, after touring round the world, has returned to make a great success in Mr. George Edwardes' latest production.

act of reparation they ingeniously build a
house round her.

There is a scene in the second act which
is unique, whether one considers it from the
view of Mr. Barrie, who has so ingeniously
arranged the action, or from the standpoint
of Mr. Hann, who designed it with so daring
a departure from conventionality. For the
full height of the stage is divided into two.
Under the ground live and laugh Peter Pan,

to the inevitable. Up through the ground,
through the roots of trees, the children wend
their way, only to be gagged and carried off
by the pirates awaiting them on the ground
above. Peter Pan learns their plight and
goes off in hot pursuit.

In the third act, the scene on the deck of
the pirate ship could not fail to move the most
blasé schoolboy. The children are brought
up from the hold and threatened with endless

Photo by Ellis & Walery.

MRS. BROWN POTTER AND HER COMPANY IN *PAGLIACCI* AT THE SAVOY THEATRE.

the Darling children, and Peter's band. They
dance and romp and crowd round Wendy to
hear the tales she tells. Above ground,
lurking in the darkness of the night, are the
Redskin savages. Presently there is a hand-
to-hand fight between the Redskins and a
band of pirates. The latter are victorious.
Below, another change is taking place.
Wendy and the two Darling children have
decided to seek their home again. Peter
is grieved at Wendy's departure, but yields

cruelty and the torment of walking the
plank. But Peter Pan comes up from the
sea, and rescues the children, who over-
come the pirates and take charge of the
vessel. Finally, home is reached again, and
the three children return to their nursery
through the window. An almost heartbroken
mother embraces them, and they live on
happily ever after. There is so much
crowded into these three acts that it would
be an easy matter to pass over some of the

Photo by Biograph Studio.

MISS MARIE GEORGE,

Who has been playing a principal part in *The White Cat* at the Drury Lane Theatre.

clever son of *Trilby's* author, is natural and convincing both as Mr. Darling and the Pirate Captain. And if one were to individualise further, Miss Pauline Chase is the most delightful of Peter Pan's little band.

What Mr. Barrie has attempted and achieved, Mr. Laurence Housman and Mr. Granville Barker have merely attempted. *Prunella ; or, Love in a Dutch Garden*, at the Court Theatre, can only be ranked as a most interesting failure. The play is described as being written for " grown-up children." But the first act only bored them, the second puzzled them, and the last depressed them. For the action of the play was never quick enough, the symbolism was not sufficiently obvious to be popular, and the story is practically a pathetic monotone with hardly any comedy relief. And yet there is a certain charm about *Prunella*. It smacks of originality, although if one were to dissect it carefully one would trace the influence of the old English morality plays on the one side, and on the other of the romantic opera,

important details. I have said nothing of the lovely creature of a dog, Nana, who acts as nursemaid, prepares the children's bath, airs their clothes, tucks them in bed, and attends to their medicine ; nor of Tinker Bell, the mystical being that rings out messages through space ; nor of the occasional drop-scenes, which are hardly necessary for the dramatist but essential to the stage-manager while the set scenes are being prepared behind.

The acting, like the play, is excellent. Miss Nina Boucicault as Peter Pan is as fantastic as Mr. Barrie. Miss Hilda Trevelyan is a sweet, sympathetic Wendy. Miss Dorothea Baird plays even better as Mrs. Darling than she did as Trilby ; and Mr. Gerald du Maurier, the

Photo by Bassano.

MR. JAMES WELCH,

Who succeeded Mr. Dan Leno in the Drury Lane pantomime.

THE LAST SCENE IN *LITTLE BLACK SAMBO*, AT THE GARRICK THEATRE.

Photo by Ellis & Walery.

Photo by Ellis & Walery.

THE OPENING SCENE IN *LADY JANE'S CHRISTMAS PARTY*.
Mr. Tom Gallon's one-act play at the Garrick Theatre.

with a suggestion of Shakespeare. Mr. Laurence Housman is known as the author of *An Englishwoman's Love Letters* and of some beautiful poetry full of the finest feeling. Consequently, when in the development of the play the author leaves prose and breaks forth into poetry, he is irresistibly charming and artistic. But though he has this gift, he is lacking in the instincts of the dramatist. There is much music to accompany these verses, but no singing. Yet if the play had been written in collaboration with one of our leading dramatists, and the music were arranged so that the poems became songs, *Prunella* would be far more commendable.

The story, though spread over three acts, is trifling. Prunella has been brought up apart from the world under the strict care of the most prim of aunts. Pierrot comes along, kisses her, and the whole of her life becomes changed. She goes away with Pierrot and his companions Romp, Coquette, Scaramel, Hawk, and the rest. In time he tires of her, and wanders over the world,

only to meet her again destitute, when the old love returns. Miss Thyrza Norman (Mrs. J. H. Leigh) played Prunella with some feeling, but Mr. Granville Barker's interpretation of Pierrot was hardly pleasing.

At the Garrick Theatre two Christmas plays have been presented. *Lady Jane's Christmas Party*, "an old-fashioned episode in one act," has been written by Mr. Tom Gallon. It is nothing more than an episode, and scarcely above the conventional. Sentiment is by no means forgotten, but having regard to the particular season of the year, it may be permissible. Jane, a kitchen maid, played by Miss Nellie Bowman, is sitting by the fire on the evening of Christmas Day reading out of a book of fairy tales. Charlie Brandon from "upstairs" is spending an equally lonely Christmas at "Miss Cropper's select establishment for the sons of gentlemen," and comes into the kitchen. A half-starved circus troupe passes the kitchen door, and they are invited in. After being fed, and having in return amused their host and hostess with a part of their entertainment, there is a knock at the door, and Sir James Brandon comes in to take Charlie home for the holidays. Of course he gives a sovereign to the circus troupe and a promise to find a place for Jane in his household. And so the curtain comes down.

The two-act musical medley that followed *Lady Jane's Christmas Party*, and entitled *Little Black Sambo and Little White Barbara*, has been adapted from two Dumpy books by Mr. Rutland Barrington. There is very little consecutive story, but as the children for whom this was written will not look for a plot, inasmuch as there is plenty of fun provided, it is not necessary to be exact in criticising. Miss Nellie Bowman plays Little Black Sambo with much cleverness. Mr. Frank Lawton, who will be remembered as having played for a long time in *The Belle of New York*, and Miss Madge Titheradge assist in making the play go with a good swing. Miss Iris Hawkins as Little White Barbara is one of the cleverest child-actors to be seen at present on the London stage, and her career should be interesting.

The new production, *Butterflies in Fairyland*, at the Hippodrome can legitimately be described as gorgeous. The ring is of course again filled with water, and coloured

fountains play round white living sculpture which rises from the flower-strewn lake. Far behind at the back dances the ballet, and at a further distance still, comes down a torrent from a fountain. There is, besides, an artistic flying ballet which comes out from the stage over the heads of the audience. The effect of the brilliant colouring of the dresses and the many varieties of lights and butterflies is extremely beautiful.

Two more new theatres were added at Christmas-time to the rapidly increasing list of London's places of entertainment, and

Photo by Ellis & Walery.

A SCENE FROM *PRUNELLA*,
The new play at the Court Theatre by Mr. Laurence Housman, author of
An Englishwoman's Love Letters.

Photo by Beresford.

MR. J. M. BARRIE,

The author of *Peter Pan*, the most delightful of this season's plays.

arrangement for the convenience of Royalty. On entering the theatre the Royal party will step into a richly furnished lounge, which at a signal will move softly along a track formed in the floor, through the salon, and into a large foyer which contains the entrance to the Royal box. The lounge car remains in position at the entrance to the box, and serves as an ante-room during the performance.

On the site of the old theatre a new Lyceum has been built up. The interior has been beautifully decorated after the style of the Louis XV. period, and as many as three thousand people can be seated. An excellent innovation has been made to get away from the customary music-hall programme by obtaining from the Grand Opera, Paris, and the Royal Theatre, Brussels, the best operatic singers. At the opening performance a selection from *Rigoletto* was given with great success.

yet several more are being built and two others being planned. The Coliseum in St. Martin's Lane is the most daring venture up to the present. The interior is palatial and magnificent, and the experiment is being tried of giving four performances each day. The Coliseum is not a music-hall nor is it quite on the lines of the Hippodrome, though it has characteristics common to both. The stage is, like the rest of the theatre, on an enormous scale, and is over ten thousand feet in extent, so that it will be possible to produce the most ambitious spectacular effects with every semblance of realism. By an ingenious device, instead of waiting for the scenery to be changed, the stage is set in motion and swings round until another scene, already prepared, comes into view. The presentation of the Derby with horses galloping in an opposite direction to the moving stage is very effective. Originality is prevalent throughout the theatre, for there are writing-rooms, tea-rooms, lifts to take the audience to the top of the house, an information bureau, a ladies' boudoir, and an ingenious

Photo by Ellis & Walery.

MISS PAULINE CHASE,

Who plays so charmingly in *Peter Pan* at the Duke of York's Theatre.

THE ART OF
MRS. STANHOPE FORBES.

BY MARION HEPWORTH DIXON.

I T must now be close on fifteen years ago since a Hibernian art critic deplored, in the columns of a contemporary, that he no longer discerned the canvases of Miss Elizabeth Armstrong on the walls of Burlington House. Is it necessary to say that the canvases were there? As a matter of fact the lady's work had undergone no other metamorphosis than the simple one of being signed by a different name, Miss Elizabeth

Photo by Henry Dixon & Son.

PORTRAIT OF MRS. W. FORBES.

(From the painting by Mrs. STANHOPE FORBES.)

Armstrong having married Mr. Stanhope Forbes, the champion of the Newlyn school of *plein air* painting, in the preceding year of 1889. A mistake so ludicrous would hardly be worth recording, were it not that an almost identical error has crept into the press during the last few months. Thus Mrs. Stanhope Forbes has been recently described as a young Canadian, who, visiting England with her mother, was attracted to Newlyn, where she

met the husband who was destined to influence her life-work.

Now Mrs. Stanhope Forbes's career was

the attention of the discerning, who instantly
saw that in Miss Elizabeth Armstrong they
had to deal with a painter who saw with her

FIREFLY.

(From the painting by MRS. STANHOPE FORBES.)

chosen, and she had already made her mark
among contemporary painters, when she met
the leader of the Cornish school. With her
very first exhibits the young artist attracted

own eyes, and could portray what she saw
with more than masculine force. As early
as 1883 the artist's pictures were eagerly
sought out in the various exhibitions to

Photo by Henry Dixon & Son.

A KNIGHT.

(From the painting by Mrs. STANHOPE FORBES.)

and the painting entitled "Little Sister"; Mrs. Stanhope Forbes emulating the practice of Mr. Robert Macbeth in reproducing the latter painting in the more stringent medium of black and white.

The artist's life, in a word, has been so strenuous a one, so full of a rounded and sustained achievement, that it is difficult to say where her far-reaching capacities should end. Whether as a designer, a painter, a teacher, a writer, we find Mrs. Stanhope Forbes's work stamped with a thoroughness and a distinction which mark her out as one of the specially endowed. I have used the word "distinction" in describing the peculiar quality of this artist's output, and no other epithet so nicely describes her clear-

which she sent her work, while in the spring of the same year her canvas "Summer" showed such mastery of her tools as to lift her, at a bound, to a foremost place among the women artists of her time. Her powers, indeed, were so ripe and her capacity for work so prodigious, that three years later we find the painter exhibiting no less than four pictures at Burlington House. Among them was the work called "After Dinner"

cut handling. An admirable draughtswoman, to whom an error in drawing is anathema, Mrs. Stanhope Forbes has so thoroughly grasped the synthetic method that she attains her efforts by the simplest means. Realising that it is not so much what is put into a picture, *as what is left out*, a drawing by Mrs. Stanhope Forbes is frequently conveyed in a dozen lines. Not that she scamps her work. She can be penetrating, she can be intricate. No one can be more deliberate and painstaking when elaboration of detail is requisite. At such a time the smallest twig on a tree, the tiniest petal in the heart of a flower, may engage the artist's attention for hours.

But it is not after all by mere laborious toil that the suffrages of the public are won. The pedant in art has rarely anything but a small and crooked following. What the public cares for supremely is, and first of all, individuality in an artist, and, in the second place, sympathy in his understanding of human nature. As the critic Mr. Roger Fry so finely says, "Our first concern is whether the artist has been able to communicate his likes to us." Now, this is precisely what Mrs. Stanhope Forbes has proved herself competent to do. Her ultimate analysis of the thing seen is not only feminine, in the best sense of the word, but joyous and stimulating. However difficult it may be to diagnose

Photo by Henry Dixon & Son (From the painting by MRS. STANHOPE FORBES.

A WIND-SWEPT AVENUE.

common in the picture called " O wind a-blowing all day long, O wind that sings so loud a song." For Mrs. Stanhope Forbes's art is an instrument of many strings : a wistful chord is as well within her compass as a sprightly one. In a semi-humorous little note to the catalogue of her exhibition she admirably shows her understanding of the small people who posed for her " Model Children." Their erstwhile eagerness, their desperate ambition " to be put in a picture," are amusingly touched on, as is their subsequent distress and restlessness under the ordeal of posing for hours.

Less trying to the artist must

Photo by Henry Dixon & Son.

THE MINUET.
(From the painting by MRS. STANHOPE FORBES.)

the charm of a particular talent, it is obvious that a passionate love of outdoor life and a tender regard for all children are the mainsprings of Mrs. Stanhope Forbes's powers. Her secret, in fact, those who run may read. One has only to glance at such a picture as "Here we go Gathering Nuts in May," recently seen on view in town, to realise the grip and *verve* which the artist brings to her work. What a merry group of youngsters here tread the springy grass, as hand in hand they bound forward on their joyous errand ! Another note is struck in the outline of the tender little maiden who wanders across the

have been the accomplishment of the long-cherished plan of writing and illustrating a book on the West Country. The time of King Arthur is the period chosen, and many and brave are the knights who figure in her picturesque pages. Of the many excellent drawings in *King Arthur's Wood* " Sir Gareth and the Damsel in the Wood Perilous " and " The Black Knight of the Black Lawn " are perhaps the most successful. That Mrs. Stanhope Forbes could wield the pen as well as the brush has long been known to her admirers. In the autumn of 1899 the artist recorded her impressions in *The Studio* magazine of a spring spent with her husband in the Low Pyrenees which was more *piquante* than anything I remember written by a professed scribe. Take the following thumb-nail sketch :

" Perhaps it was because we came on our village just at the magical minute when the last red gold of the sun was dying from the hills ; perhaps it was the troop of handsome bare-footed girls who bewitched us. They

JONQUIL.
(From the painting by MRS. STANHOPE FORBES.)

were crossing the old Roman bridge erect and dark against the pale sky, their sickles at their waists, bundles of fresh-cut grass on their heads. 'Addios!' they called back to the strangers in a chorus of civil and kindly welcome." And again the description of the *bonne à tout faire* : " Marie's French was excellent, though she was a true-born Basque, and her manners perfect. We were grateful to her for being so good to look at ; for her brisk and blithe capabilities, her intelligence and perfect temper. How satisfactory to all our senses was the vision

we had of her when, in coming in late from work on nights which were chilly, we could see her in her bright-coloured bodice, moving alertly to and fro among the wavering lights and shadows of the big kitchen ! The fragrance of burning beech logs mingles with that of the juicy capon or joint of tender *agneau*. Marie turns the spit, and the flames leap up and are reflected on the copper *casseroles* and burnished tins."

The same delight in travelling, the same delight in recording the picturesque scenes witnessed in her wanderings, remain with Mrs. Stanhope Forbes to-day. But many things conspired to keep the artist tethered to the spot where she had set up her household gods. Curiously enough, Mr. Stanhope Forbes is less a wanderer at heart than is his Canadian wife, who, it may be mentioned here, first picked up the rudiments of her art in the Students' League, New York. There is, moreover, the cherished child of their imaginations, the Newlyn Art School, which Mr. and Mrs. Stanhope Forbes established some four years ago, and which keeps their interest keenly centred in the Cornish fishing village where they are trying their new experiment. For since the collapse of

Photo by Henry Dixon & Son.

"IF I WERE AS ONCE I WAS."

(From the painting by MRS. STANHOPE FORBES.)

Photo by Henry Dixon & Son.

THE DREAMLAND PRINCESS.

(From the painting by MRS. STANHOPE FORBES.)

Bushey, it is hardly necessary to say that no artists of equal prominence in England have hitherto opened an *atelier* on lines made familiar to us by every second painter on the Continent. Perhaps something in the Royal Academician's birth (he is French at least on one side) suggested the idea of acclimatising so useful a fashion. Certain it is that Mrs. Stanhope Forbes is never happier than when wending her way down at an early hour from

"Trewarveneth" to the Meadow Studios, where, posing her model, she starts an eager band of students off on a hard week's work of painting. Nor does the artist at any time flinch from practising what she preaches. A tireless advocate of *plein air* methods, she not only works out-of-doors the whole day (having built a painting-hut for severe weather), but insists on her more advanced pupils following her example. More beautiful surroundings for these open-air instructions it would be hard to imagine. St. Michael's Mount, rising above Harbour Bay, juts out just below this *al fresco* studio. Sometimes, too, the velvet twilight of a little wood is sought, a wood deep and mysterious, with strange, silent pools reflecting the overhanging crags and intersected by tiny by-paths carpeted with bluebells. Who would not be an art student indeed under such happy conditions?

But one may also now turn to the artist's academic work, which has found so many admirers for her in Piccadilly. For a certain note of life and movement, of joyousness and gaiety, is noticeable in nearly every canvas to which the artist has put her hand. At times she loves to turn to mediæval themes depicting now an armoured knight, and now a Court fool, but under all a passionate love.

Photo by Henry Dixon & Son.

ALEC, SON OF MRS. STANHOPE FORBES.
(From the painting by MRS. STANHOPE FORBES.)

THE TRUTH ABOUT MAN.

By a Spinster.

ILLUSTRATED BY FACTS FROM HER OWN PRIVATE HISTORY.

The author of " The Truth About Man" is a well-known novelist, who prefers not to reveal her identity. In her opening chapters she subdivides Man into the Irresistible, the Admirable, and the Marriageable, discourses on the unattractiveness of the Ideal Woman, and analyses the effect of Love upon mature Man. She then proceeds to give advice to other Spinsters on the use and management of Man the Lover.

As he believes that the views of " A Spinster" may not be shared by all the readers of THE LADY'S REALM, *the Editor has decided to offer prizes, month by month, for the best criticisms of " The Truth About Man." Particulars will be found on page 20 of the advertisements.*

CHAPTER VI.

The Spinster goes on to speak of the "Holy Estate of Matrimony," and applies some of her previous conclusions to the relation between Husband and Wife.

I SUPPOSE the time will never come when there will be anything like a complete understanding between Man and Woman; but I may safely affirm that we understand him, on the whole, far better than he understands us. The reason of this is not hard to find. In the first place—to our credit—we are far more discerning than he is, far more sympathetic, and a thousand times more anxious to learn. Man has very little desire either to improve himself or to know what we are really like. He is even annoyed, as I have stated before, if we try to illuminate him as to our nature ; having no desire to see us as we are. He much prefers to stuff us with his own sawdust, and dress us up as puppets to his fancy. Quite the nicest and best of men are like this : they never make the least attempt to find out how we feel, what motives sway us, and why we act as we do under certain conditions. One has only to read the work of one of our greatest authors, Thomas Hardy, to see the idea that average man has of woman. Hardy's heroines are all precisely alike in one respect—they are mere personifications of caprice. Their actions are ruled by no rational sequence of

ideas, but are a series of wild leaps and bounds in all directions, generally of the most unexpected and impossible character. This, you may be sure, is Man's general notion about us—and why? Because he never studies us at all ; he simply follows our movements with his eyes, as we watch the gyrations of a bird, and never troubles to inquire what are the vital causes of those movements. He has taken the trouble to study the habits and instincts of fowls and bees, because unless these creatures are understood they cannot be managed with profit ; but Woman doesn't matter. She must learn to understand him, or else blindly obey without understanding, so Man seems to think. He will always tell you that any attempt at comprehending us would be waste of energy, as the achievement is impossible ; but this is not the truth. He will not try because *it is too much trouble !*

On the other hand—to their credit—they are easier to read than women, because they are simpler, less subtle, complex, and contradictory. In spite of their bare-faced humbug they are not so schooled in the art of deception as we are—they don't *have* to be. Unless a woman conceals her true feelings, her real self, she has no power whatever over Man, over the world, over her destiny ; she is nothing but a dupe, a tool, and a laughing-stock! There is an old poem that runs as follows :

Our life is like a curious play,
Where each man hideth from himself ;
" Let us be open as the day,"
One mask doth to the other say,
That he may better hide himself.

I think this applies more to us than to Man. Woman appears generally most open when she has most to conceal. It is necessary for her to put on a candid, guileless look, and to adopt a demeanour that will suit the graven image Man has carved in his mind of her. Then when, abruptly, the mask happens to fall, he is confused, and thinks there is no reason for anything she does. The thing seems causeless and fortuitous, as every natural phenomenon has always seemed to the ignorant. But oh, if Man would only take the pains to master a few square facts about her, if he would but try sometimes to imagine himself in her place, how quickly he might solve the mystery of the Sphinx, the secret of the inner heart of Woman !

But he won't try. He will concentrate his whole mind on a mathematical problem, on a bit of intricate machinery, on the writing of a stage plot : he will not give so much attention to the reading of a woman's soul as he will give to the unravelling of a ball of thread. " 'Tis strange ; 'tis wondrous strange ; 'tis pitiful," yet so 'tis, and I expect 'twill be, unless the Superman to come has more curiosity and more sympathy than the present genus. But, if we are to believe Nietzsche, he is to have even less, so far as we are concerned !

Now I think that this extraordinary failure to comprehend the heart and needs of Woman is shown most plainly by Man in the marriage relation. And perhaps it is here that we, too, find our greatest difficulty. For there is one thing no woman can ever understand, and that is—the abrupt change in her husband's manner towards her soon after, and sometimes during, the honeymoon. She can never discover why, from being the most perfect of mortal women, cherished, caressed, adored, she is suddenly of no consequence whatever. Before the wedding endearing words were continually poured into her ears, the ejaculation " I love you ! " was dotted through the hours, with " darling,"

" sweetest," angel," and so forth until she had sometimes begun to think her lover was growing mad for love of· her. After the wedding all this ceases without any apparent cause. She feels herself to be the same woman she was before, her love has probably increased, her capacity for feeling is stronger than ever. The appetite for affection, and affectionate demonstration, roused before marriage by her sweetheart, has become a definite craving, and she longs hungrily for the tender speeches to which she has grown so accustomed. Imagine, therefore, her bitter disappointment, her abject sense of forlornness and misery, when she finds that her husband, now that he has become entirely possessed of her, shows no inclination whatever to fondle her any more, and very often repulses her attempts at endearment. She is no longer the " precious darling " that she was before, he does not want to kiss her every half hour, as he did, and his interest in her seems to have vanished as if by magic !

Why is it ? And how should she understand when her own inclinations have changed so little ? She is far more anxious for outward signs of his love than she ever was before ; why, then, does he not desire such demonstration ? It is a mystery that baffles and tortures her. She begins to wonder what she has done, whether it is her fault that he has changed so radically, and, above all, she agonises under the fear that her husband is tired of her and loves her no longer.

Is this surprising ? Ask yourself, Man : if you love a woman, and she suddenly turns a cold shoulder upon you, are you not prone to conclude that her love for you has waned ? And yet you will tell me that it is absurd to expect a lover's rhapsodies to continue after marriage, that a man can love a woman dearly and deeply without expressing his affection in any way, and that, when once he has confirmed his love of her by the supreme act in which he bestows upon her the honour of bearing his name, she ought to take everything else for granted. This is all very well, but it's humbug, notwithstanding. For if love does not need to be expressed, why, in the name of goodness, have you expressed it *ad nauseam* during the months of courtship? Why, after you and the maiden have plighted troth, has it been necessary to tell her so often that you loved her, and receive assurance of that love's return? No! be candid and tell the truth. You've got her fast and bound, your desires are satisfied, and you don't want to be bothered with any more love-making. If your wife suffers, it is because she is foolish and exacting; you are content, and why cannot she be the same? Thus the first year of married life is generally the most unhappy in a woman's history; and, very often, in a man's also.

I have seen so many of these cases, so many misunderstandings, such pitiable, unnecessary suffering, that I have wondered a good deal if something can't be done to set this crooked matter straight. It is to Man's own interest that he should try to make the change between his ante-connubial and posto-connubial conduct less pronounced, to be a little less fervent before marriage, a little more affectionate after. For if he does not, he will continue to have a sighing, unhappy bride, to see a sad face at his table, and, in some cases, to be oppressed with tears and reproaches. It does not need a great revolution in his behaviour to bring about a happier state of things. Man has but to exercise his imagination and put himself in the woman's place to try and imagine how she feels. Why not? There is not so very great a difference between their essential natures. And how does he know that in his next incarnation he may not be born feminine? It is a monstrous pity we cannot change places now and again!

(To be continued.)

The first prize of one guinea for the best reply to " A Spinster's" criticisms of the November instalment is awarded by the judges to Mrs. J. B. Hobman, Cowley, Chesterfield. The second prize of half a guinea is won by Miss Ernestine Morse, 149, Haverstock Hill, N.W. The essays sent in were generally interesting, though some were inclined to wander away from the main issue. Each of the above competitors showed herself possessed of a real knowledge of Man's Nature, and the criticism adjudged to be the best, and part of which is printed below, will be read with interest.

ALTHOUGH I am bound to admit that I am one of those unfortunate women who are not to be accounted an authority on the male sex, because married to one of them; still, by virtue of the time when I also was a "Spinster" and a "Free Lance" and looked at Men from the outside with a magnifying glass, I may perhaps claim to give an opinion. Even now my "duties," though they may not leave me time to take the extensive bird's-eye view of mankind taken by the writer in THE LADY'S REALM, provide me with ample opportunity to obtain a practical if not a "scientific" insight into the masculine character.

I do not intend to make use of the inhuman methods of vivisection adopted by your correspondent in dividing and subdividing the species, nor do I think it possible to cram so varied a class into three or four little pigeon-holes; but, roughly speaking, one may safely say that there are Men's Men and Women's Men, and that it is only of the latter, as a rule, that spinsters have any experience. After a woman is married, if she is wise enough to encourage the visits of her husband's bachelor friends, she finds that there is a large proportion of men who carry with them, for perhaps the whole of their lives, that feeling of wholesome contempt for the feminine sex which is so freely and openly indulged in by the average schoolboy. It is in these men, that one finds the genuine attributes of their sex.

Good, honest, straightforward fellows, staunch friends or open enemies—not over-conceited or super-sensitive themselves, and expecting others to bear friendly criticism—genuine and generous, what wonder that they are contemptuous of and completely nonplussed by the superficiality and unreality of feminine methods, or disdainful of women's friendship, with its capriciousness, its little meannesses, and its frequently insincere or diplomatic motives! Doubtless these misogynists are included by the "Spinster" in the class entitled "The World's Good Fellows," for they certainly retain a great reverence for their own ideal of Womanhood. But far from having no opinion of themselves and remaining bachelors from motives of unworthiness, I maintain that it is of women that they have no opinion, and in whom they have no confidence; and until the sex realises that there must be a great deal more "Truth about Women" the "Spinsters" will find that their choice of husbands will still rest between the empty-headed Male Flirt and the "Mercenary Getter-on."

CAREERS FOR WOMEN.

VII.—SANITARY INSPECTING.

BY RACHEL MONTGOMERY,
Author of " What a Health Visitor Does."

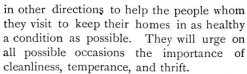

DURING the last eight or ten years the creating of women sanitary inspectors, or health visitors, has been taking place all over the country. London heads the list with twenty such women. Birmingham makes a good second with twelve health visitors and a superintendent, Liverpool coming third with eight lady sanitary inspectors. Certain towns where there is great need for work of this kind have not yet become sufficiently up-to-date to have even one lady visitor.

In some cities the women are appointed as sanitary inspectors, and in others as health visitors. The work is practically the same, though as the sanitary inspector has greater authority the position may be somewhat more satisfactory.

The duties of a lady inspector are many and various. In the town in which the writer works the following printed instructions are given to each newly appointed member of the staff :

"The women health visitors are appointed to visit from house to house under the directions of the medical officer of health, calling attention to the necessity for cleanliness of the house and its surroundings, giving advice as to the rearing of children and the nursing of the sick, distributing and explaining handbills on the prevention of infectious diseases, and doing all they can

in other directions to help the people whom they visit to keep their homes in as healthy a condition as possible. They will urge on all possible occasions the importance of cleanliness, temperance, and thrift.

"Each visitor is expected to make herself acquainted with her own district in order to discover which localities need to be systematically visited, and to visit from house to house in such localities as often as possible."

But besides systematic house-to-house visiting, a great number of " special " calls have to be made. Every " slum " baby is visited as soon as possible after the registration of its birth, advice being given to the mother both in regard to her own health and that of the child. During the summer months, when a large number of children under one year old die of infantile diarrhœa, each case is visited and inquiries are made about the milk supply, the kind of feeding-bottle used, etc., and observations are also made as to the condition of the house. Special cases, as neglect, sickness, overcrowding, etc., are also frequently reported from the schools, neighbours, or other persons, and these, too, have to be visited.

In addition to the indoor inspection, when the house must be gone through from cellar to attic, the court and outhouses, including the drains, must be examined. There are also other duties connected with the work which must be felt to be understood, such as the genuine desire to raise the people, even if it be ever so little, and to exercise a good moral influence over them. In visiting, the procedure is something like this : The health visitor knocks at the door and politely says, "May I come in ? " She then, having received the necessary permission, inquires the name, number of children, adults, lodgers, sickness (if any), entering these facts and her own remarks in a book carried for the purpose.

It must not be imagined that the lady inspector is always received with open arms. Dirty, overcrowded people do not welcome sanitary reform; and the position she holds is, to say the least of it, peculiar. She is sent out by the local authority to visit the houses of the poor, inspect the bedding, etc., and yet, legally, she has absolutely no " right of entry." The writer has come to the conclusion that in sanitary, as in other matters, " the law is a hass." That admission is gained to so many houses—a refusal very seldom occurs—is largely due to the fact that the people are under the impression that the lady inspector *must* be admitted. The writer came across a rather amusing instance of this recently while inspecting the three-roomed house of a man living quite alone. He earned his living partly by restoring old pictures by some mysterious secret process, and making them look like new. No one was ever allowed to go up his stairs, he explained, adding cheerfully and philosophically, " But I can't prevent *you*." He further explained, confidentially, that he might have got married, only it would never do for him to have a wife bringing in other inquisitive women to see his work !

Ignorance of the law, however, is not the only reason why lady inspectors are received into the homes of the poor, as very much depends upon the lady herself and her manner of treating those with whom she comes into contact.

In order to obtain a post as health visitor or sanitary inspector, it is absolutely essential to hold a certificate of sanitary knowledge— preferably the certificate of the Sanitary Institute or that of the Sanitary Inspectors Examination Board. The advantage of the latter certificate is that it enables one to hold a position in London or elsewhere, the former (Sanitary Institute) qualifying for the provinces only. For these examinations there is an entrance fee of £3 3s. and £4 4s. respectively. A course of instruction can be obtained at the Sanitary Institute, Margaret Street., London, W., full particulars of which can be ascertained upon application to the Secretary, the fee for the course being £3 3s. The National Health Society, 53, Berners Street, London, W., also prepares students for these examinations, and grants diplomas; while in Liverpool a good course is held in connection with the University, at a charge of £2 2s.

The subjects to be studied are comprehensive. They include mensuration—that is, the measuring and calculating the cubic space of different-shaped rooms, halls, workshops, etc.; hygiene, including air, water, and ventilation; meat inspection; drainage and house construction; infectious diseases and methods of disinfection; and last, but by no means least, sanitary law.

Certificates in hospital work or sick nursing are a decided help in obtaining a post, and experience in visiting among the poor is also very desirable. In fact, it may be stated as a general rule that where such work is only being commenced in a town, experience is a *sine quâ non.*

In speaking of qualifications, it need scarcely be said that tact is an all-important one. It has very truly been observed that the cry of the poor is to be let alone, and undoubtedly they look with suspicion upon any one who ostensibly goes about endeavouring to " improve " them.

Another qualification is a cheerful courage, for it must be admitted that the work is depressing in the extreme. Its great charm— if " charm " it can be said to have—is the constant variety and the opportunity it affords of getting into close contact with what is commonly known as " human nature." Any woman undertaking work of this kind should be possessed of good physical health. She will have to be out in all weathers. And not only that, but the constant striving that good may result from her work takes it out of one to a very great extent. The best age for a woman to undertake work of this kind is between twenty-five and thirty-five. Advertisements frequently have stated as an age limit for applicants, thirty-five — sometimes forty.

The · Realm · of · Society ·

IN February people have already received their invitations to the first Courts, and pleasurably excited débutantes and their anxious mothers are very busy attending to the thousand and one details connected with this important event. The early Courts are somehow specially dedicated to the Young Person; but of course, in these days, although it is courteously intimated by the officials of the Lord Chamberlain's office that those desiring to attend may state the date which would be most convenient to them, they are, on the other hand, as often as not informed that some other date has been fixed upon as the one on which they will receive the commands of the Sovereign. As there are perhaps, a hundred débutantes to be presented and not more than thirty or forty at the outside are invited to each Court, it follows that half the number make their first curtsey to their Sovereign only in May, when they have already danced gaily through the early portion of the season.

Lady Eileen Wellesley, the second daughter of the Duke

Photo by Lafayette.

LADY DALRYMPLE.

Photo by Langfier.

THE HON. MRS. AILWYN FELLOWES, WHO IS A
CLEVER AMATEUR ACTRESS.

the vaults at Apsley House. It always figured at the Waterloo banquets and graced the supper table at the famous Coronation ball given by the Duke of Wellington when Queen Victoria came to the throne. Lady Eileen Wellesley is very pretty—fair, with blue eyes and a lovely complexion. She is taller, although not so slender, than her elder sister, Lady Evelyn, who four years ago married Mr. Robert James, eldest son of Lord Northbourne. She does not ride or drive, as, before her father succeeded to the dukedom, her principal home was in London. But she is very fond of horses, and with more opportunities will probably hunt some day. Lady Eileen draws very well, and is a fair linguist; she speaks German better than French, and is now in the throes of mastering the " Lingua Toscana." As a child she was a most graceful skirt dancer, but has given it up of late.

Ewhurst, the smaller family estate, is about twelve miles from Strathfieldsaye, and is preferred by the present Duke and Duchess to their statelier home. They have made it charming inside and out, but most of the shooting is at the larger place and the guns have a long drive before and after the day's sport. There has long been some talk about letting Strathfieldsaye, but up to now it has

and Duchess of Wellington, who is so very young that only last season she was included in the Queen's garden party for children at Buckingham Palace, on the occasion of Prince Edward's birthday, is one of the youthful band about to make their appearance in society. If the Duchess of Wellington gives a dance or two, as she probably will for her débutante daughter, Apsley House will once more become a social centre in London, after having been practically closed for a great many years past. In fact, I think I am not mistaken in saying that the last time the celebrated Spanish plate was used was on the occasion of the Waterloo banquet, given by the Iron Duke the year of his death. The plate is a unique possession, presented to the great Duke by the Spanish Government in recognition of his services to Spain during the Peninsular War. It is so massive that the centre piece stands five feet in height and requires several men to lift it out of

Photo by Lafayette.

LORD BERGHERSH.

Photo by Langfier.

VISCOUNTESS FALMOUTH IS A DAUGHTER OF LORD
PENRYHN. HER LADYSHIP ENTERTAINED THE
KING ON HIS LAST VISIT TO CORNWALL.

had taken place in the historical home of the
Cecils for many years past. Her mother, the
widowed Lady Airlie, has a town house in
Elvaston Place, where she generally is in
residence when not at Cortachy, and when her
services are not requisitioned by the Princess
of Wales, to whom she is lady-in-waiting.
Lady Kitty has been brought up principally
at Cortachy, the beautiful old family place
in Forfarshire, where her grandmother, the
Dowager Lady Airlie, planted the first tree
in the now luxuriant and flourishing "Garden
of Friendship" when she married the seventh
earl of the "bonny house" in 1851. At
Cortachy, too, is the grave of a favourite
charger, whose gallant master, the late Lord
Airlie, lies in South Africa, out on the veldt
where he fell at Diamond Hill. The weird
story of the ghostly drummer boy, who
marches round the castle wall, with his
warning of misfortune to the House of
Ogilvy, is well known throughout the whole
of the north. There are different legends as

not found a tenant.
Strathfieldsaye was a gift
of the British nation to
the Iron Duke, and is
held by his descendants
on the quaint condition of
the reigning duke presenting a flag to the Sovereign
on Waterloo Day.

Another débutante
who is expected to be
present at one of the
earlier Courts is Lady
Kitty Ogilvy, sister of
the present and eldest
daughter of the late
Lord Airlie. Lady Kitty,
who is in her eighteenth
year and is a very charm-
ing young girl, made what
may be called her first
appearance in society at
a little dance given for
her by Lord and Lady
Salisbury at Hatfield
House just before Christ-
mas, the only one which

Photo by Lafayette.

THE NEW VISCOUNT RIDLEY.

to the origin of the Airlie ghost, the most generally credited being that a drummer boy was forced into his drum and hurled from the castle walls—an episode sufficiently ghastly to account for any number of apparitions. Forfarshire is especially favoured in the matter of " spooks," for not far from Cortachy is Glamis Castle, which is literally bristling with mysteries, and harbours a full half-dozen domestic spectres within its walls.

Miss Clementine Hozier, the daughter of Lady Blanche Hozier, and a first cousin of Lady Kitty Ogilvy, who also comes out officially this year, bids fair to become one of the new beauties who are gradually replacing their elders in London society. She is charmingly pretty, with a flower-like face, and a great deal of the charm of her mother, who was the eldest sister of the late Lord Airlie. Miss Hozier is often with her grandmother, the Dowager Lady Airlie, and up to now has lived chiefly in the country with her mother.

A débutante, who, like Lady Kitty Ogilvy and Miss Hozier, comes from across the border, is Miss Iona Macdonald, only daughter of the Lord of the Isles. Miss Macdonald comes of ancient Highland stock on both sides of her house, her only English forbear being her late grandmother, wife of Godfrey, third Lord Macdonald, who was a Wyndham of Cromer, in Norfolk. Miss Macdonald's mother, the present Lady Macdonald, was a daughter of the late Colonel Ross of Cromarty, and a granddaughter of the much-married Laird of Tulloch, by his first wife, who was herself a Macdonald of the Isles. Lady Macdonald has been very little seen in society of late years, but is usually at her house in Chesham Place in the winter, and will probably take her daughter out this season. Miss Iona Macdonald, who rather resembles her beautiful aunt, Lilian Lady Cromartie, with the same dark eyes and ivory white complexion, is a good musician, and sketches very cleverly. Armadale Castle, her home in romantic Skye, where she passes most of the summer, is beautifully situated on the sea shore. It is rather a fine castellated building, and the gardens are remarkable, like so many on the west coast, for the great fuschia hedges,

some of them standing ten and twelve feet high, and the almost tropical luxuriance of the vegetation. The place is generally let for the shooting season and is ideal for sport of all kinds, with its deep-sea fishing, boating facilities, and yachting anchorage.

Although she does not come under the heading of débutante, as she has been out for one or two seasons already, Lady Susan Yorke, the only daughter of the new Lord Hardwicke, will have to be presented once again, her father, Captain John Yorke, having succeeded to the family honours on the death of his nephew, the late Lord Hardwicke, in November last. Lady Susan is a remarkably clever amateur actress, a talent she has probably inherited from her uncle, Mr. Alexander Yorke, who is wonderfully gifted in this respect. She has made quite a name for herself in the leading feminine rôle of that amusing play, *His Excellency the Governor*, in which she has appeared many times in the cause of charity or for the entertainment of her friends. A year or two ago, she made a great hit in Mr. Alexander Yorke's clever little comedy, *Love me, Love my dog*, which was performed for some charitable object at one of the London theatres, in the presence of a large gathering of royalties and a representative London audience. Lady Susan is rather below the middle height, with quantities of beautiful fair hair, and is very popular among her girl friends. Lord Hardwicke, her father, known for so long as Captain John Yorke, is in appearance cut out for the career he adopted, as he is above all things a typical sailor. He and Lady Hardwicke occupy a large house in Rutland Gate, and their summer residence, Sydney Lodge, Hamble, is a pretty little white building on Southampton Water. Lady Hardwicke was Miss Oswald, of Auchencruive, in that most sporting of Scottish counties, Ayrshire, and is connected on her mother's side with the Farquharsons of Invercauld and other well-known Scottish families. She and Lord Hardwicke are both very fine bridge players, and are rather notable gastronomes. Lord Hardwicke takes an interest in the School of Cookery in Exhibition Road, and is a connoisseur in all cookery matters.

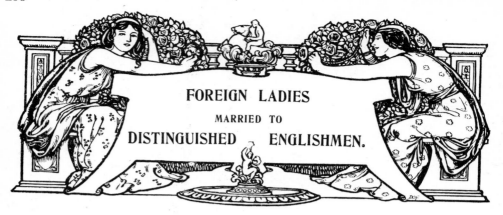

FOREIGN LADIES
MARRIED TO
DISTINGUISHED ENGLISHMEN.

ARE Englishmen less desirable as husbands than foreign men? This question naturally suggests itself to my mind when I note the extraordinary disproportion between the number of Englishwomen who have married out of their own country, and of foreign women who have become the wives of Englishmen. Italian princesses, French marquises, and German countesses who are Englishwomen by birth may be met with by the score; but in England the foreign ladies who have married men occupying prominent social positions might be counted almost on the fingers of both hands.

Abroad, English wives are to be found not merely in diplomatic circles, the members of which, by the circumstances of their calling, mix constantly with women of nations other than their own, but in every section of Society, whether in town or country. On the other hand, it is only the most cosmopolitan among our countrymen who

have selected foreign ladies as their partners for life. The average Englishman has probably never set foot in an Embassy in London, and when he goes abroad herds persistently with his own kind, frequents only the English club, and in hotel reading-rooms shelters himself behind the impregnable fortress of the *Times* if he discerns any alarming symptoms of friendly advances from the foreign foe. Are the men of other nations more enterprising, that they are able to woo and win the fairest and most desirable, as often as not, of John Bull's daughters? Is it insurmountable shyness or hopeless insularity that is responsible for the fact that there does not appear to be a corresponding inclination on the part of Englishmen to seek for their wives among foreign ladies? Or may we lay the flattering unction to our souls that the charms of their own countrywomen are paramount?

This view, however pleasing

Photo by Lafayette.

THE MARCHIONESS OF TWEEDDALE.

Photo by H. W. Barnett.

LADY LAW.

general Society than is the case now that he has ascended the throne : "Wherever I go, and whomsoever I see, there is no one like the Princess." Never since she came among us for the first time as the bride of the Heir - Apparent has English sentiment changed towards the lovely Royal lady whom the late poet laureate greeted in lines which voiced the feelings of the whole nation :

Saxon, and Norman, and Dane are we,
But all of us Danes in the welcome of thee.

It so happens that one of the greatest, if not *the* greatest, of our social leaders, the Duchess of Devonshire, is not only a foreigner, but has been the wife of two

to our national *amour propre*, is scarcely borne out by even a superficial glance at the best known among the ladies who have become Englishwomen by marriage. Above and beyond all others—*hors concours*, as our French neighbours would say—is our own gracious Queen Consort, who in point of beauty and charm stands unequalled. Perhaps the truest word ever spoken of Her Majesty fell from the lips of King Edward himself in the days when, as Prince of Wales, he went out more into

English dukes, as her first husband was the seventh Duke of Manchester. Countess Louise von Alten was a singularly beautiful young Hanoverian lady when she married the then Lord Mandeville in 1852, although perhaps less absolutely lovely than her sister, the Countess Bludoff, who was one of the celebrated European beauties of the day. As Duchess of Manchester she was most popular, although her hospitalities were naturally not then on so splendid a scale as that on which they have been conducted since she has reigned over Devonshire House in Piccadilly and stately Chatsworth, the Palace of the Peak. Her parties in London are usually the most salient feature of the season, and her famous fancy ball in the Diamond Jubilee year was the topic of conversation for weeks beforehand and weeks after it took place. The Duchess is one of the most assiduous frequenters of Newmarket, and a devotee of bridge. She is also a very keen politician, and is never quite happy when her husband is not in office. She is *persona grata* at Buckingham Palace, and two of her daughters, Lady Gosford and Lady Alice Stanley, are members of the Household of Queen Alexandra, who stood sponsor to the Duchess's great-grandson, little Lord Mandeville, last year. She has from time to time replaced the wife of the Minister for Foreign Affairs in the duty of presenting distinguished foreign ladies at Court; but it is a fact worthy of record that so great a lady should never have been Mistress of the Robes. Perhaps some future administration may see her in that position. The Duchess of Devonshire is a remarkably clever woman and a brilliant conversationalist, although she speaks English with some trace of foreign accent. She rarely, if ever, goes to Germany,

and is not very much in touch with her German relations. In London she is distinctly a power, and can do much to make or mar aspirants for social honours.

Lady Esher, wife of the present Lord Esher, whose name came so prominently before the public in connection with the Army Commission, possesses a very charming personality. Tall and svelte, with the perfect figure that distinguishes most well-born Belgians, she is always dressed in admirable taste, and wears her clothes well. She is fond of the theatre, and, with Lord Esher, is an inveterate "first night" *habituée.* Lady Esher is very popular in diplomatic circles, her father, M. Sylvain Van de

Photo by Elliott & Fry.

LADY ARNOLD,
Widow of the late Sir Edwin Arnold.

Weyer, having been at one time Belgian Minister to the Court of St. James. By a strange coincidence the late Lady Esher was also of foreign birth, her father having been M. Louis Mäyer, of Lyons.

Lord and Lady Esher are much given to quiet entertaining, and when they are in town scarcely a week passes without their giving cheery little luncheons and dinners at one or other of the restaurants. Lord Esher, who used to be very well known about town as Mr. "Reggie" Brett, is literary and artistic in his tastes, and is the author of several clever pamphlets. He has always been honoured by the personal friendship of King Edward, and since the new reign has been brought a great deal into contact with His Majesty in his capacity as Secretary to the Office of Works—the renovating of Windsor Castle and Buckingham Palace having been carried out under his direct supervision. Lord and Lady Esher have two sons, of whom the second is in the Coldstream Guards, and two daughters, Miss Dorothy and Miss Sylvia Brett.

The Countess Manvers, widow of the late peer, was with her sister, the late Lady Stair, daughter and co-heiress of the Duc de Coigny, whose name conjures up visions of stately Versailles, rustic Trianon, and the ever-living romance surrounding the Court of Marie Antoinette. The chivalrous devotion of the Coigny of that day to the ill-fated Queen was seized upon and exploited by her enemies, who chose to consider the harmless coquetries of a young and thoughtless woman as evidences of a guilty intrigue. Thoresby, Lord Manvers' seat near Ollerton, is one of the most beautiful places in the "Dukeries," and is famous for the wonderful oaks in the park, one of which is supposed to have been the trysting-place of Robin Hood and his

Photo by H. W. Barnett.

THE COUNTESS TOLSTOY
The Hon. Mrs. Philip Stanhope.

"merrie men." Lady Manvers, who in manner and appearance has all the charm of the great ladies of the *ancien régime*, is half Scotch on one side of her house, her mother having been the daughter of Sir Hew Dalrymple Hamilton.

The Marchioness of Tweeddale, although practically English, having spent her whole life in this country, is of Italian extraction, her father having been Signor Vincenzo Bartolucci, of Cantiano, Rome. Lady Tweeddale, who possesses the delightful Christian name of Candida, is still a very beautiful woman, showing considerable evidence of her Southern ancestry in her dark eyes and hair, regular features, and great charm of manner. Both in London and at stately Yester, where she has more than once entertained the Prince and Princess of Wales, she has shown herself a successful hostess. Yester, like Muncaster and Edenhall, boasts of a "luck," which has not, however, taken the usual form of a drinking vessel, but is neither more nor less than a dried pear, the possession of which is said to secure prosperity to the family.

Lady Tweeddale, who married Lord Tweeddale in 1878, the same year in which

Photo by Langfier.

THE HON. MRS. E. STONOR.

he succeeded to the marquisate, has three sons (the eldest of whom, Lord Gifford, is in the Guards, and is one of the eligible young men of the moment) and one surviving daughter, Lady Clementine Hay, who married Mr. Waring a year or two ago. Another daughter of Signor Bartolucci, an elder sister of Lady Tweeddale, also married in England—first, Admiral Sir Astley Cooper-Key, who died in 1888, and secondly, Mr. Maurice Ansell.

Lady Sligo, widow of the third Marquis of Sligo, was a French lady, Mlle. Isabelle Raymonde de Peyronnet, daughter of the Vicomte de Peyronnet. She is one of London's well-known hostesses and the giver of charming balls, chiefly for young people. She has no son; but her twin daughters, Lady Mary and Lady Isabel Browne, are among the most popular girls in Society. Lady Sligo is tall and distinguished-looking, with a crown of pretty grey hair, and in the evening wears very beautiful diamonds.

Mrs. Wombwell (*née* Boyer) is another French lady whom all London knows; but although she has lived for so many years in England, she has retained the appearance

Photo by Lafayette.

THE LATE LADY ESHER.

French. She is the mother of Lady Carnarvon, whose marriage was one of the events of the season of 1895. Lansdowne House was taken for the wedding, and Lord and Lady Carnarvon commenced their married life laden with magnificent gifts. Lord Carnarvon is an all-round sportsman; he is one of the finest shots in England, and his *demêlés* with the police over the speed at which he drives his motor-car are a matter of history. Mrs. Wombwell's eldest son, Mr. Frederick Wombwell, is eventual heir to the baronetcy of his uncle, Sir George Wombwell. Lady Effingham, mother of the present peer, was another of the handsome Boyer sisters, and married her late husband in 1865. She lives very quietly in her house in London, and does not care much for Society.

Countess Tolstoy, who is so well known in London, still calls herself by the name of her first husband, although she has been the wife of Mr. Philip Stanhope, brother of the present Lord Stanhope, for the last seven-and-twenty years. She is a Russian lady of considerable fortune, and since her second marriage has lived almost entirely in England. She and her husband occupy a charming house in Carlton Gardens, where they are among the most delightful of hosts and hostesses, their dinner parties being very much sought after.

Mrs. Edward Stonor, the widow of Mr. Ambrose Ralli, was a Greek, and married in 1899 Mr. Edward Stonor, brother of the late and uncle of the present Lord Camoys. Since her second marriage Mrs. Stonor, who is

and manner of a foreigner, and speaks English with a strong accent. She has never really assimilated with the country of her adoption, and has remained typically

extremely pretty and very much admired, has been going about a good deal in London Society. She is very musical, always beautifully dressed, and has charming manners. Her sister-in-law is the Marquise d'Hautpoul, who was Miss Julia Stonor, the daughter of one of Queen Alexandra's favourite ladies-in-waiting, who died many years ago. Mr. Stonor is interested in many things, amongst others in the importation of foreign partridges into England, and he and some of his friends have shares in a game-farm in Hungary, where the birds are bred.

Lady Colvile, wife of General Sir Henry Colvile, was Mlle. Isabelle de Préville, daughter of M. Richaud de Préville, who himself had married an English lady. In fact, Lady Colvile may almost claim to be an Englishwoman, as she was brought up entirely in the English colony in Pau, where she made her *début* in Society, and speaks our language without a trace of foreign accent. Before her marriage she usually spent part of the year at the Château de Mondrans, her father's place near the picturesque little town of Orthez, through which the Gave rolls its deep green waters, teeming with trout, and affording excellent sport to the English visitors from Pau, in spite of merciless poaching. Orthez, curiously enough, to this day contains a large proportion of Huguenots among its inhabitants. The huge tower, now a grey and ivy-grown ruin, which frowns down on the little burg at its feet, was once the home of the Calvinistic Jeanne d'Albret, who, if tradition does her no wrong, had a rough-and-ready way of making proselytes, which may account for the anomaly of a Protestant stronghold still existing in the very heart of Catholic Béarn. If a burger

refused to conform to the tenets of the Calvinistic faith, he was taken to the top of the tower and hurled into space without more ado.

Lady Colvile, who was herself brought up a Protestant, is a very clever and charming woman, who has travelled much, and recorded some of her adventures in distant lands, her book, *The Black Man's Garden*, having had quite a vogue when it came out. She

THE DUCHESS OF DEVONSHIRE.

is artistic as well as literary, and her *repoussé* work in gold and silver is very much beyond the average. In appearance she is slightly above medium height, with a slender figure and deep blue eyes, which are in pretty contrast to her dark brown hair. Lady Colvile is known to her intimates as "Zélie," although Isabelle was the name bestowed on her at her baptism.

Sir Henry Colvile, in addition to his military record, was at one time a great athlete. He is reputed to have once made a wager that he would walk down Pall Mall towards Charing Cross carrying a canoe on his shoulders, take train to Dover, row across to Calais, and return by steamer that same evening to London in time for dinner. Tradition further says that Sir Henry won his wager, thereby adding considerably to his fame as an oarsman, and not a little to his reputation for eccentricity.

Another charming recruit from the south-west of France is Mrs. Hope Vere, who was a daughter of the late M. Auguste Guillemin, and a descendant through her mother of Napoleon's famous Field-Marshal the Duc de Montebello. All her young life was spent under the shadow of the Pyrenees at Pau, where she first met Mr. Hope Vere, who used to spend the winters there with his mother, Lady David Kennedy. Since her marriage, Mrs. Hope Vere has lived principally at Blackwood, the larger place, Craigie Hall, in Midlothian, being almost always let. Blackwood is a white harled house, like so many old Scotch country residences. Some portions of it date back as far as the eleventh century, a winding stone staircase in an ancient tower being one of the most interesting features. There are some good pictures in the drawing-room, which is long and narrow in shape ; but the hostess generally uses the hall, which opens directly on to the front door, as a sitting-room. The house is not really quite large enough to contain the numerous guests who are hospitably entertained there all through the autumn ; but as Mrs. Hope Vere is the most charming of hostesses, and Mr. Hope Vere the most genial of hosts, their invitations are always much in request. Blackwood is situated about eight miles from Hamilton

Palace, right in the heart of the unsightly Scottish black country, but just around the place itself the scenery is quite pretty. A burn runs through the glens, where there is very good trout-fishing to be had.

Mrs. Hope Vere is a tall, graceful woman, with a clever, expressive face and large grey-blue eyes. She is universally conceded to be one of the best-dressed women in England, and looks so young that it is difficult to believe that her daughter, Miss Rachel Hope Vere, is out. She goes a good deal to Cannes in the winter, where she is usually the guest of the Grand-Duke Michael and Countess Torby, who have frequently stayed with her at Blackwood.

Mr. Hope Vere ("Jim" to his many friends) looks as young as his wife, with his fair hair and clean-shaven face. He is a thorough sportsman, a very good shot, and is never so happy as when at Blackwood.

As Mlle. Jeanne de Fougères, Mrs. Edward Clayton was perhaps more universally admired, when she first made her appearance in London some six or eight years ago, than is often the case with a comparative stranger. Without being regularly beautiful, this charming French lady is essentially striking, with her great height, magnificent figure, and superb carriage. She possesses in the highest degree that rare talent of moving and walking well. She is a most charming reciter, not only in French but in English, which she speaks so perfectly that it is difficult to detect her nationality. Mrs. Clayton is also a very good musician, and her delightful little musical parties were often honoured by the presence of the Duke and Duchess of Connaught.

Sir Edward Law, who has had a varied career, his public life beginning as Commercial Attaché at Teheran, found himself at one time attending to financial affairs in Greece, and there married a handsome Greek lady, Mlle. Katherine Hatsopoulo. Lady Law is a clever, interesting woman, very musical, and with pronounced literary tastes. She is now in India with her husband, who occupies the responsible post of financial adviser to the Indian Government.

OUR HUNDREDTH BIRTHDAY.

WITH this Number THE LADY'S REALM celebrates its hundredth number.

The first issue of THE LADY'S REALM was made with the November number of 1896—just eight years and four months ago. From the first THE LADY'S REALM set before itself a very high standard, and one which has never been reached by any other magazine or illustrated journal. For the beauty of its illustrations, the excellence of its printing, and the quality of the paper, THE LADY'S REALM is known all over the world.

A Unique List.

But besides the superiority of its appearance, THE LADY'S REALM can boast of such a list of distinguished and honoured names of authors as has been obtained by none of its contemporaries. Royal writers who have contributed to our pages are found in Queen Margherita of Italy, the Queen of Roumania, the Princess Gagarine, the Princess Radziwill, the Princess Doranski, and Prince Alexis Dolgorouki. Practically all the leaders of English Society have given us of their best literary efforts from time to time. The list is a long one, and it is only necessary to mention such names as the Duchess of Somerset, the Duchess of Buckingham and Chandos, the Duchess of Sutherland, the Dowager-Duchess of Newcastle, the Countess of Warwick, the Countess of Cromartie, the Countess of Munster, the Earl of Desart, Lord Kilmarnock, the Lady Violet Greville, the Lady Arabella Romilly, Lady Jeune, and the Hon. Mrs. Alan Brodrick.

There is scarcely a well-known author that has not been represented in THE LADY'S REALM. Such writers as Sir Walter Besant, Sir Edwin Arnold, Miss Marie Corelli, H. Seton Merriman, Ouida, S. R. Crockett, Stanley J. Weyman, F. Frankfort Moore, Ellen Thorneycroft Fowler, E. F. Benson, "Rita," Sarah Grand, Miss Braddon, George Gissing, Adeline Sergeant, Mrs. B. M. Croker, Katherine Tynan, have all contributed to THE LADY'S REALM.

Looking Forward.

It is pleasant to dwell on the success of the past, but there will be in the future conduct of THE LADY'S REALM the same regard for the tastes of its readers. Whatever subject is of interest in a home of refinement will continue to find a place in THE LADY'S REALM. The best English black-and-white artists are now engaged in making illustrations for the pages of this magazine. Mrs. Katherine Cecil Thurston, whose last book, *John Chilcote, M.P.*, has caused so much sensation, and was considered the novel of the year, is hard at work on her new novel which will appear very shortly first in THE LADY'S REALM. The story will be found to be full of fascination and suspense. The same amount of attention that has been paid to such subjects as Art, Society, and the Drama will be continued. During the present year the best pictures by some of the world's greatest painters will be reproduced. More space will be devoted to the subject of the Toilet and Beauty Culture; and the recent Beauty articles, which were so much appreciated, will be followed immediately by another practical series dealing with "The Care of the Hands."

THE EDITOR.

BY E. KEBLE CHATTERTON.

AMID the medley of meaningless musical burlesques, scant comedies, and un-witty farces, it is pleasant to hear of Shake-spearian productions becoming successful both æsthetically and financially. It is the fashion in some quarters, just at present, to denounce the adequate mounting of a play that shall do full justice to the picture conceived in the mind of the dramatist. For a long time Shakespearian plays were wont to be provided with the most meagre scenery and costumes of all. Why Shakespeare and dulness should be thought to go hand-in-hand is not easy to discover. Perhaps the reason may be found in the fact that Shakespeare aroused recollections of the schoolroom, or that because Shakespeare is a classic he is respectable, and because he is respectable he is dull. It is a curious note of the English character that complete pleasure can only be sought in the most frivolous and the least worthy.

But now that we have left far away behind the sombre heaviness for ever associated with the Early Victorian period—a time of insincerity in almost all the arts, when Academicians insisted on painting their grass brown, and refused a breath of *plein air* in the surroundings of their portraits— we are allowed to give greater freedom to

Photo by Ellis & Walery.
MISS GERTIE MILLAR AND HER SWEEP-BOYS AT THE GAIETY THEATRE.

our imagination and to breathe into the life-less bodies a new vigour and inspiration. No one is more convincing than Shakespeare, no one is comparable to him in his observation and knowledge of human nature. Nor is this confined to either sex or to any social rank. Shakespeare's kings and queens,

his buffoons and braggarts, his topers and coquettes, love-sick maidens and manly men, are creatures of the wide world and not of the seclusion of the study. When in one week one sees, as at the present time in London one may, a couple of Shakespearian productions, a play by Mr. Barrie, a musical comedy or two, a problem play, besides a legitimate light comedy or so, it is forced on oneself to be analytical. Putting aside all insincerity and conventionality of thought, what is there in Shakespeare that fascinates so overwhelmingly? Primarily, as I submit, it is his humanity and his deep sympathy with humanity in all its phases—its plotting and scheming, its love-making, its sorrows and its jests. There is, too, that light-ness and delicacy of touch by which a character is indicated by the fewest possible words. There is that exquisite store-house of golden English — a national heritage that, in a period of slang and half-penny papers, is invaluable. But to me it is the sense of Romance and the poetic feeling in Shakespeare that is the most compelling of all his virtues. Poetry can never die, human sympathy can never be eradicated, and Romance can never be murdered by commercialism. These three are immortal, and so long as they are not made to seem unattractive, any

Photo by Langfier

MISS SARAH BROOKE AS QUEEN KATHARINE IN *HENRY V.*

dramatist or manager can keep all the playhouses of the world filled from the roof to the floor. So it is that since by taking the smallest liberties here and there with the text, throwing aside unnecessary mannerisms and effete conventionalities, four plays of Shakespeare have been given to crowded houses during the last few months. *The Tempest* at His Majesty's, *The Taming of the Shrew* at the Adelphi, have already been noticed in these columns. Now, at the time of writing, *Much Ado About Nothing* is to be seen at His Majesty's, and *Henry V.* at the Imperial.

Much Ado About Nothing has been produced with every regard to that which is artistic, as is the custom at His Majesty's. The costumes and the armour have been designed by Mr. Byam Shaw, one of the most imaginative and romantic of our present-day artists. Mr. Raymond Roze is responsible for the music, both in this and in *Henry V.*, as he was in a great measure in *The Tempest*. Gradually Mr. Roze's art is nearing the summit of perfection. He is most obviously permeated with Wagner, with his delight in the clash of contrasts, the counterpart of which, in modern literature, is aptly found, I think, in Mr. G. K. Chesterton's essays. But Mr.

Photo by Langfier.

MR. LEWIS WALLER AS KING HENRY V. IN HIS SUCCESSFUL REVIVAL AT THE IMPERIAL THEATRE.

Photo by Ellis & Walery.

THE NURSERY SCENE IN *PETER PAN.*

Roze has also something of the mystical
sense and the same love of melody as
Wagner. His incidental music in the plays
we are considering is, as it should be,
symbolical and explanatory of the action of
the play. In *Much Ado About Nothing*,
especially in the scene in the garden of
Leonato's house, it is beautiful. In
Henry V. it is grand and stirring, suggestive, of course, of the regal and military
spirit of the play, and the clashing of the
will of the English nation against the
French. Perhaps some day Mr. Raymond
Roze may be induced to compose an opera

Photo by Ellis & Walery.

"THE NEVER, NEVER, NEVER LAND."

The second scene in *Peter Pan.* Peter's band await his return. Their home which is under the ground, is
reached by descending through the trunks of trees.

THE STRIKING SCENE ON THE DECK OF THE PIRATE SHIP IN MR. J. M. BARRIE'S PETER PAN.

that will not be deemed unworthy at Covent Garden.

In Mr. Tree's production the acting is generally good. Least of all, though, one likes Mr. Tree, for, in spite of his versatility, he is unsuited to the part of Benedick both in figure and by nature. Mr. Tree is, above all things, graceful in speech and manner, refined in gesture, and almost dainty. Benedick's character is quite the reverse He is big, blustering, and boisterous, as I understand him. He is the man of the world, who enjoys the good things of the world, but certainly not

Photo by Ellis & Walery.

MISS ELA Q. MAY,

Whom Mr. Barrie names as the author of
Peter Pan.

her elocution and gestures were excellent. Miss Miriam Clements, owing to Miss Viola Tree's illness, took the part of Hero, and made of it a great success. Mr. Laurence Irving's "Don John" was entirely suited to him, and his appearance was happily in keeping with the character.

The church scene, which is one of the most difficult to manage on the part of the dramatist, but which is one of the grandest and most dramatic of all of Shakespeare's, was marvellously accurate in ecclesiastical detail. Mr. Telbin is to be congratulated on

the æsthete, which Mr. Tree almost made him to be. The success of the evening belongs to Miss Winifred Emery (Mrs. Cyril Maude), whose return to the stage after so long an illness is the more welcome. Her Beatrice was the author's Beatrice, and that is the best that can ever be said of any actor. It was splendid comedy and most natural, and

making the best of even so large a stage as that of His Majesty's in this scene. The grouping of the wedding guests, the almost photographic resemblance to a typical Continental church, and the lighting of the whole, were triumphs to be attributed to the stage management. It is here that Mr. Tree has made an innovation with the author's

A scene from the realistic spectacle at the Coliseum, reproducing *The Derby* with actual racehorses and crowds of spectators.

Photo by Ellis & Walery.

MISS LEE,
Who is one of the most graceful actresses in *The Orchid*.

text. It will be recollected that after the dramatic incident when Claudio has denounced and refused to wed Hero, Shakespeare immediately follows up with a love scene, not devoid of humour, between Benedick and Beatrice. It has always seemed to one a little out of place inside the sacred walls of a church. Obviously, of course, Shakespeare introduces this humourous incident as a contrast to counteract the melodramatic incident that has immediately

and gives to its interpretation animation and depth of character without being unnecessarily coarse, on the one hand, or, on the other, "stagey." Mr. Waller's enunciation and action in the immortal speech "Once more unto the breach, dear friends," and his acting generally in the camp near Agincourt, were powerful and his appearance majestic. Miss Sarah Brooke, in the small part of Katharine, was good. The revival of this play is more than opportune at a time when

Photo by Ellis & Walery.

MRS. LANGTRY AND MISS BEATRICE FERRAR IN *MRS. DERING'S DIVORCE* AT TERRY'S THEATRE.
The Hon. Susannah Verner has called on Mrs. Dering to gather information as to Captain Dering's character.

preceded it, else otherwise *Much Ado* might lose its right to be called comedy. But Mr. Tree has wisely, as every one must agree, introduced another small drop-scene, representing the precincts of the church where Benedick meets Beatrice as she comes out of the cathedral.

Mr. Lewis Waller has revived the production of *Henry V.* which was seen at the Lyceum in December, 1900. There is not the same elaborate mounting as at His Majesty's, but the acting is very good indeed. Mr. Lewis Waller is again Henry V., and Mr. William Mollison again plays Pistol,

the air is filled with the sounds of war and the rumours of wars.

Passing on to musical comedy, Mr. Seymour Hicks's newest play, *The Talk of the Town*, has about the same amount of plot as any of its predecessors of this class. There is a comedian's part for Mr. Walter Passmore, which has been well written up to suit his humour and of which he makes every use. Miss Agnes Fraser and others sing well, and Mr. Robert Evett and Mr. Henry Lytton are as popular at the Lyric as they used to be at the Savoy. The play is beautifully mounted, one might say almost

Photo by Lafayette.

MRS. LANGTRY,

Who has been appearing at Terry's Theatre in *Mrs. Dering's Divorce.*

overdressed, and the stage is filled to its utmost capacity with beautiful women and handsome men. By the additional assistance of the colouring of lights and scenery and melodious music played briskly there is little else to be desired on the part of the kind of audience for whom productions such as these are provided. But there is one innovation new to English musical comedy which one is not sorry to see, and which has probably been found in the American musical comedies. Instead of the members of the chorus remaining still or with hands upon hips languidly casting their eyes around the theatre, as is generally the English custom, in *The Talk of the Town* they are working hard the whole time. The result is that a

Terry's Theatre, can be found in describing it as an indifferent play indifferently acted. Since Mr. Pinero began to write what are now familiarly known as "problem" plays, there have been many imitations. *Mrs. Dering's Divorce* would seem to be another instance. Mrs. Langtry is hardly a great emotional actress, and lacks the art of either Madame Réjane, Signora Duse, Miss Olga Nethersole, or Mrs. Patrick Campbell to enable her to play the part of Mrs. Dering satisfactorily. There was a noticeable lack of emotion which was essential to the interpretation, and which would have been supplied by either of the other actresses mentioned. The one enjoyable piece of acting was that of Mr. Leonard Boyne,

Photo by Campbell-Gray.

THE BEAUTIFUL FLYING BALLET AT THE HIPPODROME.

song goes much better and the sight is one of continuous action in place of unbecoming inactivity. Will other producers please copy?

The only candid criticism of *Mrs. Dering's Divorce*, which Mrs. Langtry has given at

though the part was hardly good enough for his ability. In the play itself there is not one powerful scene, and the technique displayed is of the simplest, especially in the drawing-room scene at Lady Grampier's, where a bridge party is assembled,

Photo by Lafayette

THE AGE OF INNOCENCE.

A Little Walk in Chelsea.

BY VINCENT BAYES.

IT has often struck me that the only compensation for the discomfort, the fatigue, and the essential boredom of a walk through the streets of London is that you can make some effort to penetrate the mystery of the generally grim, frequently grimy, walls that encompass you. To pass through Upper Berkeley Street at luncheon-time, for instance, is hardly in itself an exciting pleasure ; yet you add a little zest to it by reflecting that Mr. Max Beerbohm is probably eating his asparagus at No. 48, as you go by, and Mrs. Cornwallis West her cutlet at the corner house a few doors farther on. For each man carries the prying instinct within himself, more or less fully developed ; and before now I have derived amusement from mounting to the top of a green omnibus at Victoria Station, at eight o'clock on a summer evening, and driving up Grosvenor Place to observe what the residents of that distinguished thoroughfare are having for dinner ; for, in the summer, your Londoner dines between the lights, as it were : his blinds remain up, though the electric light is switched on, thus affording a good view to the curious passer-by.

Should you, therefore, finding yourself in Sloane Square, decide on a short walk westwards and prefer the riverside to the Hans Crescent and Pont Street quarter, it is not uninteresting to note that the long wall which you skirt in the King's Road, after passing the first row of shops on the left, conceals from sight the Duke of York's or Royal Military School, where the sons of soldiers of the regular army are trained to become soldiers of the regular army in their turn. At the end of the wall is Cheltenham Terrace : let us go down it. On the right stands Whitelands

CARLYLE'S HOUSE, 24, CHEYNE ROW.

Georgian railed wall. Here the boys go through their musical drill on Thursday afternoons, bursting into song whenever the band breaks into the Soldiers' Chorus from *Faust* or the more national "A-'untin' we will gow!" As a matter of fact, the school, which is at some future date to be moved into the country, turns out more bandsmen than soldiers proper. The little fellows play excellently, especially at church parade on Sunday mornings.

We turn to the right down St. Leonard's Terrace, which faces the huge cricket-ground of Chelsea Hospital and the front of the famous hospital itself. Mr. Bram Stoker, for many years Sir Henry Irving's acting-manager and now a well-known novelist, lives at No. 18; Lady Susan Milbank, an aunt of the Duke of Leeds, at No. 21. Many of the houses in this terrace are old-fashioned and have a quaint attractiveness of their own; they are often "modernised" when they change hands: I hope that they are not allowed to suffer in the process. The broad turning that leads to the King's Road is Royal Avenue, called, like the King's Road itself, after Charles II. Here, the story has it, the Merry Monarch's courtiers used to gallop up and down the fenced space in the middle, while

College, a peculiarly ugly building, in which young ladies are taught to be schoolmistresses. On May Day of every year, these young ladies, lightly clad and flower-crowned, perform shivering evolutions in their garden and end by electing the best - behaved of their number Queen of the May for the year. They can be heard singing quite six yards off. Their chapel, which stands in the garden, is adorned with stained - glass windows by Burne-Jones. Opposite, on the left, is the chapel of the Duke of York's School; and we see the main building and the grounds through a rather handsome

GARDEN CORNER, CHELSEA EMBANKMENT.
The residence of the late Mr. James Staats Forbes.

the King and Nell Gwyn inspected the progress of the Royal Hospital hard by. The late Dion Boucicault's widow lives in Royal Avenue, as does Miss Kate Grant, the original of Hubert von Herkomer's most famous portrait.

Redesdale Street takes us from St. Leonard's Terrace to Tedworth Square, of which the corner house, No. 15 was, till lately, occupied by Mrs. Langtry, who is now married to Mr. Hugo De Bathe, the heir to his father's baronetcy. And the turning out of the middle of the south side of the square is Tite Street, where Mr. Herbert Paul, the historian, lives, at No. 13, and many well-known artists: Mr. John

THE QUEEN'S HOUSE, 16, CHEYNE WALK.
This was built by Sir Christopher Wren for Queen Catherine of Braganza. It was for a time occupied by Rossetti.

The house has its own theatre, in which, in Lady Shelley's time, some twenty years ago, was given that famous private performance of *The Cenci* which suggested to Mr. Grein the founding of the Independent Theatre, which, in its time, became the parent of the Stage Society and the New Century Theatre of to-day. Retracing our steps and proceeding westwards, we observe that nearly all of these exceedingly beautiful modern houses (Shelley House itself is a little spoilt by its *nouveau art* bell and door-knocker) are occupied by persons of note. At No. 2, Rayleigh House, lives Mr. Richard Strutt, Lord Rayleigh's brother; at No. 3, the River House,

S. Sargent, R.A., at No. 33; Mr. Jacomb-Hood, at No. 26; and Mr. Edwin A. Abbey, R.A., at Chelsea Lodge, No. 42. The White House, No. 35, was built for Mr. Whistler: it is now occupied by Mr. Harold Mostyn, Lord Vaux of Harrowden's younger brother.

We emerge on the Chelsea Embankment. A few doors to the left is Shelley House, now the residence of Mr. St. John Hornby.

Mr. John Westlake, K.C.; at No. 4, Julia Marchioness of Tweeddale, with her second husband, Major William Evans-Gordon, M.P.; No. 5 is known as the Old Ferry House: there was a ferry from here to the opposite shore before the embankment was built; No. 6 as the Sun House: the sun forms part of the carving; No. 7, Monkswell House, is the town house of Lord Monkswell, L.C.C., who was Under-Secretary for War in Lord Rosebery's Ministry. That gorgeously handsome house, No. 8, known as the Clock House, is occupied by Mr. C. P. Huntington; the Marquess of Ripon lives at No. 9, next door; Sir Mountstuart Grant-Duff at No 11; the Earl of Lovelace at Wentworth House, No. 12. Beyond Swan Walk is the Botanic Garden, or "Physick Garden," presented by Sir Hans Sloane to the Apothecaries' Society, on condition that fifty new varieties of plants grown within its walls should be furnished every year to the Royal Society, until the number so furnished amounted to two thousand. It was famed for its fine cedars, planted by Sir Hans in 1683, of which only one survives.

The next house, No. 13, known as Garden Corner, belonged to the late Mr. James Staats Forbes, and still contains his unequalled collection of pictures of the Barbizon and modern Dutch schools. No. 15, Wistow House, is occupied by Mr. Thomas Freemantle, Lord Cottesloe's eldest son and heir; No. 16, Carlyle House, by General Sir Alfred Turner. No. 17, the Old Swan House, on the site of the Old Swan Tavern, is a rival of the Clock House for sumptuous beauty: it was designed by Mr. Norman Shaw, R.A., and is the residence of General Euston

Sartorius, V.C. All these handsome houses on the Chelsea Embankment present our modern red-brick architecture at its best, and, with their due south aspect, overlooking the river and Battersea Park, form as "desirable" a row of "town mansions" as London can afford.

Cheyne Walk, which follows, standing farther back from the river, behind a small public garden, contains mostly old houses, nearly all of which possess an historic interest. No. 4 was the home of Maclise, the painter, and, subsequently, of George Eliot, who died here in 1880. Count d'Orsay lived at No. 10; Sir Colin Scott-Moncrieff lives at No. 11; Lord Monteagle of Brandon at No. 13; Captain Edward Eaton-Ellis at No. 14, which until recently was occupied by Mr. Herbert Horne, the architect, poet and art-critic. No. 15 is the residence of Mr. Leonard Courtney, the former Chairman of Committees of the House of Commons.

No. 16, the Queen's House, is one of the most interesting houses in Chelsea. It occupies a portion of the site of the old Chelsea Manor House, where Queen Katharine Parr lived in her day and Queen Elizabeth in hers and Sir Hans Sloane in his. The old house was pulled down after

THE CLOCK HOUSE, CHELSEA EMBANKMENT.

THE WHITE HOUSE, CHELSEA.
Built for Mr. Whistler.

half-wild animals; the curious will find a selection of them depicted, with a host of the occupants and visitors, in that charming caricature in *The Poet's Corner:* "Dante Gabriel Rossetti in his back garden." Rossetti lived at the Queen's House from 1864 until his death in 1882. I am not sure if it was ever occupied by Whistler; but the late Mr. Haweis was its tenant till his death, and added the statue of Mercury to the ball on its

his death and the present Queen's House was built by Sir Christopher Wren for Queen Catherine of Braganza, whose cypher, "C.R.," still adorns the gate and railings. Subsequently, it was occupied by Dante Gabriel Rossetti, the poet-painter, with his brother, Mr. William Rossetti, Mr. Swinburne and, I think, Mr. Hall Caine. Mr. George Meredith, who was to have been a further co-tenant, withdrew at the last moment: the hopelessly Bohemian inadequacy of the domestic arrangements frightened him away. There was an enormous garden at the back of the house in those days (the garden is still a large one), in which Rossetti kept an extraordinary menagerie of wild and

SHELLEY HOUSE, CHELSEA EMBANKMENT.
This house has its own theatre, in which the famous private performance of *The Cenci* was given.

gable apex. It is now in the occupation of a physician.

At No. 18, the residence of Lord Ebury's sister, Miss Victoria Grosvenor, stood the famous Don Saltero's coffee-house, opened in 1696 by Salter, a barber, who was christened Don Saltero by Vice-Admiral Manlove, one of his patrons. The house and its curious contents were described by Sir Richard Steele, in *The Tatler*, in 1709. No. 20 is the house of Mr. Clifford Meller, who is the president of one of the modern Jacobite societies. It is an interesting old house, with beautifully panelled rooms and a fine garden. Mr. Meller keeps on the white-coated, kilted Highland footmen who did duty during the lifetime of his wife, the late Lady Helen Meller, (she was

THE OLD SWAN HOUSE.

decorated with a memorial tablet designed by Mr. Walter Crane.

But a pilgrimage there would be beyond the limits of this little walk, which must end at 24, Cheyne Row, where Thomas Carlyle and Jane Baillie Welsh Carlyle, his wife, fought and made friends, liked and disliked each other so long and so heartily during the greater portion of their married life. Have not these inspiring matters been made public quite recently by industrious and conscientious biographers? Here you can enter, on payment, and see the philosopher's hat and his bath, Jane's chair and her work-basket and the famous double-walled room which failed to keep out the noise of the "trebly-curst" cocks and hens in the next-door garden. Here you

a Lady Helen Stewart, aunt to the present Earl of Galloway), and who still cut a picturesque figure among their old-time surroundings. Mr. Arthur Dyke Acland, M.P., lives at No. 28 and, a very long way farther, some distance past Old Chelsea Church, at No. 119, is the cottage where J. M. W. Turner, the painter, secluded himself in 1851 and where he died at the age of seventy-nine, known to his neighbours by the style and title of Admiral Booth. It is a rather pretty little house, approached by sunk steps behind a set of wooden palings, and it is

can descend to the basement kitchen, where Carlyle and Tennyson smoked their long clay pipes. Here you can go up to the panelled sitting-room, where Carlyle was bored by Harriet Martineau—shall I quote you his description?—" that too happy and too noisy distinguished female, who did nothing but make me miserable. She is a formulist, limited in the extreme, and for the present altogether triumphant in her limits. The all-conquering *smallness* of that phenomenon, victorious mainly by its smallness, and which not only waves banners in its own triumph, but insists on your waving banners too, is at all times nearly insupportable to me. She said among other things that she had once met a man who seemed not to believe fully in immortality. The trivial impious sayings of this extraordinary man were retailed to us at boundless length. Then the martyr character, the hyper-prophetic, altogether splendid and unspeakable excellence of Dr. Priestley; the regiment of American great men; the etc., etc. *Ach Gott!* I wish this good Harriet would be happy by herself."

Surely never was man more bored in Chelsea than this unfortunate philosopher!

What, when our walk is done, is the last impression that we retain of Chelsea? A memory of old houses and modern houses more beautiful than in most other parts of London, with, behind and between, long rows of squalid slums; of indifferent curiosity-shops; of an infinity of open green spaces of a more public or national character than the squares on the north side of the town; of the river with its endlessly shifting effects of light and darkness; of hawkers' barrows in the King's Road; and of soldiers, soldiers, soldiers: soldiers of the past at the Chelsea Hospital, soldiers of the present at the Chelsea Barracks, soldiers of the future at the Duke of York's School. For the rest, I would, perhaps, walk in Chelsea oftener did I not live there. Built upon a swamp, it is a miasmic, if picturesque, quarter of the town, " dank, dank, dank," as Whistler once described it to me, sunless, foggy, and pestilential. Still, it has its charms.

THE DUKE OF YORK'S MILITARY SCHOOL, CHELSEA.

THE TRUTH ABOUT MAN.

By a Spinster.

**ILLUSTRATED BY FACTS FROM HER OWN
PRIVATE HISTORY.**

*The author of " The Truth About Man" is a well-known novelist, who prefers not to reveal her identity.
In her opening chapters she subdivides Man into the Irresistible, the Admirable, and the Marriageable,
discourses on the unattractiveness of the Ideal Woman, and analyses the effect of Love upon mature Man.
She next proceeds to speak of Matrimony and considers the relation between Husband and Wife.*

As he believes that the views of " A Spinster" may not be shared by all the readers of THE LADY'S REALM,
*the Editor has decided to offer prizes, month by month, for the best criticisms of " The Truth About
Man." Particulars will be found on page* 20 *of the advertisements.*

CHAPTER VII.

The Spinster calls attention to the success of the Plain Woman in the Matrimonial Market and gives a few pertinent reasons for the same.

IF there be one thing more than another that is apt to surprise the giddy young beauty who looks round upon society with observant eyes, it is the number of exceedingly plain women who are married.

We all begin by assuming that beauty is the first qualification necessary to inspire love, and even when we grow older and begin to understand that the glamour of a pretty face soon wears off when there is nothing behind to sustain it, we experience some amazement at first sight of an ugly woman married to a quite passable man. Knowing, as we do, that there are so many good-looking women always ready and willing to marry, it seems strange that men should ever wed the distinctly plain ones. Yet who does not know, among his or her friends, quite a large number of wives who could not in their palmiest days, by any stretch of imagination, have had the least pretensions to good looks ?

But what is stranger still is the fact that downright ugly women often carry off matrimonial prizes in the very teeth of handsome rivals. (I use the word " matrimonial prize " in two senses : the accepted one—meaning the man who can give his wife a coveted position in society, and the other, less material one, of a Good Fellow.) Such instances must occur to any one who thinks of them, and it would be quite easy to quote some among our best-known men and women to-day. I need not say anything about the ugly and repulsive men who often marry pretty women—they are a common or garden variety ; and there are so many reasons why women find it desirable to annex husbands that we do not wonder at such curious aberrations of taste. It is the sight of a plain woman married to a man who might have chosen from the ranks of beauty that perplexes us, and we are still more perplexed when we find her able to keep him faithful and devoted without any of those apparent charms and seductions we imagine to be Woman's only power.

Why is it ? I have come to no strictly logical conclusion, but it seems to me the strength of these women lies in their will, especially their will to please, which they cultivate to a tremendous extent. By sheer force of resolution they fascinate and command Man, who is gradually losing this supreme quality. The ugly woman is not led astray by vanity and the silly flattery of every man she meets. She is able to concentrate her entire attention upon the one object of her life, and I believe there are few plain girls who do not set their hearts on marriage. You see, it is their only way of showing that *they count*, that they are not wholly unattractive and of no importance. If a distinctly plain woman does not marry, men are prone to believe that it is because she never has a chance. It is an utterly absurd belief and has no foundation in fact; but you will find that many people—and all men—hold it religiously. This is another of Man's astounding inconsistencies. Although he marries ugly women frequently, declares that beauty is only skin deep, and affects to despise those who use artificial means to make themselves look beautiful, you will never convince him that the reason some plain spinster of his acquaintance has remained unmarried is not simply and solely because of her unprepossessing face. Not one man in fifty can shake off this *idée fixe*! But then, of course, most of them believe that when a woman doesn't marry it is because she has never been asked. This is part of their faith, agreeing with their crusted conviction that a woman unmarried is a woman marred. A few of the more enlightened have given it up, but it still holds good of the majority.

How can they continue to think so when they see the women who have refused them grow into old maids? asks some one.

Dear reader, a man always forgets he has been refused. In five years after the event he has persuaded himself that he never asked Mary to be his wife, though he has still an uneasy feeling that *she* thinks he did.

But I am straying from the subject in hand, the Plain Woman. We must remember, in considering her as a wife, that some quite ugly women are gifted with mysterious powers of attraction for the opposite sex. It is impossible to read history without realising this : for we are distinctly told, in many instances, of uncomely women who have ruled the destinies of men and nations. As it is a point which none of our sex can ever properly comprehend, we need not waste time in speculating upon it. Let it suffice us to know that there is a certain physical or mental magnetism in certain women for all men that no other woman can possibly feel, any more than we can hear sounds below or above a definite pitch.

We don't, in fact, know anything at all about the matter. We only see that plain women can nearly always marry if they like, and most of them *do* like. The reasons I offer are divided into four :—

1. They are, in many cases, possessed of a peculiar charm which can neither be analysed nor expressed.
2. They learn early the value of self-control, self-effacement, sympathy, tact, and diplomacy.
3. They cultivate will-power and the art of pleasing.
4. They make up their minds to marry— *somebody*.

It is of the utmost importance to the plain girl that she should not be self-conscious. The only ugly women who are really ugly in Man's eyes are those afflicted by a morbid sense of their own defects. He can forgive an indiarubber face, an ungainly figure; but he has no mercy on a woman who asks his pity, or who is afraid of the impression she is making on him. The first art a plain woman, or indeed any woman, should master, is the art of appearing self-satisfied. A man will always take her at her own valuation.

The girl of unprepossessing exterior who is not troubled with qualms about herself has really a better chance than the pretty girl, in some respects. She is not led into foolish flirtations and fatuous love affairs by every Lothario who comes along. Knowing from the first that she must not depend upon the little airs and graces of the Coquette for her conquests, she avoids all that is likely to bring her into ridicule, or into futile competition with her prettier friends, and is careful to do nothing which may repel the solid marrying man. Her dress is studied with a view to attracting no special attention, and yet suiting her to perfection. She must never show her emotions in any way, never suggest that she feels left out in the cold, never look disappointed or utter reproaches. Her *rôle* is to be pleasant and jolly under all circumstances; and you will find it is the "jolly" girl, pretty or ugly, who gets her programme well filled at dances while a number of her sisters decorate the walls!

The useless, waterfly sort of man, who flutters about the beauty continually, never bothers himself about the plain girl, and this is greatly in favour of her ultimate success. For it is he who spoils the chances and wrecks the happiness of an enormous number of young girls every year. His name is legion; he swarms everywhere and his charm is undoubted. Personally, I find him the greatest sport, and would not be without him for worlds. When once you know him, and do not seriously believe a single word he utters, he can be most amusing and companionable. He is a kind of camp-follower, goes always with the crowd, courts only the girl that he sees other men courting, is seen only with the woman who can do his taste credit in public by a smart appearance; so that his society is flattery—of a kind! Mothers watch him anxiously; fathers loathe him; and lucky is the woman who does not attract him. Lucky, I mean, if she be playing to win.

The plain girl soon recognises that she may never be coy, arch, airy, pert, or indifferent. Prettiness may be all these things, but ugliness has a different part to play. It is to be always agreeable and sympathetic, for while beauty is born to be flattered, plainness is born to flatter. There is no creature on earth that can flatter as subtly as an ugly woman and no creature so susceptible to her flattery as man. Æsop's crow, who was seduced to sing with a lump of cheese in its beak, must certainly, in spite of the chronicler, have been a cock bird! There is no exaggerated and bare-faced compliment a man will not swallow greedily, if it be served up by a woman. He suspects it from the lips of another man, but is so innately convinced that woman, his inferior, is always secretly worshipping him and longing for him, that he will bolt every sugared pill she offers. And his complacency under the process of swallowing is something delicious to witness! More men have been conquered and enslaved by the magic art of flattery than by all the beauty and wit of the world! To the woman who can flatter subtly and adroitly, no career is impossible. She may govern nations!

Thackeray has given us a brilliant example of the wily, cajoling woman in his Becky Sharp. If ever there was a satire upon Man *Vanity Fair* is that satire. It is singular that Man does not seem to have discovered this, does not seem to have realised that he is being held up to ridicule in it. He admits that Becky is "a bewitching little devil," that Amelia is a dull bore, that Rawdon Crawley is a weak dupe and tool, that George Osborne is equally feeble and helpless in the hands of this clever woman; but you will never hear him remark what a poor show Man makes in the book, how he gives himself away on every possible occasion!

Becky Sharp was neither pretty nor rich; her opportunities were few, but she made the most of them. And the chief weapon in her armoury was—what?

Flattery! Not such very delicate or subtle flattery, either, but of the kind that is laid on with a trowel. Yet there is not a man in the entire book who can resist it, and, in showing this, Thackeray has been faithful to masculine human nature, has painted a portrait of Man that is absolutely life-like. He knew that however men may differ individually, they are all to be worked by the woman who understands how to pull their wires. Becky Sharp understood how to pull their wires. She disguised her real self under a pleasant, unchanging mask, cultivated a constant, careless gaiety, and studied with all her might to find out the vulnerable spots, the pet vanities and weaknesses of the men with whom she came in contact. Then she started to nurse and foster tenderly those vanities and weaknesses till she became perfectly irresistible. Man adored her—all kinds of him adored her, as they always do adore Becky Sharps. " For God hath made them so ! "

(To be continued)

In considering the criticisms of the second instalment of " The Truth about Man," the Editor has found the papers sent in by two competitors to be of equal merit. He has therefore decided to divide the amount of the first and second prizes between these two competitors. A cheque for fifteen shillings and ninepence is therefore being sent to Mrs. Thompson, Woodlands Park, Altrincham, Cheshire, and to Miss Nish, 12, Onslow Road, Fairfield, Liverpool, a selection from whose essays will be found on The Editor's Page.

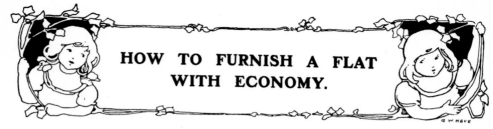

HOW TO FURNISH A FLAT WITH ECONOMY.

BY ARDERN HOLT.

FLATS have transformed all our modes of living and our conceptions of home life. They accord with the feelings of the twentieth century. Whereas our ancestors troubled themselves greatly as to posterity (for which, by the way, we owe them our gratitude), we do nothing of the sort. We live for the moment, determined to get the best out of life.

But, on the other hand, flats have proved kindly promoters of matrimony. When less than a hundred a year will provide a home with taxes and *tout compris*, and £100 down will go a long way towards furnishing, many a young couple are tempted to launch into a life together, and trust to Providence for the future.

Some of our leading furnishing firms have issued elaborate lists of what can be done on a given sum, and these estimates begin under £100 ; and are so detailed and well illustrated that would-be purchasers can judge for themselves. Having thoroughly primed themselves, with the knowledge thus acquired they can betake themselves to these large upholsterers, and see a flat home fitted up entirely for the sum mentioned. One word of warning, however. It is true in each room hangs a card, showing what articles are included in the bargain ; there are, besides, many knicknacks, pictures on the walls, and even a piano which you would not find enumerated. But as most young folk start in life with a large array of wedding gifts, these fill up the gaps as far as decoration goes very well indeed. A flat of this modest description consists of a hall, dining- and drawing-rooms, a bedroom and servant's bedroom, bathroom and kitchen well supplied with the necessary utensils, china, glass, electro-plate, and cutlery. Linen and blankets are all included ; and when you come to consider the sum, it is perfectly wonderful what you get for the money, bearing in mind that the furniture is up-to-date and so pretty that the owners need never be troubled by any sense of want of beauty or inappropriateness.

Nearly £50 out of the sum are taken up with the fittings of the bedroom and drawing-room ; the dining-room costs under £20. £15 or £16 supply the kitchen needs. It is wonderful

A SUGGESTION FOR A BED-SITTING-ROOM.

how far a few pounds will go. Blinds are left out, but carpets and lace curtains are included. An expectant bride and bridegroom should have at least another £50 in hand to settle themselves thoroughly comfortably, but without this they would be much better off than their grandparents, who spent double and treble the sum.

If they had to be content with the £100 only, they would find themselves, besides actual furniture, the possessors of fireirons, brass curtain rods and . fittings, fenders, coal scuttles, and much beside, which, furnishing in the ordinary way, run away with so much. Fumed oak and rush-bottomed chairs, quite in the twentieth-century style, make the dining-room look

and two under-blankets might need augmentation when the nights were cold. But beside the white quilt there is a down one. A change of sheets is included, pillow-cases, a dozen and three towels, glass, tea-cloths, and dusters ; so that if it happened that the owner arrived from foreign lands, he could step into his flat and find all to hand that he must have, even to dinner and breakfast services and glass. The kitchen list would be invaluable to an inexperienced housekeeper, for everything that is absolutely essential to plain living is there, even to flat irons, an egg whisk, coffee canister and knife-board, steps, plate and shoe brushes, not forgetting a tin opener.

In an ascending scale of cost our views as

A DRAWING-ROOM IN A FLAT.

homely, and the easy-chairs and settees, the drawing-room as well as the other chairs, are covered with pretty light tinted stuffs which would not disgrace much more ambitious rooms. The eye is pleased at every turn.

In the lists every article is priced, so that those who would like to spend a little more on certain items can do so. The mirrors and the writing-table are all designed to meet wants such as those who have been catering for the public for years recognise as being most acceptable and practical for the majority. The bedsteads are mostly black and brass, with a cleanly wire-woven mattress. Linoleum covers the floor where carpets are not provided. The house linen just meets the necessities of flat life, but might well be expanded : two pair of blankets

to the requirements of furnishing a home in a flat undergo many alterations. Even £200 make a wonderful difference. You may turn your thoughts then towards another bed-room and hall ; and corridors are carpeted, or at all events covered with felt, and there is a great expansion in the matter of the dining-room. If a man . has not a den of his own, he would look for a writing-table and bookshelves here. These bookshelves are often introduced over the sideboard, and a woman of taste will mingle china or bronzes with the volumes, which considerably lighten the aspect of the room. Those pretty dumb waiters, *viz.* round tables in two or three tiers —a relic of the past—have been resuscitated, and set in a corner to supply the place of a serving-table, and a couple of easy-chairs in the most comfortable, ample styles add to the comfort of the inmates.

In furnishing a flat you have not only to think of the expense, but of the limited space, and to combine as many items of furniture as you can when the rooms are small. The dressing-table, chest of drawers, and the looking-glass should be all in one ; the wardrobe should have a pier glass, and a boot cupboard should find a place under the washing-stand. In the hall one piece of furniture should represent a hall table, umbrella stand, and looking-glass, the sides having big hooks on which to hang coats.

There is no fear, in the hands of a good furnishing firm, that what you buy will not please the eye ; the danger always is that the articles may have no lasting virtues, and with young people starting in life this is all-important ; for as time goes on, and their area of existence widens and the income increases, the means of spending enlarges also, and to keep buying the same things over and over again is a mistake. If the furniture be good, it will always have its uses. Light coverings to chairs, settees, etc., are all very well, as far as looks go, in the country ; but in murky London and other towns they become shabby directly.

There is no doubt that a great deal of thought and trouble are saved by furnishing *en masse* ; but given time and a fair margin of money, the purchaser finds his reward if he picks up as many antique pieces of well-made furniture as he can, for the upholsterers in days of old gave patient, painstaking work, brought ingenuity to bear, and were most clever in making each piece " a double debt to pay."

It is a saving and a convenience to choose for curtains, in a limited space, those that easily draw across the window, and do not descend to the floor, but end with the panes. Where it is possible to arrange a species of alcove for the bed, with a curtain to draw across, you get the appearance of a sitting-room. It seems consistent with our life that every one should possess a room apart. The daughters and sons of the house much appreciate it, and with a little ingenuity it can be arranged as shown in the sketch.

It is always well when furnishing to arrange in one's mind beforehand the particular style or period that shall predominate. In bedrooms there is much to be said for the French school, with the rich-looking mahogany beds having ormolu mounts and ornamentation that generally take the form of floral garlands. The modern looking-glass is mostly made with side wings, so that the whole effect of the profile

and back can be seen. Fitments, when space is an object and a consideration, have much to commend them, and in these French rooms are frequently introduced ; but they have to be planned so that they can be moved, or they become the property of the landlord.

Quaintness and comfort go hand-in-hand in the Jacobean dining-room, with a Baldichino or alcove to the fireplace, and comfortable seats, so that you may enjoy your " ain fireside " to perfection. The chairs would be of that graceful form that have the tall narrow backs, and as often as not are of canework set in a carved wood frame.

I must bring to your notice a most excellent introduction for covering the walls of bathrooms, *viz*. Emdeca, which is a metal in sheets, that can be cut with scissors to any size, but on the wall it looks like tiles. It has the advantage that, unlike paper, it does not become discoloured with the heat of the steam, and it preserves its pristine freshness to the end. It is stuck on to the plaster with a special solution. In all well-arranged bathrooms now there is a fixed basin, with hot and cold water, which empties itself, and a towel airer. This consists of substantial metal tubes, in the shape of a horse, on which the towels are placed, and as the tubes are heated they dry them at the same time.

One old fashion is being revived, *viz*. for the locks of the doors not to be sunk in, nor mortised, but laid on the outside. Small glazed cupboards are let into the wall, to hold china on either side of the fireplace. Great pains have been taken to revive the old chintzes or to introduce chintz patterns on to cretonnes in unison with the periods of Chippendale or Sheraton. This always gives an old-world aspect to a room. A clever notion where there may be an unsightly cupboard door is to cover it with close-fitting chintz, both inside and outside. This can be easily slipped on and off. A glance at the two illustrations will emphasise the information given ; both are sketched with some amplitude. It is always easy to leave out, and my aim has been to show to the fullest extent the capabilities of flat furnishing. Corner washing-stands of the old type, now so often adapted to the display of old china, are invaluable for their original purpose, and, though scarce, they are to be had, and corner wardrobes also. A bookcase and writing-bureau combined have many virtues ; and if a couch is convertible into a bed—and there are many such to be had—it gives an opportunity of putting up a friend for the night which otherwise would be impossible.

From the original drawing by John Cameron.

APRIL GUSTS.

The Russian Grand Dukes.

BY MINKA VON DRACHENFELS.

IT is a well-known fact that the Tzar is very considerably influenced by his uncles and cousins the Grand Dukes of the Imperial House, and that the many mistakes that he has committed are owing to their bad advice. It is certainly true that two of the Russian Grand Dukes especially sway His Majesty, and these two Princes are not the most respectable members of their house. Taking them as a whole, it is impossible to admire the Russian Grand Dukes, nor can they be numbered amongst the patriots of the country. There are, however, exceptions. The Grand Duke Constantin-Constantino-witch, a grandson of the Tzar Nicholas I., and who is the son of the late Grand Duke Constantin-Nicholjewitch of Russia by his marriage with the Princess Alexandra of Saxe-Altenburg, a younger sister of the Queen of Hanover, has a splendid character, and during his entire life has tried hard to bring about reforms in Russia. His Imperial Highness, who is married to his cousin the Princess Elizabeth of Saxe-Altenburg, and who is the father of seven children, has liberal views. His family life is faultless, and he spends his time in works of charity, and in the endeavour to use his influence for the good of the people. It was the Grand Duke Constantin who called a

meeting of the professors and teachers at the St. Petersburg University lately to discuss with them how to prevent further bloodshed and to appease the people; but His Imperial Highness received a severe blow, for several of those whom he had invited—men to whom he had given his friendship, and who, he knew, were good patriots—were arrested by the police.

Russia is at present a hopeless country, and those who are working for her salvation can hardly hope themselves to see good results from their work.

The Grand Duke Vladimir, who covered himself with shame by his order to fire on the workpeople assembled before the Winter Palace on the twenty-second of January, is the senior uncle of the Tzar, and until the birth of the Tzare-witch he was, after the Grand Duke Michael-Alexandro-witch, the next heir to the throne. As such he had immense power, and he is also an extremely clever, ambitious man, wonderfully handsome, and with the most charming manners imaginable. He was formerly thought to have great sympathy with the working people, but is known to have an antipathy against all those who are engaged in trade. His wife, a Princess of Mecklenburg-Schwerin, has always been noted for her

THE GRAND DUKE BORIS.

works of charity, and during the war she has been prominent in everything that has been done to mitigate the sufferings of the soldiers Of late, however, her character has changed very much. It was a great blow to her when she was obliged to be privately received into the Greek Church, and since that time she has become quite changed.

The Grand Duke and Duchess Vladimir have a family of three sons and one daughter. The eldest, the Grand Duke Cyril, it is said, hopes eventually to be able to marry his cousin the Princess Victoria Melita of Coburg, formerly the Grand Duchess of Hesse; in fact, it is confidently said at Coburg that he is already married to her, and that they are only waiting for a favourable opportunity to make their marriage public.

The second son of the Grand Duke Vladimir, Boris, bears a very unpleasant character, and there have been many ugly stories told about him which hardly bear repeating. When this promising Prince visited America, it is said that Mrs. Roosevelt refused to receive him on account of the scandals attached to his name.

THE GRAND DUKE CYRIL, SON OF THE GRAND DUKE WHO IS THE ELDEST AND DUCHESS VLADIMIR.

The only daughter of the Grand Duke Vladimir is married to Prince Nicholas of Greece, and seems fairly contented in her new home.

The next uncle of the Tzar, the Grand Duke Alexis, has an unhappy love-story. As a young man he fell in love with a lady of the Court, much his senior in years, and ran away with her to Germany. He was, however, starved out, as all supplies were stopped, and was eventually obliged to resign his wife and return home. The unfortunate heroine of this love-story was given in marriage to another man, who received a large sum of money with her, and she died a few years ago in Wiesbaden. The Grand Duke Alexis never forgot her, and has not married again. Her son by him has been brought up in Russia and is now married. The mother was allowed to go to her son's marriage, and was always treated with great respect.

The Grand Duke Paul, the youngest uncle of the Tzar, has lately made a morganatic marriage without the permission of the Tzar, and in consequence has been banished from Russia, so that he has at

how incapable her son was, and used her power to try to persuade him to follow in the footsteps of his father.

The eldest sister of the Tzar, the Grand Duchess Xenia, is a woman of the noblest character, but she is not clever, and her many family duties (she has six children) keep her fully employed, so that her influence in politics is not felt. Her Imperial Highness is, however, beloved by every one, and she does all in her power to ameliorate the condition of the poor and suffering. The youngest sister of the Tzar is energetic, and is at the head of the Red Cross sisters sent out to nurse the sick and wounded in Asia.

We now come to the cousins of the Tzar, the children of the only surviving child of Nicholas I., the Grand Duke

present no influence in the councils of the Emperor Nicholas.

Of all members of the family of the Tzar, his mother had, until quite lately, more influence with him than any one else, and it is a matter for regret that this influence has not continued, for, although she is opposed to reform and wishes to maintain Russia as it was in the reign of her husband, she is at least very humane, and would never have counselled a massacre like that which took place on Sunday, January 22nd. Her Majesty was, until the death of her husband, entirely taken up with her family duties. She was a most devoted wife and mother, and did not concern herself with politics, though she took a vivid interest in all her husband's work. It was not until after the death of Alexander III. that his widow began to busy herself with State affairs, for she then saw plainly

J. J. CROOK '04.

THE FIRST PHOTOGRAPH ABOVE IS THAT OF THE GRAND DUKE DIMITRI-CONSTANTINOWITCH, THE SECOND REPRESENTS THE GRAND DUKE DIMITRI-PAULOWITCH, AND THE THIRD IS THE GRAND DUKE NICHOLAS-MICHAELOWITCH.

Michael-Nicholjewitch. He was married to the Princess Cecilie of Baden, who gave him a large family of sons and one daughter. His eldest son, Nicholas, is unmarried; the second, Michael, made a morganatic marriage with the Countess Sophie

THE GRAND DUKE NICHOLAS-NICHOLJEWITCH.

THE GRAND DUKE PETER-NICHOLJEWITCH.

Dukes are rendered powerless and the officialdom, as it now exists, is a thing of the past. From the Grand Dukes downwards, one is told that there is a system of dishonesty amongst those in office and who hold State positions. No man expects to live on his

Merenberg, now Countess Torby, and lives with her in England and France; the third, George, is married to the only surviving daughter of the King of Greece. The Grand Duke Alexander is the husband of the Grand Duchess Xenia, the eldest sister of the Tzar. He has great influence with His Majesty, and unfortunately his influence is not for good. He is opposed to progress, as he considers that Russia is not yet ripe for it, and his counsels are much the same as those of the Grand Duke Vladimir. After Alexander comes the Grand Duke Sergius-Michaelowitch, who is unmarried. The only daughter of the Grand Duke Michaelowitch is the Grand Duchess Anastasie of Mecklenburg-Schwerin, whose youngest daughter is now engaged to the German Crown Prince.

The great fault that has been brought against the Grand Dukes is that they are most of them, with the exception of Grand Duke Constantin-Constantinowitch, self-seeking. They are accused of embezzling large sums of money intended for charity, and, so far, these charges have not been denied. Their lives, it is said, do not bear inspection, and it is openly asserted that there is no hope for Russia until the Grand

salary. Bribery and corruption are the rule in Russia, and it will be necessary to make a clean sweep should the Empire wish for prosperity.

The only surviving brother of the Tzar, the Grand Duke Michael-Alexandrowitch, has an amiable and strong character, with the great wish to act uprightly with all men; but his health is very delicate, and his influence with his brother is by no means so great as that of the Grand Duke Vladimir. In all, there are no less than thirty-one male members of the House of Romanoff, and twenty-two Princesses of the Imperial House.

In order to understand properly the Russian Grand Dukes and the Tzar, it is necessary to consider the education that they have received. A Russian Prince, although he lives in the twentieth century, has the morality of the Middle Ages, and as regards "mine and thine" his views are very primitive indeed. The Tzar looks upon himself as appointed by God to rule Russia, and he regards it a sacred duty to leave the country to his son as he found it, with none of his privileges and rights as an autocrat abridged. From infancy the Russian

Grand Dukes are brought up to consider that their will is law, and that they are alone privileged to do anything that seems right to them. They have many virtues, but they have not yet learnt that those in lowlier positions have also the right to live, to be happy, and to have liberty.

The present unfortunate state of affairs in Russia has turned all eyes on that gigantic empire, and many dark places have of late been made light. That an autocratic monarchy should exist in the twentieth century is an anomaly, and only the keen student of Russian history can understand how it is possible that the present state of things could have lasted for so long.

But Russia is not only European ; it is also Asiatic, both in regard to territory and the population and modes of thought of the inhabitants. This alone makes such a mighty empire almost impossible of being wisely governed by one man ; but until the last eighty years there were but few complaints, and the people were for the most part contented with the ruler given to them.

With a better education and the greater facilities of travelling which now exist, the people have learnt that there are other countries in which it is much easier to live than in their own beloved Russia, and the Russian Princes have also learnt that it is possible to enjoy life with more variety

THE
GRAND DUKE VLADIMIR.

THE
GRAND DUCHESS VLADIMIR.

outside their own dominions. They have also learnt what Western luxury and extravagance mean, and have grafted the vices of Europe on their own peculiar Asiatic vices, so that the rampant, but it was of a more simple kind, and differing from the complex form which now exists and which is eating out the lives and strength of the people.

THE GRAND DUKE ALEXIS.

present state of things in Russian society is much worse than it was even in the time of Catherine the Great. Then immorality was One great failing amongst the Russians is their great superstition. The Tzar, as well as many of his relations, is believed to

THE GRAND DUKE MICHAEL-
MICHAELOWITCH.

Hesse, is an excellent wife and mother, but she is not clever, though she has many intellectual tastes. Her chief thought is to keep her husband happy and in good health, and she encourages him to be as much as possible with her and to find his greatest pleasure in his nursery.

An amusing story is told about an interview that Admiral Rojdestvensky had with him shortly before he left Russia. The Admiral was relating to his Majesty a long account of the ships and men under his command, when suddenly the Tzar remarked with a smile, " He weighs fourteen pounds."

The astonished Admiral then found that his Imperial master's thoughts were in the nursery. He naturally congratulated the proud father, and then continued his report.

be under the influence of any charlatan who may come to the Court and announce himself as a good medium. His Majesty firmly believes all that he hears from the spiritualists, and many of his foolish acts have been attributed to the advice of a certain French medium, who has a great influence over him.

The peculiarly delicate health of the Tzar makes him all the more open to suggestion, and like all weak men he is also very obstinate, so that it is more difficult for judicious advisers to gain his ear. More than one honest courtier has fallen into disgrace because he has had the courage to tell an unpleasant truth to the Tzar.

The present Empress of Russia, Alexandra-Feodorowna, *née* Princess Alix of

THE GRAND DUKE PAUL-ALEXANDROWITCH.

BY E. KEBLE CHATTERTON.

SHOULD an actor be versatile? Should he, in order to uphold his right to be called an actor, be able to adapt himself to any part, be able to succeed as well in tragedy as in farce, be as acceptable in *Othello* as in *The Private Secretary*? The ideal actor would be able to bring his skill to any *rôle* in such a manner as to sink his personality entirely in the character he is seeking to interpret. His tragic acting would no more reveal his own personality than his comedy playing. Each would be a separate and distinct piece of work, complete in itself, independent, and neither would be mutually reminiscent.

But the ideal actor does not exist, and, considering the limitations of human ability, it is doubtful if he has ever been seen by any one. For it is the tendency in every advance towards perfection to specialise. In economics one calls it division of labour; in the sphere of acting we are accustomed

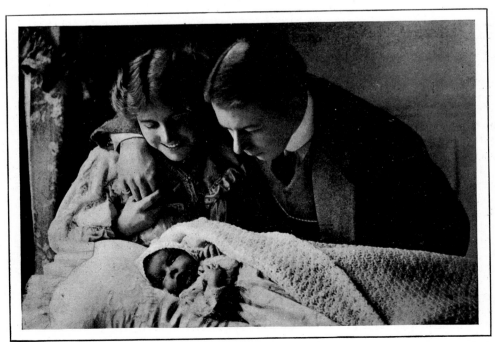

Photo by Ellis & Walery.

THE LATEST THEATRICAL *DÉBUT*.
(Mr. and Mrs. Seymour Hicks with their infant daughter.)

to label an actor either a tragedian or comedian or a character-actor. If he is not one, he must be another, for he cannot be all three: so popular opinion allows. Not infrequently, however, the poor player is neither of the three when he comes to be proved, but merely a shrewd business man who happens to lease a West-End theatre and to occupy the centre of the stage and the chief attention of the limelight in all the most dramatic situations. But if he has shown any talent in one branch of acting, his popularity will rise or fall only according as he plays such parts in the future. It is not always the fault of the actor that he must for ever specialise. Personal talent counts for something, physical appearance counts for more; but it is public opinion which counts for nearly all. He who has paid to come in by the box-office has a right to select the playing.

But to those who are not above learning something more of their art, the wonderful acting of Mr. Henri de Vries at the Royalty Theatre must come as a spray of water to a

Photo by Stage Pictorial.

MR. HARRY LYTTON AND MISS AGNES FRASER IN THE SWING SONG AT THE LYRIC THEATRE.

Photos by Bassano

MR. HENRI DE VRIES, THE CLEVER DUTCH ACTOR.

The first of these three characters represents the police-sergeant, the second the prisoner's aged father-in-law, the third the prisoner's idiot brother in *A Case of Arson* played at the Royalty. Mr. Henri de Vries interprets each *rôle* in turn with the greatest skill.

parched lawn. "I wish all our English actors, both great and small, were here to watch de Vries," I overheard a well-known playwright remark. The play is *A Case of Arson*, in subject-matter and treatment similar to *La Robe Rouge*, which was given at the Garrick Theatre as *The Arm of the Law*, and which was referred to in these columns a year ago. Before the examining magistrate is brought John Arend, a cigar manufacturer. There has been a fire at Arend's manufactory. There is something mysterious and difficult to explain in connection with the outbreak. Unfortunately, Arend's infant daughter happened to be in the factory at the time of the outbreak, and was burned to death.

Photo by Bassano.

A CASE OF ARSON.

By a clever move the examining magistrate extorts from John Arend an acknowledgment of his guilt.
(Mr. Henri de Vries at the Royalty Theatre.)

MISS DELIA MASON
(Who sings so delightfully in *Lady Madcap* at the Prince of Wales's Theatre).

Photo by Stage Pictorial.

MR. WALTER PASSMORE IN HIS AMUSING SONG, "MY LITTLE BROOD," IN *THE TALK OF THE TOWN* AT THE LYRIC THEATRE.

The legal procedure is impressive, the examining of the magistrate searching and irresistible. Seven witnesses are called, each distinct in character, appearance, manner, and voice. Mr. Henri de Vries played each in English without betraying either his own nationality or his personality. Here, as nearly as possible, is the ideal actor. He

Photo by Stage Pictorial.

A GROUP OF DUTCH GIRLS IN *THE TALK OF THE TOWN.*

Photo by Ellis & Walery.

MISS JEAN AYLWIN
(Who is appearing at the Gaiety Theatre)

plays the sad, sorrow-stricken manufacturer, who has lost his child and his money. He next appears as the idiot brother, one of the most wonderful examples of acting ever seen

manufacturer is brought in again. The magistrate's skill is too powerful for him, and he is finally compelled to admit that he is himself the cause of the fire. The

Photo by Ellis & Walery.

THE FIRST SCENE IN *THE LADY OF LEEDS.*

Colonel Claverhouse Hodge and Lord O Gorman, having been rejected by Miss Chitty, persuade
Jerome Robinson (Mr. Weedon Grossmith) to aid in their revenge.

in England. The illustration on another page will indicate the make-up for this part. There is in the idiot's voice something of the melancholy and morose, in his eyes a vacant stare, in his hands a twitching and a restlessness. The cigar manufacturer's father-in-law comes next. Old, infirm, deaf, and a trifle garrulous, he undergoes his examination as the others. As a violent contrast, the police-sergeant follows with his heavy tread and military bearing.

An affable and corpulent inn-keeper, a fussy and sycophant little grocer, and a none too respectful house-painter come before the magistrate in turn. Finally, the cigar

acting of Mr. de Vries, like the construction of the play itself, has been growing gradually stronger and more powerful. There has been tragedy and comedy, and farce and sentiment. Now at last the cigar manufacturer breaks out into a fury. Quiet and subdued he becomes again at the awful thought of the death of his little daughter, mortified at the prospect of the prison cell. He is led away into custody. Last of all is introduced the miserable idiot, who vainly tries to shield his brother by taking the blame on himself. The play, by Mr. Herman Heyermans, would never become popular in this country. Its *motif* is too sad and heavy, but it is particularly suitable for this clever seven-part actor.

One could not ask for a greater contrast than *The Diplomatists*, the two-act farce by Mr. Sydney Grundy which preceded *A Case of Arson*. It would seem to have been written by the author in the days of his youth, before his hand had learned its cunning. It is crude and amateurish in conception, weak in construction, and even thoroughly bad, with one or two exceptions in the last act. The characters have long since passed out of date and out of sympathy, and the acting did not succeed in inducing the audience to appreciate

height of their deceit is reached in the second act, when both the suburban doctor and the retired draper come to discuss the question of settlements. Neither parent is in a position to endow his child, but both are undesirous of betraying the truth. Finally a despised friend of the Protheros, John Jackson, a jobmaster, solves the difficulty by bestowing, not merely his blessing, but a sufficient sum to be a settlement on the young lovers. He is also charitable enough to arrange with the man in possession at the Jocelyns', and the curtain ends the play happily. *The Diplomatists* is not worthy of

Photo by Ellis & Walery.

THE SECOND SCENE IN *THE LADY OF LEEDS*.
Jerome Robinson, whilst endeavouring to act as gondolier to Miss Chitty (Miss Nancy Price), has succeeded in capsizing the gondola.

it any the more. The plot of *The Diplomatists* is concerned with a handful of suburban people with very suburban minds. Dr. Prothero, a Clapham doctor, has little or no practice, but a winsome daughter Muriel. She receives an offer of marriage from Arnold Jocelyn, the son of a retired draper. Both the Jocelyns and the Protheros worship at the shrine of Superiority, and the

bearing the name of the author of *A Pair of Spectacles*, although it is founded on MM. Labiche and Martin's *La Poudre aux Yeux*.

The success of *The Walls of Jericho* had raised high hopes that Mr. Alfred Sutro's *Mollentrave on Women* at the St. James's Theatre would be at least a passable if not a brilliant play. In actual fact it turned out to

A DUTCH BOY'S COSTUME IN *THE TALK OF THE TOWN*.

From the original design by Mr. Percy Anderson.

be neither. If, as is not improbable, it is of a date prior to *The Walls of Jericho*, it is regrettable that a playwright should be inclined to put forth what is immature work. There is lacking in *Mollentrave on Women* an elementary knowledge of stagecraft. To take an instance, Mr. Sutro hardly seems able to manage more than two characters at a time. If there happen to be three people on the scene, he sends one up the stage to look out of the window or to read a book, and turns the dialogue into a duologue. It is an easy way out of the difficulty, but it is not art. Moreover, there is no economy. Two characters are introduced at the opening of the first act and never seen again. It might be urged in reply that Mr. Pinero made a similar mistake in introducing Captain Hugh Ardale in *The Second Mrs. Tanqueray*. But this is always acknowledged the most forced and the least satisfactory point of an otherwise excellent play. Moreover, every work of art, whether in music, painting, or the drama, must have contrast. There is no real relief in *Mollentrave on Women*. The second act is dull and the third duller. The only

satisfactory feature is the creation of Mollentrave, who is interesting and humorous, and a distinct individual without being merely a type.

Mollentrave has raised the study of Woman to the height of a science. He has even written a standard book on his subject, and "Mollentrave on Women" is quoted everywhere. But for all that, he advises Sir Joseph Balsted, a bachelor K.C., as to how he shall dispose of his ward, with whom Everard Swenboys is in love. There is a terribly unfortunate complication : the ward foolishly imagines that it is Sir Joseph who is desirous of wedding her, and refuses to believe otherwise. In the last act, not very skilfully matters are put straight—Sir Joseph pairs off with Mollentrave's sister and the ward with Everard Swenboys.

Almost more disappointing as a play is Captain Robert Marshall's *The Lady of Leeds*, at Wyndham's Theatre. It is replete with the obvious and with stock situations.

A DUTCH GIRL'S COSTUME IN *THE TALK OF THE TOWN*.

From the original design by Mr. Percy Anderson.

Photo by Stage Pictorial.

MR. MAURICE FARKOA

(The popular actor and singer).

"THE MILL."

(From the painting by SIR EDWARD BURNE-JONES.)

MODERN MASTERS IN THE IONIDES COLLECTION.

BY TIBURCE BEAUGEARD.

WHEN the exhibition of the Constantine Alexander Ionides Collection of pictures and etchings was thrown open to the public last summer at the Victoria and Albert Museum, it was truly said that since the Wallace bequest the nation had come into no artistic inheritance so rich, so varied, and so comprehensive. The extent and importance of the present collection is shown in the fact that it comprises about twelve hundred examples of old and modern masters ranging from Botticelli, Albert Dürer, and Rembrandt to Burne-Jones, Whistler, and Degas.

"À tout seigneur, tout honneur!" Before entering more fully into our subject it is meet that we should allude, however briefly, to the Ionides family, members of which have for generations proved themselves devout and discriminate lovers of things artistic and intellectual. In William Michael Rossetti's recently published *Diary* we read, under an entry dated April 6, 1867 : "Dined with the Ionides. The first time I have been there. It was the anniversary of the Greeks in connexion with their Revolution. The members of the family seem all very intelligent, and the women especially well informed and interested in intellectual subjects. . . . Miss Ionides tells me that Homer is read entirely by accent, and the value of longs and shorts not now understood. She has herself done a hexametral, and, I understand, quantitative translation of the first four books of the Iliad. . . ."

Among the artists that were ever welcome and appreciated in the family circle of the Ionides were Dante Gabriel Rossetti, Burne-Jones, Alphonse Legros, and especially George Frederick Watts, whose lifelong friendship with the family dated as far back as 1840. It is well known that the great master of symbolism in art has represented by his brush no less than five generations of the Ionides family. The first sitters were Constantine and Mary Ionides, painted when Watts was only twenty-three or twenty-four years of age, and the last, Agathonike Hélène Ionides, the great-great-grandchild painted in 1893. Two pictures that call for special notice in this remarkable ancestral gallery are " The Baby," a representation of an infant sleeping, happy and smiling, with angels watching over him, and " Aurora " floating through the air, followed by a flight of Cupids. This series of family portraits is not yet in the Victoria and Albert Museum, having been left to the widow of the late Mr. Ionides for her lifetime.

In bequeathing his art treasures to the South Kensington Museum, the testator expressly laid it down that they were " to be kept there for the benefit of the nation, as one separate collection, to be called the Constantine Alexander Ionides Collection, and not to be distributed over the Museum or lent for exhibition." And he further desired " that the etchings, drawings and engravings shall be glazed by and at the expense of the authorities of the Museum, so that students there can easily see them."

It must be said that the members of the Board of Education have scrupulously carried

From a purely educational standpoint the present exhibition offers exceptional interest to art students, for several foreign masters are here represented who have hitherto found no place in the National Gallery, nor even in the admirable examples contained in the Wallace Collection. Ingres, Millet, Courbet, Rousseau, Degas, Daumier appear here for the first time in a British National Museum, and through the dozen or so of unique specimens of the Barbizon School we are able to trace the evolution of modern landscape painting.

Again, although the works of old masters can be studied in any public gallery in this country, the Ionides Collection comprises a number of examples the importance of which cannot be over-estimated.

A FLEMISH GARDEN.
(From the picture by HENRI DE BRAKELEER.)

out the terms of the bequest, and have displayed the pictures and drawings to admirable advantage in the first-floor gallery communicating with the Dyce and Forster Collection.

The Italian School is represented by fifteen oil paintings and about one hundred watercolour drawings, including works by Francesco Guardi, Andrea del Sarto, Mantegna, Veronese, Tintoretto, Caracci, Canaletto, Raphael, Salvator Rosa, and Michel Angelo. The "Smeralda Bandinelli," attributed to Botticelli, is interesting partly for its own sake

series of Rembrandt etchings calls for especial notice. They probably form the richest collection of the great master's works that have ever been brought together, including

THE BALLET SCENE IN "ROBERT LE DIABLE."

Degas' masterpiece is the only painting of the Impressionist School to be seen in any of our National Galleries. The composition is unique.

and partly for having once belonged to the famous Pourtalès Collection, whence it came, at one time in the possession of Dante Gabriel Rossetti.

The old Dutch and Flemish Schools are illustrated by the small early work of Rembrandt, "Abraham dismissing Hagar and Ishmael," and a fine "Interior" by Adriæn Brouwer, which, it is said, the Berlin Museum made repeated and, fortunately, unavailing efforts to obtain from the late Mr. Ionides. But in addition to these and other oil paintings by Van Ostade, Ruysdael, Konnick, Rubens, and Teniers, the marvellous

portraits and landscapes and such Biblical subjects as "Abraham's Sacrifice," "Ezekiel's Vision," "David and Goliath," "The Nativity," "Jesus and the Samaritan Woman at the Well," "The Descent from the Cross," etc. If, as we are told, Rembrandt's etchings are still technically unequalled, the unique value of the two hundred specimens now treasured up at the Victoria and Albert Museum can to some extent be realised.

The scope of this paper does not, unfortunately, allow of my dwelling at any length on the French early masters to be seen in the Ionides Collection, as, for instance, the brothers Le Nain's fine and attractive "Landscape with Figures," or Poussin's two large canvases representing in classic style "Venus arming Æneas" and

Of Dante Gabriel Rossetti's works we reproduce the well-known "Day Dream," painted in 1880, and which the artist at first thought of calling "Monna Primavera."

"PORTRAIT OF A LADY.
(By DANTE GABRIEL ROSSETTI.)

"Artists sketching among Ruins." I must rather turn to more modern times, and mention some of the works reproduced here by Burne-Jones, Rossetti, Degas, and other eminent painters of the last century.

It is a beautiful portrait of Mrs. Morris, represented holding a book open on her lap and seated among the branches of a sycamore tree. The work is highly finished, and remained unexecuted for years after the original studies had been prepared. Mr. Marillier, the conscientious and well-informed biographer of the pre-Raphaelite painter-poet, records as an instance of Rossetti's pains-

examples by Rossetti include "The Portrait of a Lady," in red and black chalk, on grey paper, dated 1867, and a characteristic pencil study of "The Head of a Woman."

HEAD OF A WOMAN.
(By DANTE GABRIEL ROSSETTI.)

taking and scrupulous exactness, that after the figure in "The Day Dream" was finished, he deliberately set to work to paint out all the lower portion because he thought that the limbs were made too short. The other

Two of the most famous productions of Sir Edward Burne-Jones, that were admired at the Grosvenor Gallery in 1882, "The Mill" and "Cupid's Hunting Fields," are now included in the Ionides Collection.

That graceful composition "The Mill" was begun in 1870, and took nearly twelve years to finish. It shows in the foreground three girls in blue, green, and brown, dancing

Among other works of the modern English school we find also two small but fine examples of George Frederick Watts : "The Bath of Daphne" and "The Window Seat."

THE MARKET PLACE OF PLOUDALMEZEAU.
(From the painting by L'HERMITTE.)

hand-in-hand to the music of a viola player, standing against a background of great water-wheels. More complex in character is the monochrome "Cupid's Hunting Fields," representing the God of Love blindfolded and falling, as if unexpectedly, among a group of fair maidens by a brook-side. In addition to these two oil-paintings we have also from the same artist a red-chalk drawing of "A Head of Cassandra," a study in pencil of "A Head of a Girl," and an important water-colour sketch, "Dorigen of Bretaigne." The heroine of Chaucer's "Franklin Tale" is depicted watching for her husband's return from a sea voyage. Through the window of the castle Dorigen sees the waves dashing against the bleak rocks, stretches her hands to Heaven, and exclaiming :

"But wolde God that al this rokke blake
Were sunken into helle for his sake !"

We can hardly classify Alma Tadema's charming "Dutch Interior," or "A Visit," among English works. The picture is dated 1868, and offers curious interest as showing the early style of the artist when he had not yet been attracted by the classic correctness of Greece and Rome.

When we come to the paintings, sketches, and etchings of Alphonse Legros, we feel again more inclined to assign him a place among the French than the English artists. Let us, however, take the *via media*, and merely state that the eminent professor of the Slade School stands between the two countries, being English by adoption, but essentially French by temperament. In the Ionides Collection, which, we have been told, Alphonse Legros helped to form, the great artist is represented by five character-istic paintings, amongst others " Le Chaud-ronnier," or "The Tinker," an admirable canvas exhibiting remarkable technique and restrained power in treatment and conception alike. Of the master's well-known etchings we have, among the two hundred and fifty exhibited, studies of Spanish monks, French churches, and rustic scenes, the famous compositions " Death and the Woodcutter" and " The Vagrant's Death," and last, but not least, a series of characteristic portraits, such as those of Dalou, the sculptor, Cardinal Manning, Sir E. J. Poynter, and Auguste Rodin.

Let us now turn to some of the masterpieces of the modern French School, and we shall realise to the full the importance of Constantine Ionides splendid bequest. For the present collection most opportunely indeed makes up for the deficiency so apparent in the National Gallery : the more

Good Samaritan " and his first sketch of " The Shipwreck of Don Juan," and by Ingres the oil-painting " Henry IV. and the Spanish Ambassador " exhibited in the Paris Salon in 1824. Then we come to some magnificent examples of the apostles of the " Return to Nature," the famous masters of the Barbizon group. Jean François Millet heads the list with his impressive " Wood Sawyers " and three other typical works, " The Shepherdess," " The Well," and an exquisite landscape, treated in his well-known direct and forceful manner. Here, too, we have three landscapes by Théodore Rousseau, that conscientious artist *par excellence* who painted an oak tree in his dear Fontainebleau with the same respect and enthusiasm as he would paint the portrait of a hero or of a god. It is sad to think that,

" A DUTCH INTERIOR."

This charming picture by SIR ALMA TADEMA is interesting as an indication of the artist's earlier period, before he was influenced by the Grecian and Roman styles.

than inadequate representation of French painters, especially of the later schools, whether of *peinture de genre* or of landscape. Here at length we have by Delacroix " The

like his friend Jean François Millet, Rousseau struggled all his life long against the pressure of poverty. So hard pressed indeed was he at one time that he sold a painting of his

"CUPID'S HUNTING FIELDS."
(By Sir Edward Burne-Jones.)

that had cost many a year of study and toil for eight hundred francs, or about £32. The same work fetched over fifty times that amount—but, as is usually the case, only after the great artist's death.

In Diaz de la Peña's "Baigneuse" we have a fine example of the painter's delightful art in the rendering of forest scenery, while in Gustave Courbet "L'Immensité" we are once more impressed with the realistic force and serene beauty the master of Ornans so often imparted to his well-known landscapes of the Franche-Comte.

But even with Delacroix, Ingres, Millet,

Rousseau, Diaz, and Courbet we have not yet exhausted the list of modern French painters represented at the Victoria and Albert Museum. Here again we can admire two exquisite pictures, "Twilight" and "Morning," by Corot, and note how feelingly the artist has expressed on canvas the ineffable charm of the

visionary glow,
Pendulous 'twixt the gold hour and the grey,

and how under his magic brush Nature appears to us paradisaical and idealised. On the other hand, Léon L'Hermitte's rustic scenes "Le Pardon de Plourin" and "The Market Place of Ploudalmezeau," bring us back to a sterner aspect of country life, the depicting of which being perhaps due to the rugged character of the Finistère scenery and the rough life of the peasantry the famous Breton painter is so fond of delineating.

Another branch of art is admirably represented in the Ionides Collection by Fautin Latour's delicate, soft-toned groups of flowers: irises, azaleas, tulips, and hyacinths. We have besides about forty specimens of water-colour works,

including three studies and portraits by Ingres; no less than four landscapes by Millet; a number of military subjects by Guillaume Régamey, and a couple of exquisite pictures by Henri Harpignies. Another

"THE DAY DREAM."
(By Dante Gabriel Rossetti.)

master whom the British public will now have an opportunity of studying at the Victoria and Albert Museum is Honori Daumier, the "French Hogarth," represented by about a dozen original drawings. Finally, England now possesses the famous "Ballet Scene in Robert le Diable," by Degas, the only Impressionist picture to be seen at the present time in any public gallery through the length and breadth of this country. "Degas' 'Ballet Scene' is a masterpiece," wrote recently a distinguished art critic. "It is a poet's as well as an observer's vision of orchestra and stage: the orchestra as a pictorial effect; the waving pictures on the stage behind it with the temporary architecture of the theatre, as a pictorial effect, too." Some of the readers of the present article may have visited lately the Grafton Galleries and seen among the Impressionist pictures therein exhibited by M. M. Durand Ruel another remarkable example of the art of Hilaire Degas, "Mademoiselle Zaza

au Cirque Fernando." A comparison between this picture and the "Ballet Scene," reproduced here, cannot result but in confirming one's opinion as to the unerring draughtsmanship and the harmonious flexibility in composition of one of the great masters of Impressionism.

Before concluding we must not omit mentioning two eminent artists of the modern Flemish School whose works have also found place among the pictures of the Ionides Collection: Mathys Maris, the painter of "The Hay-cart," and Henri de Brakeleer, whose charming "Flemish Garden" will doubtless attract many admirers. In presenting these and the numerous other masterpieces we have just described to the South Kensington Museum, the late Constantine Ionides has indeed made one of the most munificent gifts which it is the exceptional privilege of a wealthy, generous, and enlightened man to confer upon a community.

"DORIGEN OF BRETAIGNE."
(BY SIR EDWARD BURNE-JONES.)

Castles in the Air

THE day of hope is past,
    The day of love is here ;
Beat high, my heart, beat high—
    Thy knight is drawing near !

He will come on his coal-black
        charger,
    He will stop 'neath my latticed
        bower,
He will doff his helm when he sees
        me smile,—
    Ah me ! the glorious hour !

Oh, youth is merry and love is sweet,
    And this is a golden day !
'Tide weal, 'tide woe, the waning
        years
    Can rend no love away.

268

He came on his coal-black charger,
   He galloped across the moor ;
But he stopped when he saw me
      standing,
   And his face was sad and dour.

My heart — oh, my heart was breaking!
   But I stilled it with infinite pain,
And I filled all the hunger of seven
      long years
   As I gazed on his face again.

We might not speak to each other,
   And I knew that he must not stay ;
But his face was sad and his eyes
      were dim
   As he steadfastly rode away.

                         B. C. HARDY.

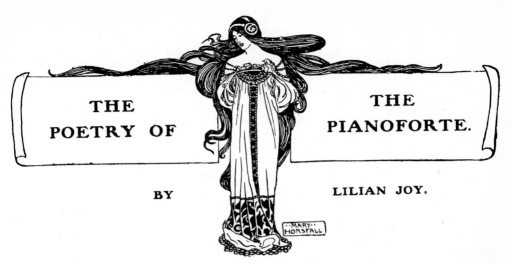

THE POETRY OF THE PIANOFORTE.

BY LILIAN JOY.

THE question, " Is the piano a musical instrument ? " propounded by Mr. Bernard Shaw in his article on " The Religion of the Pianoforte," which appeared some years ago in *The Fortnightly Review*, would probably be answered by most people in the affirmative. Another query, " Is the piano an artistic piece of furniture ? " would be equally likely to meet with a negative reply. Yet a musical instrument which gives birth to beautiful sounds should surely be beautiful, its outward form a delight to the eye as its voice is to the ear. It has always been thus with musical instruments from the Egyptian harp of four thousand years ago downwards. Yet in the midst of the present great revival in artistic furnishing, when we are surrounded by a wealth of fine objects stolen from every period, that terrible late Georgian or early Victorian atrocity, the grand piano of polished mahogany, is far too often seen. It still desecrates many an otherwise beautiful room.

The immediate forerunner of the piano, the harpsichord, was frequently a passably

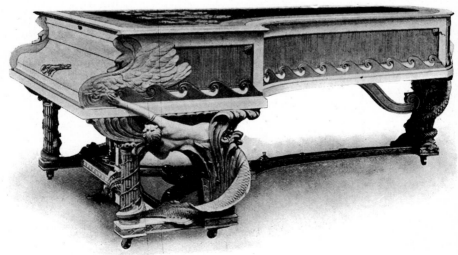

THE WAGNER PIANO.

This is one of the most remarkable pianos in the world. It was designed by Professor Koch to suggest the legend of the Rheingold.

elegant piece of furniture. And the earlier instrument, the spinet, was grace itself, consisting as it did of a flatter case balanced on slender legs.

As is usual with the introduction of a new invention, great minds met over it, and both Italy and Germany claim to be the birthplace of the piano itself. Be this as it may, the early pianos, though they certainly did not produce much music, were not so unsightly

of a lighter build, they did not need the massive supports required later. When musicians demanded greater and greater volume of sound the strings had to be lengthened and more metal introduced into the mechanism, and the modern massive grand was produced, of which the heaviest and ugliest development is the concert grand.

No attempt was made, however, to decorate

THE FRONT OF THIS PIANO WAS DESIGNED BY SIR ALMA TADEMA, AND THE PANEL PAINTED BY SIR EDWARD POYNTER.

as those of a later date. People, with the conservatism usual in the human race, did not at first take to the piano, but remained faithful to the harpsichord. It was not until after nearly a hundred years of patient investigation and experiment, and after the mechanism had been enormously improved, that the former finally superseded the latter instrument.

The first pianos were made of waxed walnut instead of the polished mahogany and black wood which followed, and being

the early pianos in any way—in fact, any ornamentation was strictly avoided. This is curious, because its precursors, the spinet and the harpsichord, were generally thus beautified, frequently with fine paintings. The same may be said of the still older virginal. One of these, owned originally by Queen Elizabeth, is to be seen in the Kensington Museum. This is of black wood patterned all over with gold; it rests in a cedar case lined with faded Genoa velvet, which must have been of a vivid red

A PIANO DECORATED WITH PAINTINGS AFTER BOUCHER.

when Queen Elizabeth tried her very considerable skill on the ivory keys.

It is only in comparatively recent times that it has occurred to people that the piano, being a most prominent object in a room, and one which from its very size requires relief, should certainly, like the antique instruments, receive some form of decoration.

No less notable artists than Sir Alma Tadema and the late Sir Edward Burne-Jones have, as is well known, used their gifts upon the adornment of pianos. Sir Edward Burne-Jones, as a matter of fact, painted two or three, of which the best known is that recalling the mythical history of Orpheus. Various scenes from this story contained in medallions go round the sides of the piano. The beautiful and characteristic painting on the front panel over the keyboard is shown in one of our illustrations. The inside and the outside of the lid are both decorated. On the inner side is the figure of Mother Earth surrounded by cherubs. The subject on the outside shows a half-length figure of Music appearing as in a vision to Poetry. An objection has been put forward that when the lid is lifted on its hinges these figures appear upside down ; but it should be remembered that the piano would probably stand against a wall, and in any case no listener would place himself on the wrong side of a piano of which the lid had been opened.

How far better is this manner of beautifying an instrument necessary to every house occupied by people of refined taste, than is the terrible practice of turning it into a supplementary table and using it as yet another receptacle for meaningless ornaments, or for vases of flowers, which are invariably upset.

The equally celebrated Alma Tadema piano was made at immense cost for an American. When he died it was sold with the rest of his possessions, and one regrets to hear that it then disappeared from sight, and was purchased for far less than its value, perhaps by some one who had no idea of its artistic worth and interest. The piano is composed of ebony, inlaid with box and cedar woods, ivory and mother-of-pearl. The surrounding band is of ivory with mother-of-pearl stars inlet, and each centred with a coral. The very music-rest is a wonderful piece of design and workmanship in carved brass inlaid with silver and copper. On the top of the lid are scattered nine wreaths containing the names of the Muses. The inner side of the lid is fitted with parchment, on which the famous musicians who played upon the keys signed their names.

An addition to the wealth of beauty in this remarkable instrument is the front panel, painted by Sir Edward Poynter.

There is something to be said against the decoration of this part of a piano. There is every point in favour of adorning the body of the instrument, which appears to listeners and when the piano is not in use. Yet surely a musician would be distracted in playing some serious music, for instance, if his eye fell upon a panel treated with some light and gay subject. Indeed, it would be difficult to find any set subject likely to be in harmony with all forms of music, which, like every great art, is as many-sided as life itself.

Such criticism seems out of place here, however, since its carrying into effect would have deprived us of the fine painting under consideration. It represents the garden of a Roman villa, where a group of maidens dance to the sound of ancient music. The construction of the picture is charming, and, indeed, so singularly

is it adapted for the purpose for which it was designed, that one can fancy it in no other position. As this work, so full of grace and movement, might have been itself inspired by the spirit of Music, so one can well imagine it in its turn inspiring

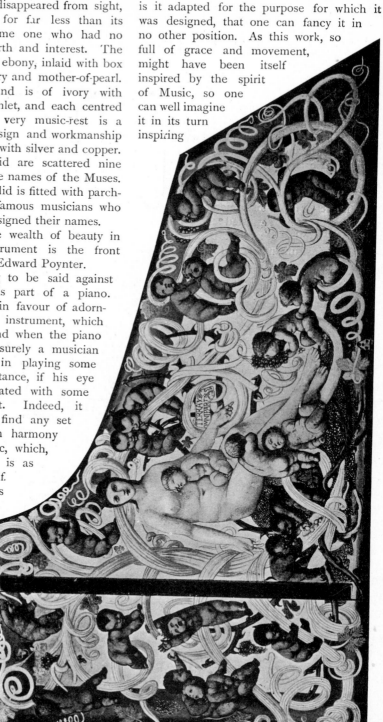

THE INNER SIDE OF A PIANO TOP PAINTED BY SIR EDWARD BURNE-JONES.

the musician who looks on it to a rapture of gay and fanciful melody.

The verdict which those most competent to judge have passed on both these pianos, however, is that the design of the general structure is hardly worthy of the decoration lavished upon it. One cannot, of course, help feeling conscious of this. Yet it should be remembered that there is bound to be great difficulty in the designing of any structure where a heavy body containing a considerable amount of metal is placed on wooden supports.

Apart from this, both the artistic beauty and interest of the instruments are so great that it is to be regretted they have not been acquired to swell the collection of musical instruments at the Kensington Museum, among which no piano appears.

One of the means employed for lessening the over-weighted, top-heavy appearance of the grand piano is the using of a number of less solid legs, which are connected at a short distance from the ground. This may be seen in our illustration of a very fine and simple grand designed by Andrew Russell. It is decorated in the French style, and has a number of medallions painted in mythological subjects by the well-known artist Hermann. The panels on the late Queen's yacht, the *Victoria and Albert*, were the work of the same hand and brush.

The popularity of decorated pianos has increased immensely during the last few years. What has retarded their coming into favour was the belief that the mechanism is sacrificed to the case. This is a most erroneous fancy, for no maker would care to save on an interior which costs hundreds, whereas the decorative case may go into thousands of pounds. If decoration is used

THE SIDE OF THE "ALMA TADEMA" PIANO, SHOWING THE CHARMING DECORATION AND CARVING.

at all it should of course be of the best, as the only excuse for its existence is its genuine beauty and artistic merit.

Royalty has set a seal of approval on this art of beautifying the musical instrument of the age. The same firm from which the Hermann piano issued designed a notable instrument for the Princess of Wales when she was Duchess of York, the sides being surrounded with paintings.

Twenty years ago one of the oldest piano-firms had a piano decorated in Vernis Martin with Watteau subjects on a background of gold. People used to come into the shop and look at it, and say, "What a gaudy thing! I couldn't have that." But the opening of the Wallace Collection has had an immense influence on public taste, and now a plain mahogany piano is not so readily tolerated in a Louis Seize room. And though there are still many who cling to this relic of the

THE FRONT PANEL OF A PIANO PAINTED BY SIR EDWARD BURNE-JONES: ORPHEUS AND EURYDICE ON EITHER SIDE, WITH PLUTO AND PROSERPINA IN THE CENTRE.

Victorian age, there are also those who insist on having an instrument cased in harmony with the rest of their furniture. One piano has indeed been copied from the celebrated King's Bureau at Hertford House.

Now we come to one of the most remarkable pianos ever built. It was designed and carved by Professor Max Koch, President

With the exception of the Greek rhythmic wave which forms a border representing the flow of the river, it is a wonderful example of purely modern design and carving. From out the river foliage which supports the sides lean Rheindaughters, to stretch graceful arms towards the swans forming the cheeks of the piano. The weight at the far

A PIANO DECORATED AFTER THE FRENCH STYLE, WITH PAINTINGS BY HERMANN.

of the Royal Academy of Decorative Arts in Berlin. It was shown at the 1896 Berlin Industrial Exhibition, where it was bought by the Lottery Committee. For a time it, like the Tadema piano, disappeared, but eventually the original makers gained possession of it. It is known as the "Wagner" piano, the whole scheme of decoration being suggested by the legend of the Rheingold.

end is sustained by a group comprised of Alberich, the dwarf, struggling with the third Rheindaughter for the possession of the river treasure.

As has been said, the idea of the decoration of a piano should always be that it is specially planned to harmonise with that of the room for which the instrument is intended.

Sir Alma Tadema designed another piano for his own use, in order to have one in keeping with the famous marbles and Eastern adornments of his house.

The very distinctive character of a Morris room certainly requires that an instrument should be in harmony with it. And William Morris was once commissioned to inlay a case or decorate it with gesso in the style for which he was celebrated. A follower of his in the revival of art craftsmanship has evolved a charming upright piano, with folding doors composed of six or eight panels, each painted with a full-length figure subject. These are intended for rooms furnished in the purely modern manner. The Kaiser Wilhelm discovered some time ago that there was no reason why a piano should not be a harmonious piece of furniture for whatever kind of apartment it might be intended, as well as an excellent instrument, and he went so far as to have a case especially designed in Norwegian style for his shooting-box. It was quite a success, the quaint candle-brackets being particularly attractive.

A French artist once collected various designs of Italian Renaissance carving and adapted them for an upright piano. The top was an exact copy of an ancient coffer,

and the curious side-handles were suggested by those on another old coffer, and so on. The front was inlet with Gorgon bronzes. This was carried out in Italian walnut by a celebrated firm, and for a long time remained on their premises. Eventually a purchaser appeared who said it was the very thing that he had been in search of for years. It now stands in a room of a London house of which not only the magnificent furniture, but the very walls and ceiling, are examples of carving of the same period. Such a piano was the only instrument possible to place in such an apartment.

Everything points to a piano being made, especially in a room where there is no bookcase, *the* important piece of furniture. Apart from the fact of its size giving it an actual prominence, the noble use to which it is put fills it with a deeper significance. It is like a piece of furniture with a human soul. Thus no care which the sister art can lavish upon it is too great, and no fitter outlet could be found for the noblest decoration that the age can supply.

The writer desires to acknowledge the courteous assistance and loan of photographs by Messrs. Bechstein, Messrs. Erard, Messrs. Johnstone, Messrs. Norman & Co., and also the help of Messrs. Pleyel.

THE BUTTERCUP
by Jeannette A. Marks

There was a tiny buttercup
That grew beside a spring;
His little dress was green & gold
And thus he used to sing:

I love the night,
I love the morn,
Heigho! I say.
The earth was bright
When I was born
Upon this very day.

It was in May he sang this song
With every Bobolink;
In June he changed his song a bit
To this, it was, I think:

I love the night,
When it is cold,
Heigho! I say.
The sun's too bright,
It melts my gold
And takes my leaves away.

And when July was come at last
The buttercup was dead.
But ere he went he left these words,
His testament, he said:

For every hour
I have a song.
Heigho! I say.
Next April shower
Will bring along
More buttercups & May.

M. V. Wheelhouse.

THE NURSERY and its DECORATION

BY SPENCER EDGE.

AFTER centuries of neglect the pendulum has swung to the other extreme, and the importance of childhood is at last realised. Whatever else may have resulted from our ultra-modern civilisation, or whatever else may be its effect on the after history of our little planet, this fact will assuredly stand to its credit. Generations ago, when it was the hey-day of maturity, irresponsible youth formed the theme on which our great-grandmothers loved to discourse. Nowadays the confessor to fifty summers is out of the race, and infallible, not irresponsible youth, makes the running. Whether this gradual recognition of the merits of the young has been responsible for the altered and improved conditions of the child does not concern us ; the happy fact that childhood has taken its rightful place in the pockets as well as in the hearts of the grown-ups is sufficient.

Nowhere is this revolution more complete than in the nursery, the home,

SOME DESIGNS FOR CHILDREN'S NURSERY WARE.

the very shrine of childhood. Time was when anything was deemed good enough for this retreat—stowed away at the top of the house, in the attic, under the very eaves—a retreat it was with a vengeance ! When we all-important elders had worn the pile off the drawing-room carpet, had loosened the legs of the dining-room chairs, had, in short, discarded the fittings of our own apartments, we were graciously pleased to make them over to the children, till the nursery became a depository of all our worn-out, broken-down belongings. But we have changed all that, and to-day the most artistic firms vie with each other in the production of furniture in which childhood may indeed delight.

In our eagerness, however, to make the *amende honorable*, we are apt to be carried at times, and in certain respects, too far. It is one thing to awake to the terrible importance of the early years of a girl or boy's life ; but it is quite a different, and, in

A DESIGN FOR THE NURSERY EMBODYING A CHILD'S
FAVOURITE STORY.

my opinion, a mistaken idea, to seek to force the pace at which they should be lived. In short, since the nursery represents the sum and substance of our views on the training and up-bringing of its inmates, we should do well to ponder on its influence while there is yet time.

None of us, I imagine, have shaken off the feelings with which our earliest surroundings inspired us. We can recall with an astonishing exactitude the get-up of the room, even the position of many of its details. We remember the outlook from the nursery window, the cupboard which held our toys, and even the colour of our favourite doll's hair. Indeed, although we do not always admit it, we have forgotten very little, and the hall-mark of our infancy is apparent in our characters to-day. Thus the child whose early days were spent amid dismal scenes, in dingy rooms to which the sunlight of cosiness and comfort was as rare a guest as the very sun himself, will surely be predisposed to pessimism, exactly as her sister's outlook will always be the brighter, and her temperament the saner, for experiences of the opposite order. In the same manner, without doubt, does the too pronounced cultivation of a child's intelligence react on its later ability. The infant prodigy—the child whose mind is invariably fed at the expense of its body—is at best but a seven days' wonder, and no one outside the pages of romance can be found to testify to its matured and middle-aged importance.

It is therefore on this theme that I would ask my readers' serious consideration, since there is to-day but little to fear from the comforts with which we love to enrich the playground of childhood, though much from the form, educational or otherwise, that they may take.

The question of a child's education is one on which we shall possibly differ. We are agreed as to the desirability of an acquaintance with the alphabet, with the rudiments of figures, and the art of caligraphy, but we are not agreed as to the age at which this knowledge should be imparted. Whilst we must confess a sneaking fondness for the genus "prodigy" (for what parent loves not to boast of her children's wonderful attainments?—wonderful, that is to say, as they are beyond their years), we hesitate to show our hand in too outspoken a fashion. We resort instead to a sort of trickery, and just as we conceal a pill in a spoonful of jam, so do we artfully disguise the alphabet, for instance, in some plausible form of decoration. Now surely this is distinctly unfair; and unless the child be of an unusually forgiving nature, it will not readily pardon us for the deception, any more than it will become attached to that particular kind of jam which is always to be associated in its mind with pills. Not to be misunderstood, let me explain that I am not referring to picture-books, furniture, or to any movable object of the nursery, but to the actual decorations of its walls, to the pictures, panels, dados, or whatever form the decoration may take, that day after day confront its occupants.

Now there are few children whose little heads are not saturated with romance, to whom the legendary adventures of equal legendary heroes and heroines are not of absorbing interest. The exploits of the fairies, and the more up-to-date experiences of mortals famed in rhyme, possess attractions for them which we can only realise if we ourselves were permitted such fellowship in days long past; and with these subjects, treated from the pictorial and not the educational point of view, should we content ourselves.

The accompanying illustrations contain two suggestions for the accomplishment of this idea; let me offer some explanation as to their execution. The third sketch, which embodies the whole wall from floor to ceiling, represents a series of panels, each one containing a simple decorative version of some well-known rhyme; the two rhymes depicted, Little Tom Tucker and Little Miss Muffet, being typical of a host of others known and loved by children of all ages. The panels are separated by a plain, flat "style," an upright

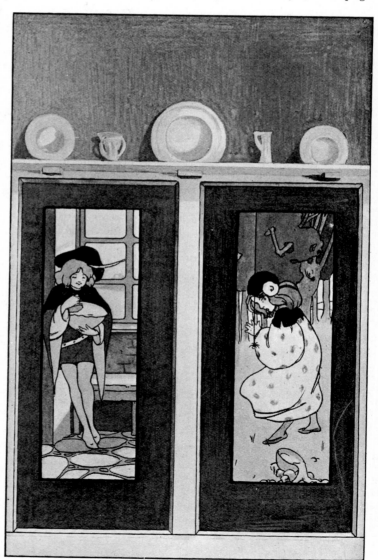

A SUGGESTED FORM OF DECORATION FOR THE WALL OF THE NURSERY.

A DESIGN FOR A NURSERY " CRAWLER."

inculcate a love of the beautiful even though all other tuition is to be avoided. To complete the picture the woodwork should be painted a dead cream white, and the deep but plain frieze space covered with a green or a terracotta paper, or canvas, as the aspect of the room and the treatment of the panels may require.

timber from three to five inches in width which rests on the skirting-board, and which, if the pictures be painted on canvas or paper, serves to hide the joining, besides adding constructional elegance to the scheme. Above them, a shelf of ample proportions affords not only a vantage-point for old brasses, copper, or pottery, but—and what is far more desirable in a nursery !—a convenience inaccessible to its mischievous inmates. Whatever be the materials used, it is hardly needful for me to say that the panels, together with woodwork, should be varnished.

The second drawing represents an alternative plan : that of carrying out the complete history of one of the children's favourite stories on all four walls. If this be done—and I can imagine no more charming or appropriate treatment for a nursery—we should contrive to have so many panels devoted to the principal and so many others to the minor personages in the story, arranged, of course, consecutively as regards the narrative, but, if possible, alternately also. In any case we should endeavour to adopt one definite colour scheme for our art gallery, remembering that we wish at least to

The furniture of the day nursery, plain, comfortable, and utilitarian, as it needs must be, we may pass by unnoticed ; but in the pottery that is required at meal-times another chance presents itself of gaining the child's interest and kindling its enthusiasm. Moreover, whilst our wall-decorations are probably not to be found ready made, nursery ware, good, bad, and indifferent, is to be had exactly on the lines we want.

Pottery apart, one other feature of the room's equipment demands our consideration ; and that is the " crawler "—a circular rug on which, as its name suggests, tiny mites may crawl, and crawl in comfort. Since this vast expanse of cloth forms, or should form, the limit of their kingdom—a limit which, by the way, they are frequently desirous of extending—it is the custom to embellish its border with simple pictures suited to their tender years. Here again we may find that both in *appliqué* and stencil-work our wants have been forestalled ; but if not, if we should once more find the educational element too strongly emphasised, let us commission some friendly artist to design a crawler after our own heart—and carry it out ourselves.

THE TRUTH ABOUT MAN.

By a Spinster.

ILLUSTRATED BY FACTS FROM HER OWN PRIVATE HISTORY.

The author of " The Truth About Man" is a well-known novelist, who prefers not to reveal her identity. In her opening chapters she subdivides Man into the Irresistible, the Admirable, and the Marriageable, discourses on the unattractiveness of the Ideal Woman, and analyses the effect of Love upon mature Man. She next proceeds to speak of Matrimony and considers the relation between Husband and Wife, and calls attention to the success of the Plain Woman in the Matrimonial Market.

As he believes that the views of " A Spinster" may not be shared by all the readers of THE LADY'S REALM, *the Editor has decided to offer prizes, month by month, for the best criticisms of " The Truth About Man." Particulars will be found on page 20 of the advertisements.*

CHAPTER VIII.

The Spinster blushingly retails a few of her Experiences with Man, the Lover, as he varies according to Race or Nationality.

I HAVE not been a great traveller in my day, and therefore cannot claim to know a large variety of men. But I have met Frenchmen, Germans, Dutch, Swiss, Turks, Greeks, Spaniards, Hungarians, Jews, Indians (Hindoos), Japanese, and, of course, Americans, Irish, Scots, and Welsh men. Most of these I have met casually in society, exchanged civilities with them in the ordinary way, and know no more of them than can be gleaned from the surface of conventionalities. My impression has been that the Frenchmen were the most excitable and alert; the Spaniards and Greeks most courtly and inscrutable; the Hungarians most artistic and intense; the Japanese most serious and polite; the Jews most versatile; the Germans and Scots most passionate; the Dutch most like Englishmen, and the Americans most fascinating. These impressions were, naturally, more or less influenced by the different individualities of the different men, but I think as generalisations they may not be far wrong.

Among all these I have known a few intimately, and it is of them I am now going to write. My analysis must, perforce, be somewhat objective; there is nothing so difficult in the world as to throw one's self into the nature of a human being who has been bred and trained under different conditions, laws, and traditions than one's own. It is hard enough for a woman to understand any kind of man, but when he is of an alien race the difficulty is increased tenfold. I can but draw an outline of each man as he has appeared to me in one light— that of a lover—and show wherein he has differed from another: not in essentials, for a man or woman in love has certain symptoms in common with every other man and woman (to say nothing of the lower animals !), and they vary only in degree or point of view. I will try to describe and analyse the slight variations.

I have been loved by three Americans, two Frenchmen, one German, one Irishman, one Swiss, three Scotsmen, and two or three Colonials, who do not count, as they are so nearly English. Of these I put the Americans first and foremost, as I consider the American man to be quite the most delightful and captivating of his sex.

In the first place he has a manner that is positively irresistible. It is quiet, self-assured, restrained, yet without the English stiffness, being extremely easy and spontaneous, inspiring tremendous confidence, inducing a sense of well-being and repose. I have never been quite able to discover what it is that makes a woman feel so safe, so natural, so altogether pretty and charming and happy as she usually does in her intercourse with an educated American. He has the mysterious power of making her satisfied with herself all the time she is in his company ; indeed, he manages to convey to her, without words, the impression that, so far as he is concerned, she is the only woman in the universe ! How he does it I cannot tell you ; it is a knack, a trick, and has probably been acquired, like the nightingale's voice, by natural selection in a country where the human male is not so numerous as he is here.

American Husbands.

I believe American women train their men well, bring them up in the way they ought to go, demand a certain amount of homage, and get it : we don't—or, rather, we have not done so in the past. There has been such competition for husbands that the competitors have resorted to the wiles of Becky Sharp, the flattery, blandishment, and ignoring of insults that has made our sex cheap and caused one of our poets to cry :

> Ah, wilful woman, she who may
> On her sweet self put her own price,
> Knowing *he* cannot choose but pay,
> How has she cheapened Paradise !
> How given for naught her priceless gift—
> How spoilt the bread and spilt the wine
> That, spent with due, housewifely thrift,
> Had made brutes men and men divine !

Written by a man, these lines, of course, ignore the fact that Man has always had the power to make of Woman what he chose by demanding the best from her ; that through his love of the worst and her natural desire to please him alone has she fallen from her high estate. But it is nevertheless true that we have "stooped to conquer" in the past, and are, many of us, doing so still. We may hope and believe, however, that as the Englishwoman becomes more powerful and independent she will be able to do without the wiles of the courtezan and insist upon her dignity, as the American woman does.

It is said that Man in the United States is not only kept in his proper place by Woman, but that he involuntarily makes of himself a slave to her interests, realising the enormous importance of her functions as wife and mother, the immense influence she wields over the welfare of the State, present and future. The American works day and night, with all his activities, to make a position for his wife, to surround her with luxury, to keep every rough chance from her path. I speak, of course, of the higher classes particularly ; but it must be remembered that the ways and manners of gentlefolk all over the world are emulated, more or less successfully, by those beneath them, and, although I know little of the American workman, I have heard that his wife is better off than our poor women. At all events it is a well-known and accepted fact that the Yankee usually strives with constant, feverish energy to amass "the almighty dollar" for his wife to spend, leading, himself, a hardworking, restricted life, and it has been said of him that he is the best husband in the world !

The Question of Money.

I am, however, not so sure that to be the wife of a man utterly absorbed in money-making is so enviable a state as we are taught to suppose. Not so long ago I read an American novel that gave a graphic description of such a *ménage*. The man was a good fellow, devoted to his wife, and extremely anxious that she should possess every material thing the heart of woman could desire. In compassing this he left her a great deal alone, and when with her was so absorbed in mental calculations that he scarcely seemed aware of her presence. She chafed and grew wretched, fearing some other woman had supplanted her ; and when at last she discovered what had engrossed all his thoughts, that her rival was a gorgeous, palatial mansion he had bought and furnished for her, the case was not mended. For her best feelings were wounded by the knowledge that he understood her so little as to imagine she would care more for a showy house than for his companionship and demonstrations of affection ; she was shocked by the gross materialism of his thoughts ; and she taught him a lesson by leaving him for a time with his costly gift on his hands, and a farewell letter to say that she, and any woman worthy of the name, would rather have her husband's society, sympathy, and attention than all the treasures of the earth.

The curious part about this study was that it was written by a man. But Man does occasionally get a lightning glimpse of his own frailties—or, perhaps, I should say, the frailties of his fellow-men. And here we have the whole strength and weakness of the American in a nutshell. He is strong in the tenacity of his purpose, in the straight, definite aim of the *idée fixe*. " What a wedge, what a catapult, is the earnest man ! " said Carlyle. The American, for all his lazy, gentle manner, his quiet drawl and whimsical humour, is an earnest man, but he is earnest in the wrong direction. He goes blindly ahead for the things that are seen, and misses the "inward invisible grace " of things unseen—the things that really matter to the soul of mankind. But this by the way. *Revenons à nos moutons*—my foreign lovers.

A Personal Experience.

I regret very much that I can only quote and give no personal experience of the American as a husband, but this is not my fault. I believe I should have been able to do so had I not discovered that the beautiful homage poured out at my feet by a certain American, once in my life, all his protestations, his caressing, tender words, his comprehensive sympathy, were equally at the service of half-a-dozen other women at the same time ! I discovered this just when I was thinking what stones I would have in my engagement ring, and weighing the respective merits of my girl friends as probable bridesmaids. But as I could not be sure how many other persons had been honoured with the same offer that he made me, I thought it most dignified to decline it without further inquiry. I do not in the least wish to insinuate that Americans usually propose to half-a-dozen girls at once, or that this particular lover of mine was a

Mormon. On thinking the matter over since, and in the light of other experience, I believe I acted hastily, and that, had I held him firmly to his word (as the woman who plays to win would have done), I might now have been the possessor of a tired, money-getting husband, a magnificent home, and a ravishing wardrobe. But I was ignorant in those days, and had not fathomed the mind of Man, still less of Yankee Man. I did not know that in his country girls are so hard to win that men say more, dare more, on a slight passion, than they dare here, where a large number of women are (or have been) eager to marry anybody available. I did not realise, either, the sense of chivalry which no striving for the dollar has been able to extinguish in the American, which makes him always tender and affectionate to every woman he meets, simply because she *is* a woman ; and I had no idea that this feeling would probably incline him to marry any girl who took him seriously, rather than wound her heart and self-respect.

My Lovers.

So I lost him, and sometimes I am a little sorry ; but my loss has been another's gain. He went back to the States and married one of his own countrywomen, who has since been over here queening it in Society—without him, of course ! She left him at home engineering his fortune and paying for her diamonds ! My other two American lovers were impossible. They were just as charming in manner, just as whimsically humorous, just as ready to take me everywhere, give me everything I wanted, and load me with lovely flowers ; but one was too commonplace, the other was married. I loved them both in a way and for a time ; but they left me with only a tender memory, which is aroused, accompanied by a certain pang, whenever I hear the soft rising cadence of the American voice.

My French lover was exciting. He could not grasp English ideas, and thought that if I consented to meet him alone I was prepared to fall into his arms. I shall never forget his surprise when I first checked his amorous ardour. He could not understand what "love" and "lover" meant to me. To him these words had a signification wholly different, and indeed so had the word *amie*. I should have spelt it *amante*, as he read it! But then a good deal of this confusion lies in our two languages, which have certain subtle idiomatic meanings impossible of translation. To begin with, of course, we have the verb "to like," which, I take leave to assert, has no real equivalent in French at all. "Je vous aime beaucoup" was the nearest Lucien (my lover) could give me for it. It seems curious that the adjective *beaucoup* should diminish the warmth of the verb, and that *je vous aime* without it should mean so much more! I learnt to be very careful what I said to Lucien in his own language (the French I had been taught at school) after his look of amazement and wicked joy when I used the word *baiser* as a verb. It appears that even a prude may take or give *a* kiss quite innocently; but *to* kiss is extremely improper!

"Quite Nice."

Of course, we have odd idiomatic uses of words too. We say "quite nice" to signify indifferently nice, so-so, endurable; we are "glad of it," "sorry for it"; we like some one "pretty well," or "ever so much"; while our arbitrary use of "shall" and "will" confuses many English-speaking people, Americans, Scots, and Irish. Every one has heard the story of the drowning Frenchman who cried, "I will die, and nobody shall save me!" and it gives a fair sample of our verbal pitfalls. Why should it mean, "I am resolved to die and refuse to be saved," when the transposition of two words, that appear identical in sense, would have been a cry for aid?

But to return to my French lover. He was an oddly complex creature; more so, I think, than any Englishman I have ever known. For in spite of his unabashed, even boasted sensuality, he was curiously spiritual (I don't mean *spirituel*) and capable of fine feeling. His imagination was very strong, very poetic; he seemed able to extract supreme delight from thinking of me, dreaming of me, writing to me. There was

no brutality in his love-making, as there so often is with the Anglo-Saxon; his passion was not half so elemental as that of the ordinary Briton; and yet I know that he never for one moment lost sight of the fact that I was a woman, as our men do in good comradeship. Friendship between a man and woman could, to Lucien, mean but one thing; platonic friendship was a mystery, an impossibility to him in his conception; yet he was one of the best platonic friends I ever had for several years. I know this sounds paradoxical, but it is, nevertheless, true, and it was not until the passion of his words and thoughts and dreams led to a moment when he must either embrace me or give me up that the baser side of his nature triumphed. Of course, such a man must never be allowed the least liberty; and as he, with all his fineness of spirit (and he really was a charming fellow), would not or could not continue to meet me on the lines I had laid down, our friendship had to cease, much to my regret.

Love's Categories.

But his point of view was amazing! It differed from that of our men, even our Lotharios, as a Dutch cheese differs from the moon. The things an Englishman would do secretly, think disgraceful, and never dare to speak of, my Frenchman would glory in doing openly and vaunting before the world. He could not possibly comprehend the reticence of an Englishman, and merely regarded it as hypocrisy, holding the firm conviction that our countrymen pretend to more virtue than they possess and that they are naturally more brutal than his countrymen, whom he termed *debile* and *effete*. He divided love into three categories—*l'amour*, *le flirt*, and *la fonction*; but I could never understand where he thought one ended and the other began. And although he claimed to set *la femme* before everything, even his own desires, that he studied her wishes before his own, I never found him less selfish than my other lovers when it came to the test. Like the rest of them, he wanted his own way entirely, and did not even attempt to put himself in my place. But that is a feat of which no man is capable, be he French, English, or South Sea Islander, so far as I am aware ; and I must not hold it against poor Lucien. For he was certainly chivalrous in his thoughts of women ; the worst would never have been scorned or snubbed by him, and he would raise his hat to the grimiest scullery-maid.

With regard to brutality in courtship I must confess I have found him right. No man can be, according to my experience, more fiercely passionate, savagely jealous, headstrong, and unrestrained than the men of our isles. Above all, the Scotsman stands as type of the primitive lover, the nearest to him who used to knock a woman down with his club and carry her to his cave unconscious. The force and vehemence of his passion are overwhelming. He *will* be master, and one cannot be quite sure whether his love is for the woman herself or for his own way ! With my last Scotch lover I came to the conclusion that he was far more intent upon getting his own way than upon winning my love. He went for me as a wolf goes for a lamb, and almost swept me off my feet with the force of his fierce desire. But at the same time he was singularly cautious—a caution that must have been instinctive, for he was in no state to reason. I mean that, while before the world he showed by every look and action the condition of his feelings, and when we were alone together behaved like a man distraught, yet he never once uttered a word that would commit him definitely to marriage, because he did not imagine his income (and mine !) permitted such a step. One can hardly believe it possible that a man could go so far, infer so much, and say so little as he did. It was really clever, and roused my admiration with my wrath. No one can play this part so well as the Scot and the Englishman. I have known the latter to propose marriage, after losing his head completely, pouring out a stream of tender epithets, and behaving like a lunatic at large, then write next day a letter beginning, "My dear Miss ——," ending "Yours sincerely," and ignoring everything that has happened. In fact, as a backslider, the Englishman is supreme. A Frenchman, a German, an American, an Irishman will say a little more than he means, and stick to what he has said when required. An Englishman or a Scotsman will say a little less than he means, and try to back out of that ! He is a cowardly wooer as a rule (I have known noble exceptions), owing his success in love generally to the magnetism of his strong will.

As I have said somewhere else, the lion is an impressive beast, and there is a good deal left in woman that responds to the cave-man's method of courtship. But the more intellectual and spiritual she grows, the more she loves to be trusted, hates and despises the man who fears she will take a mean advantage of him. Thus, in the end, though she is momentarily carried away by a fierce onslaught of his passion, she is so revolted and distressed at the cowardly lover's quick recoil afterwards that she ceases to love and respect him. It is a pity that the average Englishman, with his leonine qualities of dash and pluck so much *en evidence* among men, should show the white feather in his relations with women. But he is afraid to be honest either with them or himself, and that is the bare truth. My Frenchman was more candid, more open and straightforward with me than any of my English lovers have been. In fact, he treated me as an equal, not as a being of inferior intellect, a creature of caprice to be humoured and petted and deceived, which is the Englishman's usual notion of womanhood.

(To be continued.)

The awards in connection with the third instalment of " The Truth About Man" have been made as follows : The first prize is won by " Martha," 197, Amesbury Avenue, Streatham, London. If " Martha" will kindly inform the Editor as to her full name he will have pleasure in sending her a cheque for a guinea. " Martha's" criticism is the best sent in so far, and in the next number the Editor hopes to be able to let his readers read the same. The second prize of half a guinea is awarded to Miss Helen Smythe, 61, Cambridge Gardens, North Kensington, W.

Cookery Notes.

SWEETS SUITABLE FOR THE SEASON.

Cophetua Pâte.

Cut the peel of 3 oranges in strips and boil in ½ pint of milk ; strain the milk and then make rather a thick custard of it with the yolks of 2 eggs, 4 oz. of cornflour, and sufficient sugar to taste ; slice the 3 oranges and lay them at the bottom of a pie-dish ; sprinkle with sugar and pour the custard over ; when set, beat the whites of the eggs to a stiff froth with sugar and lemon juice ; pile on the top of the custard and brown slightly in the oven.

Riviera Pudding.

Take the weight of 3 eggs in butter and beat this to a cream ; dredge in the same weight of flour and sugar, and continue beating until perfectly smooth ; whisk the 3 eggs well and add them to the mixture with ½ teaspoonful of grated lemon rind ; butter some little moulds ; fill them 3 parts full with the mixture, and bake for ½ hour in a hot oven ; turn out ; scoop out a little of the top of each and put in a lump of greengage or other jam.

Mont Blanc.

Soak ½ oz. of gelatine in 1 gill of water for ½ hour ; then add to it the juice of a pine-apple and stir over the fire until quite dissolved ; when nearly cold add it to the whites of 3 eggs beaten to a stiff froth with 2 oz. of castor sugar ; whisk until stiff, adding at the same time some pineapple cut into small pieces ; lay some slices of pineapple at the bottom of a glass dish, and pile the egg mixture as high as possible on top.

New England Pancakes.

Mix 1 pint of cream with 5 tablespoonfuls of flour, 7 yolks and 4 whites of eggs, and a pinch of salt, to a batter ; fry them in butter and sprinkle with sugar and cinnamon.

Suprème au Chocolat.

Soak ½ oz. of gelatine in ½ pint of milk ; dissolve it over the fire ; add 2 oz. of grated choco-late carefully, and the same amount of castor sugar ; boil for about 10 minutes ; make a custard of ½ pint of milk, the yolks of 2 eggs, and a little sugar ; when done, stir it to the chocolate ; add vanilla essence to flavour, and pour it into a glass dish to set ; whisk the whites of the eggs to a firm froth with 1 oz. of sugar, drop it in little heaps on to a greased baking tin, and bake for a few minutes, but do not let it brown ; when cold, arrange on the chocolate and serve.

Castle Puddings.

Melt 2 oz. of butter with the same amount of sugar and flour with 1 egg ; then add 1 teacupful of milk, well beating the mixture : put into small buttered cups and bake for 20 to 30 minutes ; when done, turn out and place a glacé cherry on the top of each, and serve with any jam liked or some whipped cream.

Greek Almond Cream.

Blanch ¼ lb. Jordan almonds and 4 bitter almonds ; dry and pound them ; beat up the yolks of 4 eggs, and add to them ¼ lb. of castor sugar, ¼ teaspoonful of grated lemon peel, and the almonds, beating well for some time ; then add the white of the eggs beaten to a firm froth ; bake in a well-buttered pie-dish for about ¾ hour ; turn out, and when cold cover it with whipped cream, flavoured with almond essence and slightly sweetened ; cut some Rahat-Lakoum in small pieces, and place this on the cream ; serve at once to prevent the cream sinking.

Baked Gooseberry Pudding.

Stew gooseberries in a covered jar in the oven until they will pulp ; press a pint of the juice through a coarse sieve, and add to 3 eggs which have been previously well-beaten, and 1½ oz. of butter ; well sweeten ; line a pie-dish with crust ; pour this mix-ture in, and bake in a moderate oven ; a few breadcrumbs mixed with the fruit will give it consistence.

Marlborough Peaches.

Arrange some sponge cakes, ratafias, and maca-roons in a glass dish, and soak thoroughly with white wine ; boil the syrup from a tin of peaches with a tablespoonful of castor sugar, and when nearly cold pour over the cakes ; place the peaches on these, and cover with whipped cream.

THE EDITOR'S PAGE.

THE next issue of THE LADY'S REALM will be our annual Special Spring Number, and will, it is believed, be regarded by our readers as one of the best numbers that have as yet appeared.

"The Gambler."

Mrs. Katherine Cecil Thurston, to whom reference is made on another page, has written for us a powerful novel entitled "The Gambler," and the first long instalment will be given in this Special Spring Number, to be had at all the bookstalls on April 28. "The Gambler" is a brilliant story concerning Clodagh, an impulsive and very human Irish girl. Her marriage to a man of tastes opposite to her own, her life in Florence, and her revelling in Venetian gaiety, her meeting with the "other" man, and the dramatic situations in which she finds herself inevitably placed—these are related with a skill that makes "The Gambler" a worthy successor to Mrs. Thurston's last book, *John Chilcote, M.P.*

In the same number, which is also the first of a new volume, and is therefore an excellent month for new subscribers to begin reading THE LADY'S REALM, will be found a charming story which the Countess of Cromartie has been good enough to write for THE LADY'S REALM. "Under the Sea" is the title of this romance, which, besides being refreshingly real, is treated in a delightfully original manner.

The Lady Helen Forbes has written specially for this Magazine a brilliant article on "The American Girl," which will probably be widely discussed. The illustrations to this article are unique, being reproductions from neither photographs nor drawings, but from a new process.

"A Day in the Season," depicting the busy round of the Society woman, illustrated with some charming sketches, will be appreciated by our readers.

Some Interesting Features.

THE LADY'S REALM is justly famous for its exquisite illustrations. The scenes from the West-End theatres in "Plays and Players of the Month" will represent the latest new plays staged at the moment of going to press. In addition, a splendid art article will be given dealing with the work of one of the most popular painters of Society. Special permission has been granted to THE LADY'S REALM for these striking portraits to be reproduced.

A short series of amusing love stories, each complete in itself, entitled "The Birthdays of Delia," by Gertie de S. Wentworth-James, begins in the Special Spring Number.

So popular were the last papers on Beauty Culture that the Editor has arranged for these to be followed by another series dealing in a thorough and practical manner with "The Care of the Hands." The first paper will appear in the Special Spring Number, and will be beautifully illustrated.

"A Spinster" will in the same number consider the subject of Marriage from the woman's point of view. Should the man or the woman have the right to propose marriage?

The Special Spring Number, with a most artistic cover worthy of being framed, will be ready on April 28, and will contain the newest Spring Fashions and the best serials and short stories. THE EDITOR.